THE CEO CHRONICLES

THE CEO CHRONICLES

Lessons from the Top about Inspiration and Leadership

Glenn Rifkin
Douglas Matthews

KNOWLEDGE EXCHANGE

Los Angeles

Knowledge Exchange
a division of Knowledge Universe, Inc.

ISBN: 1-888232-23-4
Library of Congress Catalog Card Number: 99-63593

Book design by Susannah Auferoth

Knowledge Exchange's books may be purchased for
educational, business, or sales promotional use. For information, contact:
National Book Network, Inc., 4720 Boston Way, Lanham, MD 20706
Phone: 301-459-3366

Printed in the United States of America
First Edition: November, 1999
10 9 8 7 6 5 4 3 2 1

Table of Contents

Table of Contents

Foreword

In the leadership field, we often talk about something called the "romance of leadership." What we mean by this expression is that people want to believe that a single individual can truly be bigger than life. We want our leaders to be heroes. We want to imagine that leaders are somehow unique in their strength of character, their visionary insights, their talents, and that this unique combination in one person can explain why an entire organization did so well.

However, in the process of creating this myth, we fail to see that most leaders are a reflection of the people with whom they have surrounded themselves. Just as important, the romance blindsides us to the human being in every leader. We are unable to see that leaders have struggled like the rest of us. We are unable to see that their pathways to leadership have been filled with many trials and tribulations. We are unable to see that it is not magical talent, but the twins passion and persistence, that have carried them on to success.

In reality, leaders are like those painted Russian dolls. Within a single doll, there are six more—each hidden within the next. As we strip away our romantic notions, we see that our leaders are multidimensional and very human.

What Glenn Rifkin and Doug Matthews have done in *The CEO Chronicles* is to show us this more intimate side of leadership—the human portrait of leadership. They take us to a richer world where CEOs are not simply painted portraits of somber-looking gentlemen that line the paneled corridors of some distant executive suite. As we look at the stories contained in this book, we see that the heroism of leadership has less to do with remarkable talents and more to do with determination, a love for what one is doing, and a quest to have an impact on the world. Similarly, the insights of these leaders have more to do with personal experiences that put them into the shoes of customers and employees than with any special powers of vision and foresight.

What we also learn from this book is that CEOs come from many walks of life. These are the portraits of people from an amazing array of backgrounds who went on to become business leaders—and, by the way, with hardly an M.B.A. among them. They include a motorcycle racer, social worker, football player, and drug dealer.

But what is even more interesting is how these individuals handled the obstacles that life shoved in their ways. For some, the path was hard from the beginning, including childhoods spent in poverty—one in an orphanage. For others, the tribulations came later: being fired when seemingly on the road to success, sitting on the edge of bankruptcy, or facing the ignominious end to a once-stellar career.

What is clear from all of these CEO stories is that adversity built leadership muscles. It taught these executives the value of persistence, determination, passion, and values. As I read many of their stories, I could not help but think of the old analogy of the oyster and how it takes a gritty particle of sand and, over time, transforms it into something of remarkable beauty. In a paradoxical way, this is a book about heroes, but very human heroes who have faced life boldly and with a sense of passion. It is a collection of personal triumphs. It tells of individuals who wanted to make a difference in life. Many of these are beautiful, touching stories of lives lived well.

As I read through the book's chapters, I was also reminded of the importance of a personal vision; that leaders are indeed pragmatic dreamers. They are dreamers who want to get off their Lazy Boy recliners and start building. I thought of a story that Steve Ross, the entrepreneur behind Time Warner, used to tell about his pathway to success. He explained: "When I was a teenager and my father was dying, he gave me the best advice possible. He said, there are three categories of people in this world. The first is the individual who wakes up in the morning and goes into the office and proceeds to dream. The second category is the individual who gets up in the morning, goes into the office, and proceeds to work sixteen hours a day. The third individual comes into the office, dreams for about an hour, and then proceeds to do something about his dreams. My father said, 'Go for the third category—for only one reason. There is no competition.'"

Foreword

This book is filled with individuals from that third category, those who dreamed and then went out and built their dream. Many started simply—often without knowing about what their ideas would later become. One of my favorite stories in the book is about a CEO who began by handing out calling cards that simply read "Mrs. Norman Silverman. Please give me a chance." She went on to build an $80-million business.

The other striking feature of these human portraits of CEOs is the desire of many of them to improve the lot of others. In essence, they are building living legacies. They want to repay their success by contributing to the lives of others. One individual in the book put it so nicely: "When you reach your star, turn around and help someone else reach theirs."

I know you will enjoy this book. At the heart of every good leader is a great story, a story of who they are, where they are going, and how they changed the world in some form or another. This is a book filled with leadership stories that will hopefully inspire you the reader to see and realize your own potential as did the CEOs in this book.

Jay A. Conger
Senior Research Scientist
Center for Effective Organizations
University of Southern California

Professor of Organizational Behavior
London Business School

Introduction
Life at the Top

"Leadership is about taking an organization to a place it
would not have otherwise gone without you."
—*George M.C. Fisher*

In the world of popular culture, who is more compelling, admired,
envied, reviled, and misunderstood than the chief executive officer?
But considering all the attention that CEOs receive, we don't really
know that much about who they are and how they feel about what
they do.

In a different age, titans of business, such as John D. Rockefeller,
Henry Ford, and Andrew Carnegie, cast a giant shadow over the world
of commerce. Their names not only became synonymous with hugely
successful companies, but their bigger-than-life personas helped define
an era. Their command-and-control style also helped define the chief
executive officer for generations to come.

In the flush of post–World War II America, with business driving
the changes that swept across the nation, the concept of brilliant and
tough-minded professional managers was utterly fresh and inspiring to
a new generation coming out of graduate business schools. Eventually,
the model would spread around the globe.

These newly minted CEOs were facing competitive battlefields
that were vastly different from any business environment that had
come before. New technologies, manufacturing capabilities, capital
markets, and international marketplaces—not to mention new
organizational structures—redefined the role and responsibility of the
CEOs. They could command and control, but they did so from the top
of hierarchical pyramids that required management skills unknown to
the monopolists of the past. Most CEOs learned to climb the

corporate ladder, rung by political rung, and emerged tougher and more steeled to the task than those who had come before.

Building giant, profitable companies was a daunting task and spawned the era of the "Organization Man" and the "Man in the Gray Flannel Suit." Men (and it was almost always men) rose through the ranks, grabbed the keys to the executive washroom, and found themselves ensconced in lush, darkly luxurious corner offices on the highest floors of corporate skyscrapers. In time, a stereotype was born. Hollywood appropriated the stereotype and, in film after film, cemented the public's image of the single-minded, ruthless, and omnipotent chief executive who was often the evil foil to the hero's search for truth and justice.

Indeed, the prototypical CEO has not changed much in the minds of the general public. Organizations have changed dramatically. They have been recast, reengineered, and restructured to fit a newly wired world that has eliminated most geographical and cultural barriers. But there are still giants to cast their shadows: Bill Gates at Microsoft has been called the Rockefeller or Carnegie of the 21st century; Jack Welch, Michael Eisner, Katherine Graham, Andrew Grove, Ted Turner, Linda Wachner, Louis Gerstner, Scott McNealy, Rupert Murdoch, Lee Iacocca, Roberto Goizueta, Roy Vagelos, and a legion of other dynamic CEOs reshaped their companies, fueled unparalleled growth, and became the focus of a media spotlight that suddenly shined brightly on the fields of business dreams.

CEO biographies, ghostwritten and polished by publicity departments, topped the bestseller lists. Business magazines flourished, and cover stories on fabled CEOs and their fabulous wealth and power only served to fuel the public's fascination with these oversized figures at the top.

But something has always been missing from the scenario. Behind the guise of the pinstriped suit or Hermès scarf, there is a human being who faces life from a different perspective. These men, and increasingly more women, strive to have it all in ways mere mortal workers can't fathom. Classically driven, these CEOs invest everything in the grasp for success. While some have worked their way up and others have inherited their spots in family businesses, many have embraced a new entrepreneurial spirit that has flashed across the past two decades and changed not only the CEO profile but the office itself. Young, brilliant, aggressive, sometimes arrogant, and fabulously wealthy, they are driven by the same inner fire that drove their predecessors in a bygone era.

Most will explain it like Steve Tobias, CEO of a Detroit-based online stock trading company and one of the CEOs profiled in this book: "I think people climb mountains because they can, they run in marathons because they can. I'm a CEO, because I can. This is just what I do and what I am."

These leaders all share traits that mark them with the title CEO. It is, for most of them, most of the time, a blessing. It can be and often is a curse as well. But in a world where business increasingly is the engine that propels society, we have learned little about the inner thoughts and feelings of these special people.

What is life at the top truly like—and not just for the small fraction of the world's CEOs who gain the lion's share of the fame and attention? There are, after all, hundreds of thousands, if not millions, of CEOs running small to medium-sized businesses around the world. Most of them work in virtual obscurity and never get quoted in *Business Week* or the *Wall Street Journal*.

Behind all the trappings and the stereotypes, who are these CEOs and how does it feel to be one? Whether running a multinational giant or a ten-person family business, some things are the same. The buck, for example, stops at their desks. Even if they are backed by a board of directors and an army of senior executives and outside consultants, they alone have that final word and must make the toughest decisions in the solitude of the corner offices. Talk to enough CEOs and you understand the origin of the aphorism, "It's lonely at the top."

Ultimately, all major decisions find their way across the CEO's desk. A company's success or failure will ultimately depend on the steady and knowledgeable hand on the tiller. Leadership, as the quotation at the beginning of this introduction says, is about taking an organization to a place it would otherwise have not gone without you. Bad or ill-informed decisions eventually affect many lives and can have disastrous outcomes. Great vision and wisdom conversely can enrich lives both financially and emotionally and provide not only a place of employment but a family, a support group, and a foundation from which to build a secure future. These are not trivial things, and attention, as Arthur Miller once put it, must be paid.

Introduction

In this book, we bring together the voices of CEOs in candid conversations about their lives, their businesses, their families, their triumphs and failures, and their joys and sorrows. These profiles, all told in the CEOs' own voices, provide a very personal portrait of leadership and life at the top.

Our CEOs come from around the world, from vastly different backgrounds and different eras. They are men and women, young, middle-aged, and near or past retirement. They have built stunningly successful multibillion dollar companies, as well as small but thriving businesses of under $10 million. Their stories are compelling. One has climbed all seven of the world's tallest mountains. One is the new, young mother of twins. Another was blinded in an automobile crash and went on to start a successful software company. Another is a former National Football League star who bought an old municipal golf course and now uses golf to teach inner-city children about values, discipline, and fun.

Collectively, tens of thousands of workers depend on them for their livelihoods and futures. Some have made it big; some have lost. Some head companies you've heard of, such as Harley-Davidson, Lanier Worldwide, and Pier 1 Imports. Most run companies that you'll never hear of unless you live nearby or work in the particular industry.

Besides their title, they are tied together by one common thread: all are current or former members of TEC, a worldwide organization of CEOs. TEC, which stands for The Executive Committee, is a forty-two-year-old, for-profit organization, that began in Milwaukee and has grown to include more than 6,000 CEOs. In effect a fraternal organization or support group, TEC is a collection of regional groups that meet regularly, so that CEOs have a place to go for advice, support, and understanding from peers who are facing the same daunting challenges.

It is the very premise of TEC that spawned this book. CEOs come to TEC for a single reason: it is, indeed, lonely at the top. In these groups of fourteen or fifteen CEOs, TEC members find places where they can share their triumphs and their pain. They must drop their guards and share both professional and deeply personal issues. If they remain quiet and aloof, they eventually are asked to rethink their membership and leave.

But the sharing that is done is very real and powerful. Faced with crucial business decisions or difficult personal issues, a TEC member finds unconditional support that is both practical and inspiring. One member, who unwisely bought into a struggling business venture across the country from his home, was viewed as a pariah by the local business press and embarked on a lengthy and unpleasant attempt to right the listing ship. In the midst of this painful vilification, his entire TEC group flew, unannounced, to his side to help him work through the crisis. Another TEC member, dying with cancer, got to attend his last meetings, because the group came to his home to meet by his bedside. When he died, the members ran his business until his family felt ready to take over themselves.

A majority of these CEOs run small or medium-sized companies and thus tend to have an extra personal stake in the lives of their employees and customers. Though the glamour and spotlight tends to fall on the CEOs at the IBMs or the AT&Ts, these CEOs have driven the remarkable economic boom of the 1990s.

What becomes clear in conversation after conversation is that these CEOs believe deeply in what they are doing and in the responsibility they carry for the people who work for them. While all are driven to build and sustain profitable businesses, none are motivated solely, or even primarily, by profit. Indeed, if there is a common theme that emanates from these chronicles, it is the passion that fuels the work that these CEOs do, a passion for the business, for the product or service, for the success of the people they hire, for the community around them.

Consider Abby Margalith, the forty-five-year-old CEO of Starving Students of San Diego, a regional moving company founded by a group of unemployed students in 1973. Though she runs a thriving, conventional moving business, Margalith, for the past decade, has helped move battered women and their children from their homes to a safe place—at no cost to the family. Here is a small piece of her story:

Why do I do this? Because it's what we do best. We move people every day. More important, I believe there's more to life than just working and making money. I have an opportunity to break the cycle of violence, so for me it's more a question of how can I not do this? I consider it an honor to be able to help these women and

15

*children. Even though I never hear from them after the move, I
know in my heart that we are making a difference in their lives.
And you can't put a price on that.*

Our hope is that the stories that follow will not only provide a
vivid and enlightening view from the top, but will inspire you as well.

Section One
Overcoming Adversity

One

Between First Place and Nowhere

Ted Henter
Henter-Joyce, Inc.

In 1978, when Ted Henter was twenty-seven years old, he was fully invested in a wild and adventurous lifestyle. A championship-caliber professional motorcycle racer, Henter loved speed, excitement, and life on the edge—but all that changed one tragic night in England. After a motorcycle race at a racetrack south of London, Henter left in a rental car. He was driving back to a friend's apartment in the dark of night when he came around a turn and realized, too late, that he had been daydreaming and was driving on the wrong side of the English road. He crashed nearly head-on with a passenger car, an accident that left him blind. After three years of rehabilitation and a short period of despair, he began a new life as a computer programmer. He founded Henter-Joyce, a software company in St. Petersburg, Florida, which makes screen-reader software for the blind and visually impaired. With Henter as CEO, the business has grown into a $12-million company with fifty employees, many of whom are also blind, and a top ranking in its software category. Along the way, Henter and his wife have raised three daughters and became deeply involved in the Christian religion. A water skier since age five, Henter returned to the sport several years after his accident, and in 1991 won the gold medal in the world championships for blind skiers.

I've always been adventurous and a bit different. I was born and raised in the Panama Canal zone in Central America. My grandfather came from Europe at the turn of the century to help build the Panama Canal. My dad was born and raised there, and so was I. I graduated from high school down there and came to the U. S. to go to college.

I went to the University of Florida, and though I majored in mechanical engineering, I spent a lot of my time surfing and water skiing, and eventually I got involved in motorcycle racing. I raced professionally for five years after college and finished in eighth place in the world championships before I was blinded in the car accident.

I remember that night vividly. It was a dark country road, and I was heading back toward my friend's apartment, where I was staying. I saw a pair of headlights coming toward me, but I didn't think anything of it; I was daydreaming and not paying attention.

At the last instant, I realized those headlights were right in front of me, so I swerved to the right to get off the road. This was in England—I was supposed to be driving on the left. We collided, not quite head-on but pretty close to it. I wasn't wearing my seat belt, so I hit the windshield and cut my eyes and my face. I detached my retinas, and that caused the blindness.

In the 1970s, the British medical system was rather primitive compared with the United States'. The doctors couldn't tell if I was going to be permanently blind or not. They told me they thought my vision would clear up.

Over time, it did clear up enough for them to see that the retina was detached, and they recommended I go back to the United States and have an operation. One operation was successful at first but failed six weeks later. I regained my sight for a short time, and I was thrilled. When it failed to heal properly, I had another operation that was not successful, and that's when I had to face the music that I would be blind. Up to then, I had this glimmer of hope that I would make it.

It was devastating, to say the least, but I had been a Christian for about five years at the time, and my faith grew pretty quickly during the three-month period that I spent going through the operations and healing. When I finally realized that I was going to be blind, I had about ten minutes of outright despair, and then I realized that this was part of God's plan. I thought, "There have been successful blind people before, and there will be successful blind people in the future, and I can be one of them if I just get over it."

It took me literally ten minutes to realize that. I still wasn't happy about it, but I had a much better feeling about the whole thing. I set my mind on getting back into life and learning the skills I had to learn to be an active blind person.

It's an amazing learning experience. You need to learn skills such as walking around with a cane and safety techniques so you don't hit your head or trip off the curb or walk out in traffic. I needed to learn how to read and takes notes using Braille, and there were simple daily living skills, such as how to make a cup of coffee or a piece of toast without burning myself. Most people take these things for granted; it's quite shocking to find out what you have to learn when you can't see.

It took about three years to learn those basic skills and get over my self-esteem problem. When you're blind, I found out, people treat you like an idiot. If you're blind, you bump into things. That's how you find stuff. You have to ask what is on the menu, because you can't read it. People feel sorry for you and take pity on you. You have to be tough to fend that off, or else you start *feeling* like an idiot. You have to get over that and be comfortable walking around so that you don't look so clumsy, and you have to be able to dress yourself in reasonable clothes.

I tried to be productive and effective and worked on my motorcycles. I even invented a wheel alignment tool and received two patents. My dad and I built them and sold about 500 around the world. But I wasn't cut out to work in a machine shop. I decided to go back to school and become a computer programmer. Eventually, a friend of a friend offered me a job. He had no clue that I could do it, but he just thought he'd give me a chance. That was my first big break.

I worked hard at it and didn't charge him much, and I learned more and more. During that time, I bought some equipment that allowed a computer to talk, and I met the fellow, Dean Blaise, who built it. He made a reading machine that would read print. It wasn't very good, but it was the first one.

Dean offered me a job, so I moved my family to Maryland where he lived. By this time, we had our first child. I just had a great time at that company. It had great entrepreneurial spirit. There were about fifteen people when I started, and though I was the first blind person, they accepted me and didn't treat me like an idiot. That also helped mend my damaged ego quite a bit.

I learned a tremendous amount from the other engineers about computers and about access technology, but my family and I were homesick for Florida, so we moved back to St. Petersburg. Eventually, the company had some problems and went out of business, and that was perhaps another break for me. I did a little consulting here and there, and then I met this fellow named Bill Joyce, who was blind and rich, which is a nice combination.

He was intrigued with my ideas about computing for the blind and what we might be able to do. So he suggested we start a company. In 1987, he funded the start-up: Henter-Joyce was born, and I was in charge. Four years later, Bill decided to get out of the business and made me an offer I couldn't refuse. I borrowed enough money to pay him off, and suddenly I was the CEO and sole owner of Henter-Joyce.

At the time, there were four people and sales of about $250,000. In eight years, we've grown to $12 million and fifty employees. But we struggled a lot at the beginning. We were trying to make screen-reader technology for the blind. We were not really experienced software developers, and we released some products prematurely and that hurt us a lot. We also had some stiff competition.

But by 1995, with Microsoft Windows as the dominant operating system, we released our screen reader for Windows, and it was a very good product. Henter-Joyce took off from there, and its growth ever since has been strong and steady. We continue to improve the product, and it's safe to say that at this time, we have 70 to 80 percent of the market in the United States.

With all that said, I can still say with certainty that I never dreamed I'd be a CEO. I figured I'd race motorcycles as long as I could. My goal was to be a world champion. If that didn't materialize, I would fall back on my engineering education and work in the motorcycle field as part of a racing team. So my blindness changed my life in ways I never expected. Not only did I never anticipate being a CEO, but when we started Henter-Joyce, I never thought the company would get this big.

Not surprisingly, I've faced the same issues that any sighted CEO must face. In 1993, for example, we had a dozen employees and we were just having horrible problems. Our tech support guy was complaining about us to the customers. Our receptionist wouldn't let customers through to talk to me. It was just awful, and I was severely stressed out—and so was my wife. We were losing money and just barely hanging on.

Then luck played a hand. I had been invited to join the board of directors of a local handicapped training center, and there I met a fellow who was a human resources consultant for big companies such as AT&T, Honeywell, and the Paradigm Systems Corporation. He was very nice, and he offered me a ride home after a meeting. I explained my problems to him, and he offered to come in and survey our situation for free. He knew we didn't have any money, and he said he'd make a recommendation and not charge me for it. So he came in and pinpointed the problems right away.

We had to fire about three or four people who were the problems. We had to move some people around and have some serious, frank discussions with other people to get them going in the right direction. All of this was new to me. I thought, you hire people, they know what jobs have to be done, they go out and do it—just like I had always done. But it doesn't work that way. The realities of management were all new to a guy who raced motorcycles. So he was a big help, and today he's our general manager.

That was one of the things I learned early on. I don't want or need to be the kingpin of the business. I need to hire the right kind of people so the business can pretty much operate without me if necessary. I became interested in getting the best people I could in every area, such as software development, technical support, sales and marketing, and management. I was never concerned about giving up the spotlight. It was not a big deal for me to be the top guy. I had had enough publicity. It's nice to have, but it isn't what I work for.

What I work for is multifaceted. Part of it is the financial security. My wife and I have three kids now, and I wanted to be successful financially. But I never dreamed I'd be this successful. That part is extremely gratifying.

However, what actually got us here was the never-ending striving for excellence. Product performance was always the top concern and the goal, mainly because I, as well as others on the development team, needed this product to get *our* jobs done, to get access to our own computers. Half of our development team is blind, including the top two guys. Most of our tech support and sales engineers are blind. If we make an inferior product, we hear about it. The better the product was, the more we liked it, and the easier everything else became. We had more access to information, less effort, less stress. We were our own best customers and best critics. I felt and still feel quite sure that if we do everything the right way, then the financial rewards will come, but I never focused on them that much.

Once I understood my lack of management knowledge, I started reading lots of books on management. I read books such as *Think and Grow Rich* by Napoleon Hill and *How to Swim with the Sharks Without Being Eaten Alive* by Harvey MacKay. I read books by Brian Tracey and Zig Zigler and anything I could get about the fundamentals of business. That was how I taught myself to be a CEO.

My motorcycle racing background also played a role. I quickly learned that there is only one place to finish—and that's first. Nobody remembers the other guys. You have to be first—and you can be first by only inches or hundredths of a second, and you'll be the one they remember. I've always stressed with our staff that there is just a little bit of difference between first place and nowhere.

With that concept in mind, we don't leave any stone unturned, and we do whatever needs to be done. When you win, whether in racing or in software development, the adrenaline rush is the same. The difference is that there is much more stress in software development. In racing, it is never a matter of opinion—you either win or you don't. But in software development, it's all about opinion, "Is our product better than their product?" So there is much less in the way of a concrete winner.

I suppose there have been other important lessons from my blindness. I have a basis of comparison that most people don't have. I realize how precious certain things are, and that puts business into perspective. We had negotiated a lucrative partnership deal with Microsoft a few years ago, for example, and at the last minute it appeared Microsoft was backing out. I had to tell my development team that two months of intense work and negotiation was wasted. But rather than dwell on the downside, I felt strongly that it was okay, because God hadn't intended it to be. Two months earlier, we had not had even an inkling about this deal. We lost it, but we never had it to start with. Later that day, after I'd made peace with the situation, Microsoft called and said the deal was on. I took a lesson in that.

I'm certainly not perfect about these things. There have frequently been times when I have lost my temper from the frustration, but I always catch myself. It never turns into bitterness; it's just frustration. You learn to move on.

I've been fortunate in that I've never allowed work to take over my life as some CEOs do. Because being a CEO or businessman was not my first love, racing was. I just worked my way into this job, and I never put in the kind of hours most CEOs do that would have kept me away from my family. I've been pretty good about getting out of here at a reasonable time and getting home.

Another critical part of my recovery and my success has been my wife. We were married two years before the accident, and she has stuck with me. She could very easily have bailed out back when times were really tough, but she didn't. In fact, my wife and my family and friends were all there for me, so I've been very fortunate.

I also took up competitive water skiing, once I started feeling better about myself. When I won the world championship of blind water skiing in 1991, I took the gold medal in all three events, including slalom, trick skiing, and jumping. Jumping was pretty scary. A sighted skier skis alongside you and counts down until you hit that ramp. He pulls off to the side and you go up the ramp. It's pretty terrifying. I never did get used to it.

I've also taken up downhill snow skiing and I enjoy that as well, but the difference for me now versus before is that I used to take foolish chances and risks. I'd do almost anything—not anymore. Not only am I older and smarter, I now have so much more at stake than ever before.

Two
Lessons from the Orphanage

Patrick Kelly
PSS/World Medical Inc.

Patrick Kelly, fifty-one years old, is the founder and CEO of PSS/World Medical Inc., a medical-supply company based in Jacksonville, Florida. From 1983, when Kelly started the company with $40,000, PSS has grown into a global giant with a market capitalization of $1.6 billion. In 1997, Kelly received the Horatio Alger Award, an annual award given to dedicated community leaders who are committed to excellence and have risen up against the odds to remarkable achievements.

Despite where I am today, I never set out to be a CEO. After a tour of duty in Vietnam, I'd gone back to college and graduated with a premed degree. My wife was pregnant with our first child, so I needed a job quickly. There wasn't time to go to medical school and do an internship. I decided that selling medical supplies was close enough to the medical profession.

After my first job in sales, I went to work in 1976 for a company called Intermedco, a medical-supplies distributor, in Ft. Worth, Texas. I stayed with Intermedco until February 8, 1983. That's a date I remember well. I'd gone from being a branch manager to a vice president of sales and marketing, and I'd had a big hand in developing the business, but on February 8, 1983, I was called into my boss's office, and he fired me.

Intermedco was bought by British Tire & Rubber in 1982 and a director in London decided that we shouldn't be selling medical supplies to physicians. I had taken the company into that business. So, I was let go by my boss, Buddy, head of United States operations. Now,

27

every February 8th, we celebrate Buddy Day to thank him for firing me. There is cake and ice cream for everyone in the company, and the best part is that today, Buddy is an employee here.

At the time, however, it was a painful situation. Suddenly without a job, I reluctantly became an entrepreneur. Two of the salespeople who'd worked for me when I'd been stationed here in Jacksonville for Intermedco convinced me to come back and start a company. The three of us started Physician Sales and Service Inc. Now, fifteen years later, there are 5,200 of us.

As I said, from the beginning—when we first started talking about setting up a company—I didn't want to be just an owner of a company. I had always wanted to be involved in a team. I'd still be at Intermedco if I hadn't been fired. I just wanted to be part of a team, and I think that comes from my background, one of never doing anything alone.

When I was five years old, I was sent to live in the Virginia Home for Boys in Richmond, the seventh oldest orphanage in the United States. I lived there for thirteen years and three months, until I graduated from high school. And while 20,000 boys have lived in that orphanage, I still hold the record for the longest stay.

My father abandoned my family when my mother was pregnant with me. He just took off. My mother tried to raise me and my older brother and sister, but she just couldn't handle it financially. The orphanage had a minimum age of eight, but when she sent my brother there, she petitioned the home to let me come with him, even though I was only five. I was the first kid under eight years of age to ever be admitted there.

Being the youngest kid, I got beat up a lot. When they wanted to push somebody around, there was always Kelly. I was a scrawny kid and twenty pounds lighter than anyone else, so needless to say, in those early days, it was a major adjustment for me. But I remember having extraordinary, caring house mothers, Mrs. James and Mrs. Moore. I just remember being well thought of, and despite stereotype images like *Oliver Twist*, I had a very happy childhood there.

After getting over the trauma of that first six months to a year, I figured out pretty early in my life that I was going to be a long-term attendee there, and that's when I came to the realization I best make something good out of something unfortunate. I became somewhat of a leader, both in academics and sports. If you're raised with sixty other boys and you see a chance to be in a leadership role, you take advantage of it. It helped me later on in life.

We actually had serious regimentation and discipline at the home. You had a set time for breakfast. You had to make your bed and clean up your area. Today, I'm fastidious because of that. I can't have a messy desk. If you have to make your bed every morning and stand inspection, it gets ingrained. It wasn't military school, but it created an environment in which you come to believe the way you get out is by applying yourself and that ultimately, once you do go out in the real world, you can be successful.

When I started PSS in May 1983, I knew that I would bring a lot of what I learned from the Boys Home with me into this endeavor. One of the top tenets within our company is that you can speak up without fear of retribution. It's in our top twenty corporate values, and it's the one that our employees value most. If you think your boss is wrong, you can go over your boss's head, and it's okay. If any retribution occurs to you, then that boss won't be a boss much longer.

That was part of the process that we had at the home. It was like sixty birds chirping in a nest; if you didn't speak up, you'd be lost. So all those tenets we ended up adopting very early at PSS are things that I learned at the Virginia Home for Boys.

At the Boys Home, you shared everything. You can't have sixty brothers and be alone; it's physically and mentally impossible. So when we started this company, from the get go, I said, "Okay, I'll go in with you partners, but we're going to sell stock to the other employees. The employees will be involved in this." It really ended up being the foundation and the key to our success.

It was just a natural way of doing business. It creates a culture that's extraordinarily unique and one that the employees love. It has also created a culture that has fueled an average growth rate of 43 percent annually over fifteen years, with very, very little turnover. We were boot strapped from nothing to a leadership position in three very large segments of medical supply distribution.

One of the lessons I got from the home and from my years in business is to never be surprised by surprise, because it's always going to happen. Even though we've been pretty good at building a company, surprises come up.

One surprise was that I'd end up running PSS alone. If you look at the history of our company, there were originally three founders and a financial partner. Today there's only myself left of the four who started the company. Every departure was very stressful.

When we decided, in 1989, as a $13-million-dollar Florida-based company, to jump out and become the first national physician medical-supply company, one partner did not want to take that risk. Another partner left over the ownership of the company and how it should be split up. Should the employees own it or not? Another partner left because he became an extraordinarily autocratic manager. That's why we put the tenet in place that you can fire your boss. He was one of the first fired bosses in the company's history.

One of the first things I did when I was running the company alone came from a book I happened to be reading, *Moments of Truth* by Jan Carleson. It said, in essence, that if people look to me to be the boss or the leader, we'll have difficulty growing. So we decided that a CEO in this culture is the one standing in front of the customer, making the decisions relative to taking care of that customer.

To me, a truck driver, a purchasing agent, a customer service rep, a sales rep, and I can all be CEOs. We got to a point where we could see that the people who were making the decisions had confidence in their decisions and, for our leadership team, it became very easy to see where we needed to go. Now, every employee has a calling card with CEO on it.

When an employee is standing in front of the customer, the customer can't look to me to make the decision. The employee has to make that decision. So we have a culture in which a sales rep can sell a product to a doctor today, but if the truck driver shows up tomorrow and the doctor says, "Get this out of here," the truck driver needs to say, "Yes, sir." He's to load it in the van and bring it back, no questions asked. Our employees know that, and they're taught that in the process. That's why we call them CEOs.

We've also created a culture of promoting from within. You could be a truck driver for us today and be running our largest division tomorrow, which is something that really happened. The second truck driver we hired back in 1983 is now running a $700-million division for us. He is a high school graduate who joined this company as a truck driver. Anything is possible in this company.

So I was never really on my own, because literally from the first year, we allowed the employees to buy in. By the time we went public, most of our employees were shareholders in the company. Several hundred are now millionaires. In this organization, people know what they have to do, and they go execute.

By the way, the worst crisis was not when the founders left. We've been thrown out of five banks along the way, and every time was a extraordinary crisis. Twice we had to take across-the-board pay cuts. In 1993, 525 employees took pay cuts just to keep the bank from foreclosing on us. We were growing so fast that we outstripped our credit line. We tried to take advantage of opportunities, but the company wasn't making money, and we had a covenant in our bank loan that said if we were not profitable, they could demand the loan, which they did. We had to take pay cuts just to keep the company afloat. But people stayed; in fact, nobody left.

I never let myself get too down. I guess this is the optimist in me. As soon as one bank would shut us down, we'd go to another one. We realized there were 14,000 banks in America, and if we had to go make 14,000 pitches, we were bound to find one that would believe in us. We did. Every time.

It's just part of the reality of business that your world doesn't stop unless you want it to stop. If you're determined to succeed and you believe in your cause, you'll find the resources to make it happen as an entrepreneur. This company did.

There have been some difficult personal times. My wife and I split up a couple of years ago. We were married thirty years, but once my two daughters were grown and out of college, my wife and I just didn't have a relationship. It had been oriented around the children, and so we ended up going through a divorce. We divided the family money equally; we each received a quarter of the total, and we put the money for my daughters in a trust for them.

Today my goal is very simple. Right now, I have about $20 million dollars. I want it to grow to $100 million dollars that I can leave to a Boys Home foundation, servicing children's homes around America.

Orphanages have fallen on hard times in this country. There is a distorted view that they are bad and that placing kids in foster homes is better. A foster home is good if you are accepted by your foster parents, but not if you end up getting bounced out of that foster home. Most of the kids who are ending up in orphanages today are kids who've been bounced two or three times. It's not a kid like me, rejected once. It's a kid rejected two or three times. As a result, these kids have serious self-esteem problems. We tell them, "What has happened to you has nothing to do with you. It has to do with your real parents or your foster parents—they're the ones who fouled up. You have to focus on what you have and what your capabilities are." The Virginia Home for Boys and other homes have been very, very good at getting kids to do that. I've been proud of what the Virginia Home for Boys has done.

So four years ago, my brother and I put a scholarship in place that permanently funds any kid from the Virginia Home for Boys who wants to go to college. We guarantee them a free college education. They must stay all the way through high school and graduate, but if they do, they're guaranteed a college education.

When we started this four years, there wasn't a single kid from the Virginia Home for Boys in college. This year, we had five graduates. Needless to say, these are kids who have changed their lives, because all of a sudden, they had somebody care enough to tell them that they could succeed and to help them do it.

Three
Success Comes in Many Forms

Lois Silverman
CRA Managed Care, Inc.

In 1978, at age thirty-eight, Lois Silverman decided to start her own business. Not only was she starting her venture later in life than most entrepreneurs, but she also was entering the workers' compensation claims business, a male-dominated bastion where few if any women had had the fortitude to compete. Having worked as a full-time nurse, raised two children, and been unable to shake the undeniable feeling that she could change the world, Silverman ignored the daunting odds and started Comprehensive Rehabilitation Associates (CRA). She built her Boston-based company into the nation's largest privately held national provider of injury management and cost containment services. Without any blueprint or mentor to guide her, Silverman rented office space in Boston and began selling. She recalls handing out personal calling cards that said, "Mrs. Norman Silverman," and writing on each one: "Please give me a chance." From this inauspicious start, she built CRA into an $80-million, highly profitable business before deciding in the mid-1990s to take the company public, sell it, and then move on to other challenges. After CRA, Silverman started The Commonwealth Institute, an organization of women executives and entrepreneurs who help mentor other women in business.

In 1978, I started my own business with $20,000 in savings, my personal business cards, and a belief that I could be better at this than anyone else in the industry. I had a husband and two school-age children at the time, and some people thought I was crazy trying to do it all. But I had to do this. I was driven really. It was never about money. It was about being the best. I wanted people to say, "Lois Silverman did this." That's what drove me.

Looking back, I understand where this drive came from. My mother died when I was four years old. This was during World War II, and my father was struggling in business to make ends meet. My sister and I actually spent some time during those years at a home for children whose families could not care for them. The whole concept of a large extended Jewish family not able to take care of its children was so foreign to me. But they were all struggling too.

My father remarried shortly thereafter. My sister and I, having lived with two separate families, went to Providence, Rhode Island, to live with my father and his new wife. A few years later, my father died. I was fifteen years old.

I continued to live with my stepmother. Where else could I go? Somewhere around that time I got the attitude that I could do anything I needed to do to survive. When he was dying, my father told me to take care of the family. This is part of what made me who I am as a CEO and as a wife and mother. When I think about taking care, I think about being responsible, about wanting the best. I think about all the things that I missed in my growing years. I've just wanted to make sure that my family had all that I missed.

So I went to work. My first job was in a record store, followed by a hardware store, and then a dress shop. Through it all, I knew that I had to escape from where I was, which was a very unhealthy environment.

I didn't think I'd be able to afford college, so I decided to go to nursing school, which was within my reach. I applied to an organization in Providence called Jewish Orphans of Rhode Island. It gave me $300, which covered my tuition and room and board at Beth Israel Hospital School of Nursing in Boston.

Having had both parents die very young, I chose nursing, because I felt that I was going to save the world in some way. I graduated from nursing school at the top of my class, but I felt even then that my head was somewhere else, more interested in business than nursing. There was something in me that was always questioning, and my nursing school instructors always felt that I was going to do something other than bedside nursing. They told me that, and they were right.

I started out in bedside nursing, and when I got married and had my two children, I stayed at home. I'd been married about seven years, and I remember saying to my husband, "If I don't create something good, I'm going to create havoc."

I answered an ad in the newspaper looking for a nurse interested in working with disabled clients. The company, which is today called Intracorp, was at that time a subsidiary of the Cigna Insurance Company. I was hired on the spot and became a nurse/manager, managing people with workers compensation injuries. My job was to manage these workers comp cases and help get people out of hospitals and back to work more quickly. I was thirty-three years old at the time, and the claims industry was mostly men in their fifties wearing gray flannel suits. Despite what might have been expected at the time, they were more than willing to teach me what I needed to know.

For the first three months, I didn't do anything. I was waiting for them to send work to me. I finally asked when the work would arrive, and I was told that it wouldn't. I needed to go out and get it. So I did. I built a territory in New England to more than $2 million in just about five years, providing what we today call case management services. I talked to injured workers and found out what was stopping them from returning to work. What I realized was that it's neither the medical problem nor the job market that keeps people from returning to work, but the garbage that clutters up people's lives and doesn't let them move on.

How can you give up your workers compensation remuneration if, in fact, you have nothing to replace it? You count on it. You may be fearful of reinjuring yourself or angry at your employer. Or you may be thinking that the fellow down the street is home and receiving workers compensation, why shouldn't you be compensated for your injury as well? These are the feelings you encounter in this work. So I became a nurse coordinator, social worker, and job counselor all in one, in order to initiate a return to work.

In 1978, I got a new boss and he was really not too pleased with my assertiveness and success. I called my husband one afternoon in October and said, "I think I'm going to have to leave the company." I'd thought I was going to spend the rest of my life at that company. I loved it. But it just wasn't meant to be.

I didn't know what I was going to do. When I was walking around in the mall one day, someone I knew stopped me and said, "I thought you were working." And I said, "No, I'm going to start a company." It just flew out of my mouth. I hadn't even verbalized it to myself.

So I started this company. I asked one of the vocational counselors that I'd hired at my last job, a man named Don Larson, if would join me. We got along very well, and I thought that he was somebody I'd like to work with. If I really wanted it to grow, it couldn't be a one person operation, I thought at the time. There would have to be two of us. He was a Mr. Inside, and I was always Mrs. Outside.

So, armed with my little personal cards that said "Mrs. Norman Silverman" I told the world that I had started my company. I made up fifty cards and gave them to fifty of my customers from my former company. In short order, I had more work than I could handle. I opened offices in Boston and Portland, Maine. The work flowed in.

Not surprisingly, this had an impact on my family. My husband is an engineer, and he runs his own company as well—a sheet metal company that is a family business. It was clear from the outset that this was more than something to keep me busy. I was going to put my heart and soul into this.

It wasn't as if this was anything new. I'd been the equivalent of a regional vice president for five years by that time, and I traveled constantly. I was living in a male environment, and I was out in the evenings for dinner. My children had been latchkey kids since they were six and nine years old and had grown used to coming home by themselves, letting themselves into the house, and watching TV or doing homework until we got home.

My husband and I split the child care. If there was a child who was sick, my husband did the pickup at school, because it was difficult to reach me. But if there was a play or a game at school, I got there. If you ask my children today if they missed out on anything, they'll say they had a great time, because they didn't have a mom sitting on their back saying, "Did you do the homework?" Today, I look back and wonder, "My God, how did I do this with two young children?" But it never seemed to be an issue. Everybody in the neighborhood had children. People watched out for each other.

The real trauma came when I'd been in business for just a few months and told my husband that I would not be content with Massachusetts and Maine, the two locations I'd started with. New England wasn't fertile enough for me, and I wanted to go to

New York. At that point, he raised the roof. "How are you going to deal with that?" he demanded. I just said, "Have I let you down yet? I'm going to keep going." And I did. I had a drive to succeed, and I was going to prove to someone, whoever it was, that I was the best there was in this business.

I think if you were to speak to my children, they would say they had it all. We have a very unusual family. The kids came first. It was never an issue. But I had this boundless energy, this ability to see something up ahead and go for it, and I think that made me who I am.

I left the house before 6:30 A.M. and returned after 7:00 P.M. on most days. Saturday was set aside for my children. Whether it was shopping with my daughter or taking my son to the movies, it was kids' time. I did not have any help. So Sunday was set aside for cooking for the week and doing laundry. We had a social life too. It sounds crazy, but when I look back on it, the only person who missed out on anything was me.

I missed out on being a woman, on sharing time with women friends. I had women friends, but I didn't know how to spend time with them. I couldn't sit and just talk with a woman. If I had a friend over, I'd have to be in the kitchen cooking or doing something, because time was so compressed.

I knew two things. I knew that I was missing something, but I also knew that what I was missing took work. It took work to develop those friendships. It took work to have luncheons and go shopping. I didn't want luncheons. I wanted to do something that would feed me, feed my soul, and work seemed to do it.

We built the business quickly. In five years, we had offices in thirteen states. I was traveling from state to state to state, trying to maintain the quality of service, trying to keep the market going, trying to infuse people with my enthusiasm.

I remember when we opened up our Florida office and I went to see the manager there. I said, "How many marketing calls have you made?" He replied, "Maybe two or three." I said, "What's holding you up?" He said, "Well, I've got to manage." I said, "There's nothing to manage unless you have the business. Get out there and market." I went out with him for two days, and we saw fifty accounts.

Over the years, I've made up my "Lois-isms," statements that apply to our business. I have one that says, "Man didn't fall to the top of the mountain." Everyone wants to be a manager. Every injured worker wants to be a brain surgeon. We would say, "It's wonderful to think about what you'd like to do in the future, but we need to focus in now on getting you back to work." I have this big plaque in my house that says, "A journey of a thousand miles begins with a single step." With that I say, "Success comes in many forms." To some, success may be making a million dollars, but to me it is getting to the first 10 cents. That's success.

If you are working with an injured worker and can convince that person to get out of bed and get dressed every morning, that's success. It's not necessarily just about getting them back to work. I always believed that people want to be productive. People talk about workers compensation and about people malingering, but I don't believe that a man starts out malingering. He was working the day he was injured, and there was a work ethic there. Something happened along the way that stopped it. Our job was to help find a way back to that work ethic.

I'd like to say that everything went like clockwork and that everybody flourished and lived happily ever after, but it wasn't quite that simple. I struggled and obsessed with my role as CEO, feeling responsible for all my workers and my customers. I felt like Dorothy in the *Wizard of Oz*. Or I'd feel like the cowardly lion. Sometimes I felt my heart wasn't big enough or like my brain wasn't big enough.

I also recognized how lonely it is at the top and how lonely it is being a woman. I really enjoyed talking to men, because they brought the business side, the pragmatic side to the table, but I always thought, "Why shouldn't women be able to do that?"

I kept a pen, a magic marker, and a pad of paper by my bed. At two o'clock in the morning, I'd get up and write notes. "Did you remember to call this account?" "This employee is worried about his medical reimbursement." "This employee is not working full time." "This doctor is disgruntled."

I had employees that gave their hearts and souls to injured workers every single day, and it was my responsibility to give back to them. So, at some point in my career, rather than being focused on what was at the end of the road, I became more like a tree with branches, covering everybody, watching out for everybody.

I drove myself so hard and so long for fifteen years that in the early 1990s, I became ill with a heart arrhythmia. I think it was just all those years of intense involvement that just crashed down on me, and I couldn't do it any more.

At that point I was traveling constantly. I remember my physician saying, "Lois, until we get you stabilized, you can't go on a plane." I said, "Maybe now is the time to start looking at what I'm going to do for the rest of my life." I also had a son who came into the business. Michael was twenty-three. He worked there for two years, and one day I said to him, "Mike, is this the place where you want to spend the rest of your life?" He said, "No." I said, "Then why are you here?" He said, "Because I thought this is where you wanted me to be." After that, I felt freed up to create an exit plan.

It was an extremely emotional time. I thought, I've got to make some plans for my family. Here I had this huge company—at that time we had $80 million in revenues—but we had no liquidity. I worried day to day whether I was going to wake up the next morning. I really had this fear of dying. Both my parents had died so young. My mother was thirty-four. My father was forty-seven.

The overwhelming feeling was, "How do I get this company in order so that I can leave something substantial?" I remember thinking that I needed someone to help me take care of myself. At the same time, I realized I didn't have the answers. I learned a lot by the seat of my pants. I'd go to Barnes & Noble and buy twenty business books at one shot. When I teach women CEOs today, I say, "That's why you need a peer group and a mentor, because everybody expects you to have the answers—and who do you turn to when you don't?"

In the end, I sold 49 percent of the business to a venture capital firm, and then I took it public. Upon a subsequent merger, I stepped down as chairwoman and CEO. My partner, Don Larson, was angry that I chose to exit this way, and eventually, he left the company as well. The new company has not done as well. The stock is down, an effect of the whole health care sector being down.

I feel sad in some ways. I feel sad that a company that I built, that was as strong as it once was, is not recognized and doesn't have the kind of strength that it deserves. It's still a very good company. I feel sad that the employees who've invested so much in this are worried about what will happen in the future. It is difficult, because I built something very good, and what has happened to the company since then is not within my control.

All you can do is recognize all the good things. Losing a company is like mourning the death of a family member. You get angry and upset and don't quite believe it is happening. Then at some point, you come to some peace about the fact that you built something good, and you let go of the losses.

The bigger question was how was I going to feel when I was no longer a CEO or chairman of the company? That was my identity. Without that, who was I going to be? I hadn't learned how to play golf or bridge or have lunch with the women. What was my life going to be about? That's really why I sit on sixteen corporate and nonprofit boards today, to make sure that there isn't going to be a minute to worry about whether I'm doing the right thing. Now I can pick and choose and do the things that are most important to me.

I believe I was so needy because of my childhood, and this was a way of giving to myself, to *me*. Building the company, having children and a happy marriage, building friendships. All those things were an affirmation that I was an okay person. People have told me that I have some amazing strengths. I say, I just took my strengths and built upon them. A lot of people simply don't do that.

Four
A Highway to Success

Richard Teerlink
Harley-Davidson, Inc.

Harley-Davidson, the $2-billion, Milwaukee-based motorcycle manufacturer, is one of the great turnaround stories in American business history. In the mid-1980's, the last American motorcycle maker was on the edge of bankruptcy. A group of Harley executives that had mortgaged their homes and bought the company back from the AMF Corporation were intent on saving the vaunted Harley brand. Through determined leadership and business acumen, they turned the beleaguered company into a highly profitable success story. Rich Teerlink joined Harley-Davidson as chief financial officer in 1981 and was one of the principal architects of the turnaround. He became CEO in 1989 and lead Harley through a remarkable resurgence that culminated in a string of record-setting quarters in sales and earnings. Under Teerlink, the Harley brand gained such cachet that a whole new group of customers emerged and Harley sales soared. In fact, because of the demand and the company's focus on quality, the waiting list for a Harley got to be as long as two years. Even Teerlink's wife had to wait a year to buy him a Harley for his birthday. Teerlink left the CEO job in 1997 and became chairman. He retired as chairman in 1999, but he remains a director of the company and rides with customers as often as possible.

I don't think my story is very exciting, even though the company and its success is extremely exciting. Simply put, I don't believe in the CEO hero. I think CEOs get in trouble because they try to have their name out front and lead the charge, and leading the charge doesn't do a damn bit of good unless you have followers who believe in the mission. If you lead the charge and don't have followers who believe, all you get is compliance. I don't think any CEO is so smart that he or she can demand all the right things of all employees.

I really don't think employees care that much about big, Patton-like CEO speeches and being inspired with lofty goals. They care about whether they are going to have jobs, whether they are going to like coming to work, whether they are going to walk into an awful or a nice environment, and whether they are forced to be compliant to keep their jobs.

I know that many CEOs like the limelight and the credit, but I try not to be that way. That's who I am. I grew up with parents who believed in people. My parents were immigrants from Holland who came to the United States in the 1920s. My dad was a tool and dye maker and an entrepreneur. He went into his own business in 1946 and was very, very successful. He was successful believing in people. All along the way, he believed in people. Titles weren't the important thing.

I was twelve when he went into business. He made his business partners multimillionaires, but he left with very little, because that's the way he was.

He loved to offer counsel. He'd tell me, "When you become a supervisor, your whole life changes, because you're now no longer just worrying about you, you're worrying about all those people who work with you and for you. You're the most important man to them, because you control their lives: whether they have a job, whether they don't have a job, and how much they get paid.

"So it changes how you look at the world. You start to care about others. Do the job you've got better than anyone else can do it and you'll get another job. Worry about your next job and you'll probably get fired from your current job."

He had no financial training. He was president and chairman of his company, and every day when he walked into his office, he had three numbers on his desk: cash in the bank, what people owed him, and what he owed people. He walked out into the plant, and he knew about inventory; he could look at it and see it. He was a very effective manager. He taught me early that cash is very important. Without cash, you can't make any payments. So forget about profits; generate cash. If your company is run well today, the only way you get cash is from profits. Today it's in vogue to look at cash. But my father was thinking about that fifty years ago. My mother also taught me a lot. She was a firm believer in the Golden Rule. That was her standard.

Even though my dad was a CEO, I never thought that I would become one as well. As my dad said, "Do the job you've got, then you'll get another job." I never had to look for a job until 1981, when I decided I wanted to leave Herman Miller, the office furniture supplier, because my family didn't want to live in western Michigan. Two friends told me about the Harley buyout and their search for a chief financial officer. They arranged an interview with me, and the rest is history.

I joined something special. In 1980, thirteen Harley executives had mortgaged their homes and put their entire careers on the line to buy the company back from the AMF Corporation. I came on board just after the buyout and became CFO. It was a daunting task to save Harley, but we all felt like we were on a mission.

We worked long hours and many days a week. We were all deeply involved and committed to the total business. No one sat around thinking great thoughts. We all focused on our areas of responsibility to insure that Harley would not die.

In fact, the entire time was an adrenaline-pumping experience. It required a total commitment and a new way of thinking about doing business. There is nothing as intense and difficult as being on the brink of bankruptcy, as we were in December 1985. Having pulled it out, with literally hours to go before the end of the year, we learned a lot about adversity.

Far more intense was the recognition that we were in the process of changing our very culture as a company. We recognized that the top-down, command-and-control approach was evolving into a more people-driven culture. We also had some very tough competitors out there, and we had to keep coming to market with new and better products. We had to keep a strong relationship with our dealers, and we had to continue to focus on quality and reliability in our manufacturing turnaround.

Now keep in mind that we refinanced ourselves to get out of our bankruptcy problem in December 1985, and we went public in July 1986. Only in America can you go from bankruptcy to a public offering in six months. As you can imagine, it was pretty intense. We were driven by the thought that though we were out of the danger of bankruptcy, we had to make sure that we had a structure and that we had things designed to inspire people, both inside and outside the company, to do great things.

I learned a great deal in the eight years at Harley before I became the CEO. We had to remember where we came from, for example. Harley had been a star before—the company was founded in 1903 and had been highly successful—and then it fell. Why did it fall? It fell because of leadership. The leadership wasn't paying attention to the fundamentals. You always have to focus. "Are we doing the right thing? Are we helping the employees do the right thing?" The leader's job isn't to be out there getting gold stars but to help create a fantastic environment.

Because there is no CEO school to teach you how to run the show, you are always trying new things. For example, we moved to an employee-driven culture. For many leaders, this is a fearful proposition, because they feel a loss of power. For me, this actually supported the belief that you *get* power by releasing power.

I believe there's an intrinsic motivation within everybody, and a leader's challenge is to get at that. You get at that by showing people that they're important, not in a phony way, but by your actions. Max DePree, the CEO of Herman Miller, frequently said, "Leaders, by their actions, not by their words, set the tone in the organization."

For example, in 1988, we made our first agreement with the unions to work more cooperatively as we went forward, and that was a watershed, because while we had a good relationship with the bargaining units, this was a true commitment to a joint vision for the future. It brought the Wisconsin bargaining units together with management to share and create a plan that would further identify what we wanted the organization to be able to do. Together, we wrote statements that expressed our commitment to things such as quality products, and then we worked for the next few years to make it happen.

Then in 1991, the largest union decided to discontinue formal participation. That was a little discouraging, but we kept pursuing our goal. We recognized that we had moved to a new level and that at that level, the things we had learned along the way—conflict resolution,

44

problem solving, how to have dialogue, how to listen—those things would never go away. We had done something crucial; we had laid the groundwork. In 1996, that union, known as PACE, voted for a new partnering agreement. Now we have partnering agreements with all six unions. So that was significant.

I also learned that you never stop learning. I learned to ride a motorcycle when I was forty-six years old. I discovered it is a great stress reducer. When you're on a motorcycle, you are not hooked up and wired to something. You're driving through this beautiful country of ours, and it is inspiring. It clears your head. It feels great. So when you go back to work, your mind is clear, the clutter is gone, and you can focus on what's really important.

I was lucky, because we spend a lot of time with our customers at H.O.G. (Harley Owners Group) rallies and other events. I didn't have to find time and say, "Damn it, let me go for a ride on a motorcycle." Such events included two anniversary rides from San Francisco to Milwaukee. My wife and I still ride. Riding is part of the fabric of the company.

One of the positive things about Harley is that you have an opportunity to share your business with your family, because Harley is a big family. My wife Ann became a very integral part of representing the company out in public and very involved in the H.O.G. rallies. Like me, she went around talking to customers, taking notes on a little pad of paper, coming back and saying, "These are some of the things that I heard."

I've received a great deal of credit for my years as CEO. When I retired in 1999, I had two fantastic rewards. I specifically asked not to have any retirement parties. It's just not my style. But the dealers at our annual winter dealer's meeting arranged for a farewell party for me anyway. They initiated it on their own. There were hundreds of people in the room. The host, a Harley executive, said some nice things. And then they passed the microphone around the audience, and any number of dealers got up and said some very nice things about me, about how we are a value-driven company and how much we care about the customer. They said, "Thank you for bringing us here," and presented me with a beautiful sculpture of an eagle, carved in Italy. They've never done that before for anyone. I was very moved by this.

At another meeting of company leaders, I just showed up to say "thank you" for a great ride, and they again said some very nice things about me and presented me with a specially commissioned sculpture of our circle organization concept and a huge banner signed by the attendees. Both events were very emotional for me. I am not usually at a loss for words, but I had a great deal of difficulty speaking on both occasions. It is an unbelievable feeling to know that your efforts have made a difference in so many lives.

What I really believe is important for me, more than accolades, is that as we as a company moved to a new level, with the business, the market, and relationships, these values became embedded in the organization. They're not embedded because of me, they're embedded because people decided that's what they wanted, and they took the ball and ran with it.

My feeling is this didn't start when I became CEO. It all started in 1903. There's a long heritage of happy Harley stories that people have. The only thing that Harley had to do was make products that work, then give people an opportunity to share, and keep doing it.

So while it's a very simple to say, it's very hard to make it happen all the time. It only happens if you've got dedicated employees, dealers, and suppliers, who know where the company is going and believe in it.

What I've learned as CEO is that what's really important is not you. What's really important is the long-term viability of the company. The hope is that where we go from here is embedded in the system. I just read an analyst report about Harley-Davidson, and it really made me feel good, because it said the leadership transition from me to Jeffrey Bleustein, who is now chairman and CEO, was absolutely seamless. That's the way it should be.

The big risk when you get a new CEO is that they've got to put their stamp on the company. Many times this means making unnecessary dramatic and unsettling changes. As Jeff and I said when he became CEO in 1997, Jeff will do things differently than I will. I do things differently than Jeff does. What's important is that we share the same objectives: to serve the customer, to serve the employees, to develop mutually beneficial relationships with all of our stakeholders. In these things, we are alike. So in the end, it really doesn't matter who is CEO.

Five
A CEO Because He Can

Steve Tobias
Wolpac, Inc.

*In 1986, at age thirty-two, Steve Tobias started a company in a
small shop in Detroit making shipping containers for automotive
parts. Armed with a simple notion that he could build these durable
and returnable containers better than the competition, Tobias'
business grew into a $15-million enterprise called Wolpac, with 150
employees and 100,000 square feet of factory space. Despite a deep
commitment to his company and his employees, a commitment that
profoundly affected his own marriage and family, Tobias sold the
company to a supplier of automotive parts in 1996. Now at age
forty-five, Tobias has celebrated his twenty-fifth wedding
anniversary and is already a grandfather. Though he is now
running a successful day trading business on the Internet, Tobias
knows that his decade with Wolpac was the culmination of his CEO
experience, bringing with it deep feelings of accomplishment and
failure, joy, and sorrow.*

Every year, I took my management team and other employees on a
whitewater-rafting trip in West Virginia. In October 1994, we were just
returning from a full day of rafting when I received a call from my
wife to tell me that my building was on fire. I immediately called the
fire department in Detroit and they told me that the north wall of the
building had just collapsed.

In the morning, I took the first plane home. I arrived at the
building and it was a total loss. Everything was gone. The fire had
started in the kitchen and spread quickly. Seeing the building, I had
that same feeling as when you are speeding and a police car pulls up
behind you—that big, empty, sinking feeling that you get in the pit of

your stomach. I thought, "How am I going to get through this? What am I going to do with all of the employees?" We had about 100 employees at the time, and I had no idea what I was going to do.

About thirty employees were standing in the parking lot when I arrived wondering, "What's going to happen?" Incredibly, a few competitors drove up while we were standing there and said to my employees, "We've got jobs for you guys." It upset me, but I didn't have to react; my employees kicked their butts out of there fast.

I organized a staff meeting the following day at a local hotel and told everybody that they would continue to be paid whether they were working or not. Some of the local area companies offered me space for a few employees. One fellow across the street offered me about 1,500 square feet of space where I was able to set up a few welders. I told some of our CAD designers who had computers at home that I'd like them to work from home. The Chrysler Corporation, which was one of our main customers, offered me some office space for a few of our project managers who were working on Chrysler projects and rushed to have telephones installed for us. We ended up scattered in about eight buildings.

It was a disaster financially, but it really pulled people together. Everybody pitched in to help. Amazingly, we actually grew and added business during this time. For me, it was an unbelievable experience. In front of the employees, I was the staunch leader who said, "I can handle anything and get everything done." Then I'd go home and cry and wonder what was really going to happen. I put on the face that I felt I was supposed to put on for my employees. I didn't let them see fear or anxiety. At home, though, I showed that fear and anxiety to my wife Kathy, and she supported me and patted my back. Of course, while I was at work, she was home, worried and crying. She couldn't show fear to me, because I needed her support.

My wife has always been an incredible supporter, even when Wolpac was three years old and we were not doing well. I was working 100 hours a week. I was not taking home a paycheck so I could pay other people. My wife was home with our two girls, and she was always very supportive of me.

I once had a really good business opportunity—I was offered equity in a very large business—and she said, "You can't take that, because you have all of these people counting on you. You can't look

out just for yourself and us, you have to look out for them, too."
Shortly after that, we got a couple of very large contracts that kept us
going for another year. Then, we got even bigger contracts, and we
were making good money. But at the time that she urged me to stay in
the business, it was a very dark, dismal time.

We recovered from the fire as well and eventually moved into our
new space. I learned some valuable lessons. For one thing, I learned to
distrust insurance companies! But seriously, I learned that employees,
like everybody else, need to have something positive to focus on. I
also learned the importance of working as a team. So, from that point
forward, we spent more time making sure that everybody knew that
we were a team and were performing together, not separately.

We thought the team concept was already part of our culture, but
the ordeal made us even more aware of its importance, so we
emphasized it more in our daily operations. That emphasis helped the
company grow 50 percent over the next year and a half.

These are tough tests for a CEO. You are torn between what you
must do for you and your family, especially early on, and what you
must do for your employees and the business. You have two masters.
Your response and how you handle these situations comes from the
character that you've developed over your lifetime. I've always
believed that most people have great character except when things
get difficult. The time to evaluate yourself is when it is painful and
really tough. Did you live up to your character values? Did you
maintain your own integrity? If your answer is yes, that's when you
have respect for yourself.

For example, I had a customer call me and say that he wanted me to
fire a woman who worked for me. She was a project manager, and the
customer had asked her to complete this report—about 200 pages—for
the following day. She stayed very late, finished the report, gave it to
him, and he found one cell in a spreadsheet that was wrong. So he
wanted me to fire her. He told me if I didn't fire her, he was going to
pull all his business. If he pulled all his work, I'd be out of business.

I said, "No, I'm not firing her. She's a good employee and this was
not her fault; what she did was reasonable. She's always given 100
percent effort. I'm not firing her." He replied, "Give me cancellation
charges for my program, I'm going to cancel it." I said "Fine." We spent

the next three days getting his cancellation charges together and gave them to him, but he never followed through. He was bluffing.

People might wonder if I was ready to sacrifice the entire business on her behalf. The answer is, I wasn't sacrificing it for her, I was sacrificing it to maintain my own integrity and my own values and my company's values. There are certain lines that you do not cross. That's one of those lines. You don't demean an individual for personal profit.

I told myself that if we did what was right, we'd survive. That was always our motto: "If you do what's right, everything will work out in the end." If you fail, you still have your values and your character. If you do the wrong thing, whether you succeed or fail, ultimately you are personally still a failure.

I've never worked for big corporations, so I can't say whether this attitude prevails everywhere. I've always worked for small companies or on my own. I would like to think that everybody that I've worked for thought like that, but I know they didn't.

Of course, sometimes doing the right thing is simply not enough. About a year after the fire, I had an employee die on the job and that was the most devastating thing that's ever happened to me. She was one of our truck drivers, and she got into an accident during working hours and died. I felt very responsible for that, because first and foremost, she worked for me; she was my responsibility.

She was retrieving our small pickup truck from the dealership, where it had just been serviced. It had all new brakes, tires, everything. We always kept up everything, and we always pushed safety. She just wasn't paying attention and ran straight into the back of a stopped truck. She was a woman with six children, and I was the only one at the hospital with her all day. She died two weeks later.

I paid for the funeral. Two of her sons were in prison, so I paid the state $3,000 to allow them to attend the funeral in chains accompanied by deputies. The three youngest moved in with their grandmother, and I gave them some money to tide them over. The funeral was at a black Baptist church in downtown Detroit, I and about thirty-five of the Wolpac employees went to the church and to the funeral.

I felt guilty, because I knew she wasn't the best truck driver, and she wasn't the brightest woman I'd ever met. We also had problems with an ex-boyfriend of hers. These are the CEO decisions that make it so lonely at the top. She needed the job badly and she worked really hard, but if I were a CEO looking at this in strictly business terms, I would have fired her. I asked myself, "Should I let her stay on the job?" But I didn't have any other job for her, and I felt guilty about that.

Being with her kids through all that was extremely tough for me. I started thinking about leaving the business altogether. I thought, "I want to get out. I'm leaving. I can't do this." At that point, I started therapy and realized a lot about myself. What I know is that certain beliefs that I hold are the result of my own background and experience. They are etched pretty deep inside me.

I was born in the inner city of Detroit. My parents were married very young. My father was eighteen and my mother was seventeen. I was born just after they got married. We lived in a two-family flat with my cousins living upstairs. When I was about seven years old, we moved to Harper Woods, which is a small, one-square mile suburb of Detroit.

My father, by today's standards, was an alcoholic. He worked construction jobs and then drank a lot, and he left when I was about fifteen. After he left, I always worked and paid room and board. Most of my values came from my mother and from watching a lot of television, which sounds crazy, but it's true. I loved television, especially the shows where one heroic leader had to meet the challenge. I went to therapy for a couple of years, and the therapist said that I got a lot of my tribal mentality from television.

I went to therapy to deal with some underlying issues that I have being a CEO. Basically, I like to be the leader of my tribe. My employees are my tribe and I'm the leader of the tribe, and that's where I get my self worth. It's kind of like an old John Wayne movie— the sacrifice, the do or die thing. I was John Wayne or Vic Morrow in the television show "Combat."

My mother had an extremely strong work ethic, and she also had extremely high expectations of me. She is a tough lady. She instilled some strong values in me such as respecting other people, not making fun of other people, and standing up for your friends. She taught me to do what's right, even if it meant being beaten up by bullies at school. If you make a commitment to go to work for somebody, you work for them. She used to tell me, "Just because your girlfriend is all upset doesn't mean you get to take off from work. You've made a commitment; people are counting on you to live up to that commitment."

A CEO Because He Can

So I learned early about making my own way. I've paid for everything since I was little. I worked and saved for my bicycle. I bought my first car for $500. If there was anything I wanted, I had to earn the money to pay for it. I've worked full time since I was fourteen.

Like my mother, I got married very young, at age twenty, and that was a strong motivator. I had to support my wife and pretty soon after a daughter and then another daughter. I started working in a machine shop for $4.50 an hour and worked my way up. Our idea of a night out on the town was a stop at Tubby's Submarine Shop, which had a two-for-one special on Friday night and half off on a theater ticket. I persevered. I was working 80 to 100 hours a week at that job. I learned that if you work your ass off, good things will come.

Unfortunately, I gave up a lot during that time as well. I had my work and, later, my business, and Kathy had our family, and that was her domain. I was not allowed to have a lot of say as to how to raise the kids. It wasn't like "Father Knows Best," where the mother said, "Wait until your father gets home." It was: "When your father gets home, he doesn't get to say a thing."

For a while that worked for us. But then there came a time when I didn't have to spend as much time on the business and I wanted to participate at home, and that caused a lot of problems between me and my wife. We had several very bad years. I felt like it was not my family but her family. She would say that I wasn't there when they needed me, and I couldn't come in and make changes now.

I suspect other CEOs have experienced this. I can't say that I have regrets about it, because people are what they are. I don't know if I could have been happy not doing what I do. I know it's a lot to give up. I know that especially now that I have a grandson. I spend every Thursday afternoon with him, and everyone else has to be gone so that it's just my grandson and me.

My relationship with my daughters today is excellent, and I think that's because there was a difference between their experience and when I was little and my father was gone. I knew that he was gone because he was drinking. He'd come home with a smashed up car, and all my friends knew he'd been drinking. For my kids, it was different. I didn't go out at night. I didn't go partying. When I was not working, I was home. I think they respected that, even though they didn't like it.

But my wife was a great mother and gave a tremendous amount of time to my kids.

When I decided to sell my business in 1996, I found I needed therapy even more. I'd been offered a deal and decided to allow my key employees to vote on whether to sell or not. I said, "The offer is okay for me, I'm willing to take it, but if you don't want to sell, then I don't sell."

When they voted to sell, it really hurt. Even though my friends and all of my business associates said, "Hey, this is a good deal. Take it and go," I still felt betrayed and that I was being left behind while they moved on. I felt as if they didn't trust me to take the company further, that they'd rather go with these other people.

Obviously, I didn't have to put it to a vote, but I felt that it was affecting their lives more than mine. I'd be getting the money and be set financially. I just thought it was my job to support their security. I didn't think that it would be fair for me to take the money and say, "Tough, guys, I'm out of here."

One part of me knew it was smart to take the money and give my family financial security, but on the other side, this was my tribe. To me, they seemed to be saying, "Hey, we want a new chief. You're no longer good enough." This was devastating for someone who got all his personal self-worth from being the chief. Here was everybody saying they didn't want me to be the chief. In fact, that's not what they were saying, but that's what I perceived.

After they voted, I went to a bar and got drunk—and I don't drink. I didn't tell anybody where I was going, I just went and sat at the bar until I passed out. My general manager found me. He went driving around from bar to bar looking for me, and he found me and took me home. The next morning, I got a tattoo. I was still drunk when I woke up. I left the house really early, and driving to work, I saw a tattoo parlor and got a dolphin tattooed on my right shoulder.

I don't know why I did that—probably defiance. I thought, "I'm not part of the business world anymore, why not?" I was still angry and hurt. It took about six months of intensive, two-hour therapy sessions to feel better. Starting my new business and bringing some of my key managers with me made me feel a lot better.

I knew that a lot of things were on my mind: the departure from the business, the fear of taking new risks, the problems with my wife about the family. In fact, the issues with my wife were the toughest of all.

My wife and I are working really hard on our marriage, and it is paying off, but we came close to divorce on a few occasions. I actually went to see a divorce attorney one time, because my wife and I were having a very hard time and she had asked me to leave. I eventually found out she asked me to leave because she thought I was going to leave anyway, so she wanted to ask me before I told her.

The divorce attorney interviewed me for an hour and a half. He asked me a long list of questions about the marriage. When he was finished he said, "I don't understand. Why do you want to get divorced? It doesn't add up." I said, "I don't know." He said, "Well, maybe you ought to think about this a lot more."

I went home and told my wife. That's when she told me that she just thought I was going to leave anyway. I said, "I don't want to leave. I want this to work." We started trying to work on it. I realized the same issues would arise with anybody I was with, so why lose the history? Why throw that all away? It's all about working at it.

I go home now and have to catch myself sometimes, because I know what I'd be willing to do for my employees: how much I'm willing to listen, how much real emotional energy I put into them and the work. When I get home, I want to go and sit on the back porch and watch television. I'll be sitting back there watching television or reading a book, and I'll look at my wife through the glass doors and see her watching the same show or reading a book. I think to myself, "Why in the hell am I sitting out here by myself?"

I actually have to force myself to say, "Get up, go in there and sit with her. Even if you don't talk, just read and be together. Instead of running away, go to her." With all of the emotions that you've given out all day, it's sometimes hard to continue giving those out at home. You've got to learn to balance that and to pace yourself at work, so that you can be there at home.

People ask me why I do the things I do. I just think I do what I do because I can. CEOs can make the decision, and other people can't. I have had partners over the years. All of my partners have left, because they just couldn't handle the pressures of not knowing where the next pay check was coming from, robbing Peter to pay Paul, the self sacrifice and hours, and waking up in the middle of the night. I do all of those things. They do bother me, but they don't bother me like they bother them. I can still continue to function.

Steve Tobias

When I make a decision, I don't know if it's the right decision. In general they turn out to be right. I just kind of shoot from the hip and say, "Here's what I do and believe in, and I'll fight for this until somebody proves that I'm wrong." It doesn't mean I'm always right, but in general, I'm right. That's why I'm successful.

I think people climb mountains because they can; they run in marathons, because they can. I'm a CEO, because I can. This is just what I do and what I am.

55

Six

A Corporate Divorce

Judith A. Armstrong
ADA Technologies, Inc.

Judy Armstrong, the founder and CEO of ADA Technologies, Inc. in Englewood, Colorado, has both a masters and doctorate degree in mathematics, but her years of running ADA have spawned an intense interest in a different field: psychology. ADA Technologies is a $4-million, federally funded, for-profit company with thirty employees that serves as an incubator for research and development on small businesses that eventually are spun off into separate endeavors. Having cofounded the company with three partners, including her husband at the time, Armstrong is the only founder who has stayed with the company. The CEO experience has been marked by a painful divorce, periods of self-doubt, and the resulting belief that women have a contribution to make to corporate America and that they need to mentor each other far more in business than they currently do.

Majoring in math put me in a unique position. As an undergraduate and a graduate student, I was usually the only female in a room full of men. I spent a lot of the early years of my career in that position as well, and I chose to ignore the implications of that. Some women seemed to stress over it early on in their careers. You just have to numb yourself to it or block it out.

So I went charging down the path and paid no attention to the fact that I was the only woman, although it was there. I also knew that I had traits that let me work well in that situation. I liked the camaraderie and I had a sense of humor. I was good at being well accepted by rooms full of men. The reality of being a woman in a male-dominated profession, however, soon caught up with me.

57

Before founding ADA, I worked for the space and communications group within the Hughes Aircraft Company for eight years. I saw an opportunity that I wanted to pursue, and I went to management and said, "I want this opportunity." They said, in effect, "We'll need to bring in somebody from headquarters in California, because this is too big an opportunity, and you're not senior enough." That made it clear to me what my future there would be like.

At the time, I had a running partner, Anita, and we would run at lunch time and talk. One day, Anita said, "Why don't we find something to do together? We are already doing software and algorithms. Why don't we find something we can do at home with personal computers?" We agreed and set about finding an opportunity. We quickly found a customer who wanted a software package for timing triathlons.

At the same time, my husband Jim and one of his colleagues, Mike, were working at the Denver Research Institute, a government-funded contract research and development organization that was part of the University of Denver. They came to Anita and me and suggested that we start a business together since we were already heading in that direction.

So the four of us had some meetings and wrote a couple of business proposals. I don't think Anita was ever really convinced that she wanted to participate with anybody else beyond me, and that soon became a dividing point between us. She stayed around for only the first three or four months.

But before she left for good, we formed ADA Technologies, and the four of us decided that I should be president, because we felt there were advantages to a woman-run company if you are doing business with the government.

Anita left soon after, and then we won our first contract with the Environmental Protection Agency. We didn't all leave our jobs immediately. It was a gradual process. It took almost another year before we developed enough business for Jim to join us full time. Unfortunately, the excitement of starting a new business was tempered by our confused marriage.

It's important to point out that we had two small children while we were making this plunge. I had my first child when I was thirty-two and my second at thirty-four. It took a lot of work to get to the point where I was willing to have children. We started the business in 1985 when they were ages six and four.

Unfortunately, there was this sense of competition between my husband and me. When you are starting a company, you want to put in many, many hours to get things done. Somebody had to take care of the kids. So that set up the emotional collision that came later on. All in all, being a mom was great for me. I really liked it, and I still treasure it and identify with "being Mom." But our marriage was already under great strain.

We bootstrapped the company the whole way along, and we spent four years building the business. We had about twenty employees at that point. I tried to focus on the new company, but there had been other events earlier in my marriage that told me that this was just not a marriage made to survive. We were married for twenty-two years by the time we got divorced.

Personal events really triggered things. We had been in therapy for couples, and I was just feeling really unhappy. So I decided I was going to go back to this therapist on my own and not get into couples therapy, because I wanted to work on my own head. A lot of mathematicians have music as a hobby. My hobby is psychology.

Jim was unhappy that I was doing this alone and that he wasn't involved. So he got involved, and we took some personality tests, and we read the results to each other. That was a turning point for me. He strongly denied that the tests reflected who he was, and I thought they reflected him perfectly. A few months later, the therapist was diagnosed with pancreatic cancer and died three weeks later. At that point I said, "Enough. I've been working on this marriage for a long time. This glass is half empty and not half full." Certainly the stress of trying to build a business together was part of it, but it was the personal problems that really ended the marriage.

People ask me how I coped with all this, and I point out that I was the instigator of the divorce. I wasn't a victim. I've never had the energy to let myself be a victim. Being a victim seems so horrible to me that I can't imagine how people make that choice. It was my proactive choice to start a new life. I did things such as lose weight and exercise more. I moved out of the house. I left the kids and my husband in the house. I felt the kids would be better off in their own neighborhood.

A Corporate Divorce

I am a conflict-averse person. I've come a long way in developing my direct communication skills, but moving out of the house was a conflict-averse thing to do, although most women certainly wouldn't have made that choice. I had a sense of relief, because I was no longer trying to juggle all the 24/7 mother commitments along with the business commitments.

Though they lived in a different house, I stayed extremely involved in my children's lives. I still went back and forth all the time, and I saw them often. They'd call me on the phone frequently. Ultimately, my son stayed with his father, and my daughter ended up coming to live with me. My kids grew up in separate households, but it didn't have a serious negative impact on them. They are great kids, and their lives have worked out very well.

There were also extenuating circumstances that had an impact on all this. I was very lucky. I had gotten my Ph.D. at the University of Denver, and I had a wonderful advisor, Norm, through graduate school. We had remained friends. In July of 1991, soon after I had gotten divorced, Norm's wife died tragically in a bicycle accident in Canada. Norm was grieving for his wife, and I was working through my own emotional issues after the divorce. But we started dating in September, and this person, who had been of great significance earlier in my life, was there for me again. Norm and I got married about a year later, and we've been together since then. He continued to be a coach and mentor in a new phase of my life and in a much more intimate way. I'm sure I would have found support somewhere, but here was a significant well of support that I didn't have to wait for or develop. It was just there, almost immediately, when I needed it.

The most gut-wrenching part of the whole experience turned out to be with the business itself. The first strategy was to see if, despite the divorce, we could all work it out and have everybody stay with the business. But that proved to be too difficult. With all the stress of the divorce, I was just going to have to leave ADA. Some of my business friends said, "Judy, you're crazy to do that. You spent all these years building it. You own the right to continue and develop what you can." I realized they were right. My partner Mike and I talked, and I told him I'd really like to stay. He told me that if I left, he'd probably want to sell the business. He didn't think he could be in business with Jim.

So he went and talked to the senior managers within the company, and we had this advisory counsel meeting with outsiders to discuss the company's future. It came down, unfortunately, to Jim or me. Who would stay? Who would leave? Jim presented his view. I presented mine. We both left the room and sat at different ends of the lobby for an hour and a half. Mike stayed and talked with the advisors. Then we went back in, and the advisors presented their recommendation. They offered Jim a settlement and asked me to stay on and run the company. That was the most gut-wrenching event. In essence, we had to get divorced twice, once from the marriage and once from the business.

Jim took it very, very hard. We still have fallout from it, and certainly the business suffered because of all this. Undoubtedly, the business would be significantly different and significantly larger had the three of us been able to pull together. We had employees who became like kids in a divorce, with divided loyalties and friction between people. I give Mike credit for really holding things together. He did a yeoman's job for about a year, while I was off doing whatever it was I was doing back then—exercising, driving kids around, being untethered, and just trying to get my life together.

After the advisory board gave me its support, I never considered leaving again. I just love doing business. It was actually a very positive thing to have to focus on while I was trying to extract myself from the marriage.

Eventually, Mike went on to run ADA Environmental Solutions LLC, a spin-off of ADA that we started. Jim Armstrong now has his own business, and I have ADA. So all three of us are still functioning as entrepreneurs.

With me running ADA alone, in the last couple years, the culture has become more an extension of my personality. ADA has a very polarizing culture. It's similar to what is described in the book, *The HP Way,* which discusses the huge influence that Hewlett and Packard had over the culture of the business. When a company has a really strong culture, the culture rejects people who don't fit. So it becomes self-perpetuating. I certainly think ADA is that way. It's only recently that I've come to view it as an extension of my personality. I see it in the way conflict is handled and in the acceptance of the emotions involved in creativity, leadership, management, and everyday life.

Of course, that has presented problems. I'm living through those every day right now. I have new vice presidents, and I have one particular business area that has had repeat problems. I have some people who are unhappy and have chosen to leave, because now Judy owns the business, and they liked it better when things were more consensual. With multiple owners, there was more consensus building. That kind of informal consensus-building doesn't happen any more.

My goal is to ramp up and increase the growth and get several more $5-million and $10-million spinout businesses. I would like to believe that's not just a pipe dream.

Then there is the issue of whether or not this is more difficult for me because I'm a woman. The honest response is that stuff just doesn't ring true for me. I work hard, but everybody works hard. I'm Irish. I'm really stubborn. There have been periods of doubt, but never to the point that I was going to let those doubts win. They were always something simply to be worked through.

Being a woman CEO and experiencing all the emotions that this job brings makes you understand more about why we react as we do. Recently, somebody told me that the most common reason that women cry is because they are angry. I think that is really true of me. I've cried in the workplace. Because I've spent time in therapy, I've learned not to be embarrassed by my tears. I've owned my own tears and felt that if they needed to come, they were going to come. There was nothing I was going to do about it. So there was no point in being embarrassed about it or thinking that it made me less of who I was because it happened.

Over the last few years, I've softened a little bit and let women's issues drift into my life after having put them at arm's length for protection. I still don't identify with women's organizations. I don't like same-sex stuff, but I recently went to an economic summit for women in Washington, because I was invited to speak by one of the Senators. It was mostly women, and I saw the plight of those women. I saw how hard it is to capitalize women's businesses, because most of them are service based.

I also saw the issues that other women face that just have not had an impact on me. And I met some very powerful women there as well. I did come away with an evolving new interest, which is to get on some boards of directors of some publicly held companies that currently don't have any women on the boards.

When things have gotten tough, I've had moments when I felt like I ought to just recruit somebody to take my place in a couple of years, that I should take my money and run. But I have mentors who counseled me, and I really didn't want to do that. They made me see that I would really be happier here, continuing to build the business. And in the end, I absorbed their comments. I've recommitted myself to ADA and making it go. I'll undoubtedly need my psychology hobby more than ever as I go forward.

Seven

From Welfare to the Executive Suite

Pam Reynolds
Phoenix Textile Corporation

Pam Reynolds represents a true American success story. Forced to go on welfare after an unexpected divorce at age twenty-five, she eventually worked her way up the corporate ladder to become vice president of a successful textile company. Fired in a clash of values with new ownership, she found a partner and launched her own business. Starting from scratch, she built Phoenix Textile Corporation into the largest woman-owned company in St. Louis (until the professional football Rams moved to St. Louis from Los Angeles), with $50 million in annual sales and 120 employees. In 1989, Phoenix Textile received the "Small Business of the Year" award from St. Louis Commerce. In 1993, Reynolds was honored by Inc. magazine as an Entrepreneur of the Year. That same year, Inc. magazine named Phoenix Textile as one of the twenty-five best companies in America to work for. The company has also been featured in several business books for its innovative employee-retention techniques. Fiercely loyal to her employees, Reynolds has found those relationships to be the source of both her crowning successes and her biggest failures.

Growing up in the 1950s, I had what you might call a "June Cleaver" childhood. I came from a middle class Southern family where the father worked, the mom stayed at home, and everyone knew their roles. I expected to grow up raising children and greeting my husband at the door when he came home from work each evening. I never dreamed I would go to work, much less own my own company. But as anyone who has made it to adulthood knows, life often rearranges your dreams without your permission.

65

From Welfare to the Executive Suite

Like many in my generation, I married young. We moved to St. Louis and quickly had three children. When my husband divorced me, I suddenly found myself having to support a family. I had no job skills, no work experience, and not a clue about how to find employment. I did not know which way to turn. My parents in Atlanta offered to take us in, but even though I felt very close to them, I just couldn't go back home. To this day, I can't say why. Perhaps pride drove me, but for some reason I felt compelled to make it on my own.

Unable to find a job, I landed on welfare for eighteen months. I hated it at the time, but welfare ensured that my children had the basic necessities — including health care — until I could get a job. Today, I can look back on that experience with pride, because I proved that the system *can* work, that the taxes we pay really do make a difference in people's lives.

Eventually I secured a job as an entry-level bank clerk, opening new accounts. Three years later, I went to work for one of the bank's customers, a local textile company. I discovered I had an aptitude for sales, and over the next thirteen years, I worked my way up to senior vice president. When the owner died suddenly in a car accident, the new owners named me the next president. Here again, life threw me another curve.

I thought I had it made. I had broken through the glass ceiling; everyone in the company reported to me. I earned a substantial income, enjoyed a very comfortable lifestyle, and all three of my children had enrolled or were about to enroll in private college. What more could I want from life?

However, I soon discovered that the new owners had very different ideas about how to run a business. Having bought the company as a cash cow, they proceeded to milk it for all it was worth. They strung out vendors, found ways not to pay employees, and destroyed much of the good will I had helped to build over the years. Their management philosophy did not jibe with mine, and I let them know in no uncertain terms. I was debating whether or not to renew my contract, when they suddenly called me on the carpet and fired me, saying I wasn't a team player.

Getting fired unleashed a torrent of mixed emotions. At first I felt angry. "You can't fire *me*. This is *my* company! I'm the one who helped make it so successful." Then I felt disappointed and embarrassed. "I spent the last thirteen years pouring myself into this company. How could they not want *me*?" It felt like the ultimate rejection. But they owned the company, so they could do whatever they wanted. Needless to say, we did not part on good terms.

After the initial anger and resentment, I actually felt a great sense of relief. Getting fired freed me contractually, which allowed me to stay in the field I knew without taking a year off. The owners offered me a year's salary to not compete, but I turned it down flat. I live so much by honor that, had I signed such a contract, I wouldn't have tried to find a way around it. I would have abided by it, and lost a year of my life in the process. So after stewing for a few days, I realized that a tremendous opportunity had been laid at my door. Looking back now, I can see that getting fired was one of the best things that ever happened to me.

In truth, the notion of running my own company had begun to form in my mind long before the firing. So when they showed me the door, I never even considered going into another business. Having come up through sales and marketing, I felt like I had the wealth of the company in my heart and in my head. I knew whom to contact, and I knew that if I called, they would answer the phone. If I got on an airplane to visit a customer, I knew the customer would see me. More important, I *knew* I could run a business better than the people who had just dismissed me.

I also had accumulated more than decade's worth of customer understanding and knowledge of how the market operated, and you can't put a price on that experience. If the owners had offered me ten years' salary, I wouldn't have taken it because I had a good reputation and I had friends in the business from coast to coast. I couldn't see any other option except to strike out on my own.

What really sealed the decision was how much money people offered me to work for them. Some of the offers literally stunned me. I thought, "If *they* think you're worth that much, why shouldn't *you* think you're worth it?" Given how others valued my abilities, it didn't take much self-convincing to strike out on my own. I hooked up with my partner, Hal Dean, who was retiring as chairman of the board at Ralston Purina, and together we formed Phoenix Textile.

Despite plenty of confidence in my abilities, I had more than a thimble-full of fear and uncertainty starting out. I may take great risks in business, but I live a fairly conservative lifestyle. I don't strive for the personal Lear jets and the Caribbean getaway homes. Money doesn't drive me; it measures me. But I had three daughters to support, and I wanted to make sure I knew all the costs—physically, emotionally, and financially. I soon learned that you can never fully measure the costs until you get into the driver's seat.

I thought I knew the work of a CEO, because in my role as senior vice president and in my short stint as president, it felt like the company belonged to me. I quickly discovered that I had no idea what the job really entailed. I knew nothing about the financial end of the business—cash flow, balance sheets, inventory terms, relationships with bankers and attorneys, and all that—and I certainly didn't understand the power of using your money well. Worse, I found that as CEO I now had to report to everyone in the company. As senior vice president, I only had to report to one boss. Now, everyone wanted my time.

Perhaps the biggest surprise was watching what I considered my greatest strength become a weakness. I've always focused on building relationships, and people generally liked working for me. I wasn't necessarily easy to work for but always fair and fun. Plus, I had the ability to motivate people. As a CEO, it shocked me deeply to learn how difficult it is to work with employees. What I thought would be a piece of cake has turned into my biggest challenge. It has also turned into the source of my biggest hurts, disappointments, and failures. When it comes to leading employees, I have done it as well and as poorly as could be done. I've felt thrilled, praised, pleased, hurt, trampled, and misunderstood—every emotion you can imagine. Through it all, the hardest lesson I've had to learn is that employees don't want to be treated fairly, they want to be treated equally.

Let me explain. Early on, one of my employees had a problem with her child. I gave her some paid time off and told her not to worry about it, thinking that when she came back, her work would improve without the worry of her family. In less than a month, someone else wanted time off. This situation was repeated several more times before I realized I couldn't treat people according to the situation. I had to treat everyone *exactly* the same way or pay the consequences.

Now, I accept the fact that every decision I make has to apply to the whole company. Otherwise, I end up creating anger, dissension, and jealousy, when all I want is to do right by the employee.

Despite those painful lessons, I still feel like Phoenix Textile is a family. We truly care about our employees, and I want them to feel like they have more than just a place to work. In fact, my goal is to make Phoenix Textile a company where people can retire. That may sound strange in a world where the average worker changes jobs every few years, but I firmly believe that if you treat your people right, they will treat you right. I still have a number of employees who have been with me from the beginning, and many others have worked here twelve, thirteen, or fourteen years. We've also received recognition in a lot of books and publications for our innovative techniques for rewarding and retaining employees. So we've had our share of success in this respect, but it still hurts when someone decides to leave. I feel like I have failed in some way.

Perhaps the biggest challenge for me now is not just to maintain the family environment but to pass it on to the next generation of leadership. I'm not ready to call it quits yet, but I feel like the time has come to start thinking about those succession issues. When I started this business, people said (not to my face), "She's a great saleswoman, but can she run a company?" Now they say, "She's a great leader, but let's see if the company can go on without her." I'm determined to prove that it can. After all, I named the company Phoenix so it would rise without me.

Section Two
Giving Back

Eight

Moving to the Beat of a Different Drummer

Abby Margalith
Starving Students of San Diego, Inc.

*Abby Margalith, forty-five years old, is president of Starving
Students of San Diego, a regional moving company that was
founded by a group of unemployed students in 1973. Today, the
company has more than fifty locations. A separate licensee,
Margalith owns her own location, which handles more than 3,500
moves a year. For the past ten years, Starving Students of San Diego
has extricated battered women and children from their homes and
moved them and their belongings to a safe place without charge.
Although Margalith does not require her employees to do these
moves—which may put them in harm's way—most of them eagerly
volunteer and are proud to participate. To date, Margalith's crews
have helped rescue more than 100 battered women and children
from violent households. As a result of her efforts, Margalith has
appeared on numerous local and national television and radio
programsnot to publicize her company but to challenge others to
emulate her company's efforts and do what they do best for the
community.*

Most people start a business because they have a great idea for
some new product or service. My brother and his roommate started
Starving Students because they couldn't find work. I began my career
there answering phones. Not far from the office, there was an old
truck stuck in the remnants of a recent mud slide. The owner said we
could have it if we dug it out. After many hours of mud, sweat, and
tears, we had our truck — and a business.

We painted the name of our new company on the side of the truck
and parked it at one of the busiest intersections in town. The phone

73

immediately began to ring off the hook, and before we knew it, we had a thriving business on our hands. We didn't even have an office at the time. We worked out of our home, and we grew from there.

When I took over my location in 1983, I noticed we were receiving an alarming number of calls from women who needed to move out of a violent-home situation. To my surprise, most of the calls came from well-educated women who could afford to pay a moving company, but nobody would take the move, because no one wanted to get involved in that kind of a situation. A battered woman would call and ask, "Can you meet my father at the convenience store at a certain time, and we'll make the arrangements there?" Other movers just didn't want to take on those kinds of jobs.

One particular instance forever touched my soul. A woman called and said she had been held prisoner in her own home for two years. I worked with her for several weeks to plan the move. The day before the move, I received a call from a friend of hers saying the woman had been savagely beaten by her husband and was clinging to life in the hospital. The next day the friend called again to say the woman had died. I vowed then and there that when my company reached a position where I could afford it, I would provide these moves free of charge.

A few years later, we had grown to the size where I felt we could begin to help women and children in need. We completed a few moves, and the calls from women in danger began to escalate. Fortunately, we stumbled upon a local agency that helped us screen the calls and systematize the moves. Now, a battered woman calls the agency, and one of its trained counselors contacts us with the specific circumstances of the move. We carefully assess each move in order to avoid getting caught in an ambush situation. I want to help as many families as possible, but the safety of my men comes first. If necessary, the agency will arrange for the police to watch over the crew during the move.

I don't require my employees to work these moves; they do so on a volunteer basis only. Certain guys always ask to work them though, and no one has ever turned one down. The crews that handle these moves are street-smart and know how to take care of themselves. They don't often talk about what they see, but many times they come back noticeably shaken from the experience, especially when it involves children. Sometimes, the battered woman needs someone to actually take her by the hand, walk her out the door, and give her a ride to a safe house or shelter. Words can't express what it feels like to help people extricate themselves from a dangerous or life-threatening situation.

Why do I do this? Because it's what we do best. We move people every day. More important, I believe there's more to life than just working and making money. I have an opportunity to break the cycle of violence, so for me it's more a question of how can I *not* do this? I consider it an honor to be able to help these women and children. Even though I never hear from them after the move, I know in my heart that we are making a difference in their lives. And you can't put a price on that. I don't keep track of how many of these moves we do, but I guarantee you there are more to do than any one company can handle.

I'm just like any other chief executive officer running a successful business. Every time I solve a thorny problem or overcome a particularly daunting challenge, another one pops up to take its place. Just keeping the doors open when I bought this location was my biggest challenge. The first day I opened our office, the line of creditors stretched out the door, and they all had their hands out. Our survival came down to some very basic things: pay people when you say you're going to, treat employees and customers with respect, and keep answering the phone. Sometimes it doesn't get any more complicated than that. In fact, the biggest lessons I have learned in business are to follow the Golden Rule and to learn how to deal with the people who don't.

One of the most personally rewarding aspects of running a business is that it has forced me to grow in areas I would have never thought possible. When I took over this location, I knew a lot about operations, but I didn't know anything about banking and insurance. I had to learn fast in order to survive, so I just did it. I read books, talked to people, and soaked up everything I could. I especially learned a lot by interacting with other CEOs. I belong to an organization whose members are all CEOs, and there's nothing like getting together with a group of your peers once a month to really put things in perspective. We all run very different companies, but we all share the same types of problems. I've gained a lot of knowledge and experience from that very diverse group. Today, the parts of my business I enjoy the most—things such as banking and insurance — are the ones I originally knew nothing about.

I generally try to keep a low profile in regards to our work with battered women—partly for safety reasons but also because I don't do it to seek publicity. In fact, we performed this service silently for ten years, until a group of my peers urged me to come forward and disclose it. They felt that my example might inspire others to perform similar good deeds. So when I get asked to speak in public about our efforts, I focus less on what we have done and more on encouraging other CEOs to do what they can. As business owners, we have tools and resources beyond the reach of the average person, and so we can have tremendous impact on our communities. If my story inspires even one CEO to get involved in his or her community in a meaningful way, I will consider it a success.

I like to close my speeches by saying, "When you reach your star, turn around and help someone else reach theirs." I've been fortunate enough to reach my star, and this is my way of helping people in need reach theirs. Think what a difference it would make if more of us did the same!

Nine

From the Football Field to a Field of Dreams

Ernie Wright
EHW Management Group

Ernie Wright, fifty-nine years old, is president of the EHW Management Group in San Diego, which provides private correction and rehabilitation services for the county and federal governments. A high school All-American and an outstanding two-way lineman at Ohio State, he caused a sensation by becoming the first college football player to leave school early in order to turn pro. He went on to enjoy a stellar thirteen-year career with the San Diego Chargers and Cincinnati Bengals, serving as the team's player union representative for eight of those years. Upon retiring from football, he became a certified National Football League player's representative and soon began representing athletes from basketball, baseball, motocross, and rodeo as well. Sixteen years later, he entered the private corrections business, and today his company runs several facilities in San Diego County and does nearly $5 million in annual sales. A golf fanatic since the age of eleven, Wright has turned his life passion into a remarkable foundation that is helping to reshape the lives of hundreds of inner-city kids.

If at the time of my eulogy, all they said about Ernie Wright is that he played football, then I would consider my life a failure. I enjoyed playing, and I had a long and successful career, but for me football has always represented a means to an end. It enabled me to go to college, enjoy a better lifestyle, and visit parts of the world I never dreamed I would get to see. After I retired, it led to a successful career representing professional athletes and, in a roundabout way, introduced me to my current business. But I always knew that I could accomplish more.

In my last years as a player agent, we did a lot of investment counseling for our professional athletes, and I spent a lot of time listening to investment proposals—some good, some not so good. One day, a guy came in with a plan to have athletes finance a private jail. The profit margins looked too good to be true, so I began a thorough research process. I talked to a lot of judges and government officials about the overcrowding of the courts and jails, always asking the same question, "If I build it, will they come?" They all seemed to think the business had tremendous growth potential if managed properly.

After fifteen years as a player agent, I had grown weary of living on airplanes and in hotels. Plus, I could never carve out enough time to do what I love most—playing golf. The business appealed to me, and the time seemed right to make some major changes in my life, so I took the plunge. It has turned out to be the right decision.

As you might expect, in the for-profit private corrections business you don't just hang up a shingle and open shop. It took a lot of work to make the right connections and convince people to consider this concept of inmates paying for their own custody. I remember one judge in particular who asked, "Ernie, you're in business to make a profit. Suppose a guy whose custody is worth $2,000 to you turns up drunk. Why would you send him back to me and lose the money?" I replied, "Because if I send him back for violating your rules, you'll be so impressed that you'll send me two more." He said, "Good answer," and things took off from there. I knew the profits would come if we did the job right.

The business grew much faster than I expected. Initially, existing private work-furlough centers held twenty beds. We set a goal of increasing that to forty, but within nine months we had grown to eighty. You just have to read the papers to know our society has no shortage of people being placed in federal or local custody. The business began humming along nicely, and I finally had some time to get back out on the golf course.

One day, while finishing up the front nine, a golfing buddy mentioned his interest in getting more minorities involved in golf. We tossed the idea around a bit, but we didn't come up with anything specific. A few months later, he contacted me about a run-down inner-city golf course. The leaseholder wanted out, and if we took over the lease, we could run the course and give priority to the kids in the area, one of the more economically underprivileged neighborhoods in San Diego. We raised some money from local companies, including a $475,000 grant from the Calloway Golf Foundation, and the Pro Kids Golf Academy and Learning Center was born.

The academy is open to kids ages seven to seventeen who have an interest in learning to play golf. It doesn't cost them a penny to join, but we require that they stay in school and maintain a passing grade-point average. The kids must also adhere to a dress code and join in doing community work, such as cleaning the streets, doing yard work for seniors, and the like. As long as they abide by the rules, they can play as little or as much as they want at no charge. Initially, we started out just providing instruction on the basic skills, rules, and etiquette of golf, but it didn't take long for me to realize we had a lot more to teach these kids than golf.

It really hit me the first time we took a group of kids to Torrey Pines, a beautiful public course overlooking the Pacific Ocean, which each year hosts a PGA tournament. Not one kid in the group had even seen the ocean before, even though they only lived about eight miles away. The same thing happened when we took them to a course in East San Diego at the foothills of the Cuyamaca mountains—again less than ten miles away. None had ever laid eyes on a mountain before.

I realized then that the twenty-block area these kids live in is a world unto itself. Most people take it for granted that they can roam the world at large, but these kids never get out of their neighborhood, so it's all they know. I asked myself, "How can we expect them to become good citizens and want to go to college when their entire world consists of a disadvantaged, inner-city, high-risk neighborhood?" That's when I knew we had to do more. Sure, we can teach them how to act on a golf course, but I also believe we have an obligation and duty to teach them how to act in the world. We have to give them life skills and education, so they'll be able to afford to play golf anywhere they want because they'll have good jobs and an appreciation for what the world has to offer.

As a result of that personal awakening, we began to expand the program. We raised some more money, built a real clubhouse with a learning center, and arranged for students from nearby San Diego State University to come in as tutors. The Academy's emphasis remains on golf, but now we're trying to take golf skills, along with the requirements of honesty, respect for the rules, and respect for others, and translate them into life skills. We want these kids to be able to compete educationally and professionally, as well as athletically.

So far, the program has exceeded our wildest expectations. We've had the opportunity to take several kids to junior national golf tournaments, where they represented themselves very well. More importantly, two years ago we began a college scholarship program and there was one recipient. Last year, there were three, and this year we expect six. Nobody in that neighborhood is talking about college except the kids in our program. Hardly any of the homes have computers, and many don't even have phones. To even get the kids to dream of going to college represents a tremendous achievement.

When I started the Academy, I thought I would help get it off the ground and then move on. I was named chairman because of my efforts to secure a golf course, and being a minority was a plus. Obviously, it helps to have a minority head up something for minorities. I have served as chairman of the board since we started, and now I expect to remain in that position for a long time.

My two main priorities are making sure the board of directors is running in the right direction and devoting time to raising money for the endowment fund so boys and girls—athletes and non-athletes—can further their education. Although other retired pro athletes have helped the program, we de-emphasize the athletics. I don't want our kids emulating pro athletes, movie stars, or rock stars, because that only sets them up for failure. Maybe one out of every thousand who aspire to that level will ever reach it. So we're trying to instill more realistic goals by setting up a mentoring program that brings in people who work for a living: bus drivers, teachers, doctors, lawyers, and others who fill essential roles in the community. Our goal is to show these kids that that kind of a lifestyle is worth working for *and* that it requires further education.

Although we have come a long way at the Academy, there's so much more we can do. I want to see as many kids as possible go to college, whether it's city college, junior college, or Stanford University. I also want to explore vocational training. I want these kids to have summer jobs, whether they are bagging groceries at the supermarket, learning to fix cars, or working at the Salk Institute.

You see, I consider these kids my extended family. Beyond my own children and grandchildren, my "family" consists of any young child that wants and needs an opportunity. When they get to the age where they have to decide whether or not to be a pimp, prostitute, dopehead, or drug dealer, if they've been in our program for several years, I believe they will make the right choice. If they don't, I tell them one day they will occupy my jails. But if we give them the right guidelines and avenues to see what the world looks like, they will make the right decisions.

The one thing I love about golf, what makes it such a wonderful metaphor for life, is that it's different from other sports, where you try to cheat on the rules, argue with the officials, and intimidate the other guy. Golf isn't like that. It teaches you social skills. It pits you against the course and shows all your strengths and weaknesses in one round. You can hit a perfect shot and then completely duff the next one. You can suffer a triple bogey, shake it off as you approach the next tee, and then sink a birdie. Golf teaches you about discipline, self-control, and learning to overcome adversity. Those are the kinds of life skills these kids need to develop in order to get ahead.

I will continue to work with my extended family for as long as I can. I enjoy building businesses and doing what I do, and I'm devoting a lot more time to the Academy than I originally thought. But like I always say, someone has to do it. Why not me?

Ten

A Double-Edge Mission

Roy Soards
St. Vincent dePaul Rehabilitation Service Inc.

Roy Soards describes himself as a "social entrepreneur." He is devoted to social service but feels that financial rewards must accompany these good deeds. Soards, forty-five years old, has spent his entire professional career in social service jobs. Now, as CEO of St. Vincent dePaul Rehabilitation Service Inc. in Portland, Oregon, he admits open disdain for those who believe that people who work for the social good must necessarily live a life of poverty. St. Vincent dePaul Rehabilitation Service is a non-profit organization, with offices throughout Oregon, that trains and employs people with disabilities. At any given time, St. Vincent has more than 1,000 people with a wide range of physical and emotional disabilities working at a variety of jobs. In Soards's four years as CEO, the company has grown from $9 million in sales to more than $21 million, with profits of $600,000. He believes his model will attract more talented people into social services and will become the wave of the future for non-profit businesses.

The first thing I always tell people is what we're not. Even though we were started by the Society of St. Vincent dePaul in 1971, a Catholic charity, we are not part of their thrift store or social services program. We're an independent organization that employs and trains people with disabilities. About fifteen years ago, we realized that if we relied upon traditional government funding and charitable giving, we would never be able to expand our mission. So we started running businesses that would employ people with disabilities and, at the same time, hopefully make us enough money so that we would be able to grow and also gain a certain level of self-sufficiency. We have done that. What makes us stand out is that we have a double bottom line.

Like any business, we need to make money and have a good *financial* bottom line, but the other bottom line is our social mission: how many people with disabilities we employ. The trick with our business is that we can't be successful with just one or the other; we have to be successful in both.

More than 80 percent of our employees have a disability, including very severe mental disabilities and various physical disabilities. We have people in wheelchairs with mobility problems and injured workers who can't go back to what they were doing before. We also have people who are blind or deaf or chronically mentally ill. Some are highly skilled, others can only do entry-level work. They are all very aware of our mission and our two bottom lines. As a matter of fact, every worker in the organization knows our goal is designed around hitting those two targets.

For me, running St. Vincent's is the fulfillment of a dream and the culmination of a long, strange trip that began in Iowa more than twenty years ago. I was a journalism student at Drake University in Des Moines in the early 1970s when my life really hit bottom.

For several years, my life was focused entirely on drugs. I managed to cover it up pretty well, because I figured if I stayed in school and looked like I was doing something, nobody would notice. In truth, I hit bottom. At one point, I ended up in jail for six weeks on drug charges. I was selling drugs, doing drugs, and was facing three to five years in the Iowa State Penitentiary. Only because I was a white, middle-class guy with a good lawyer, I managed to avoid that. It was a powerful catalyst to make me rethink my whole life.

I just woke up one day and looked around. I was a young kid, and I saw that all of my friends were either in jail, going to jail, or on probation. I said, "I need to get away from this." Out of the experience of being in and out of the corrections system and being around some pretty scary people in the process, I decided, somewhere along the way, that I was going to devote my life to helping other people.

I thought, "Why are people poor?" The obvious answer was because they don't have jobs. So I figured, "Okay, what's the best way to help people?" The best way is through getting people jobs. If you're going to commit yourself to working in this field, do something that is going to fix the problem rather than just put a Band-Aid on it. That's how I got into this. I decided that that was what I wanted to do as a career. So I just packed up my bags and moved to a place where I didn't know anybody and nobody knew me, and I started over.

I moved to Oregon in 1975 and went to the University of Oregon in Eugene. I was a pretty mediocre and generally uninterested student in college. There wasn't a lot there to hold my attention. I was saved by the existence of a program called Vista, which is now called Americore, which had a program for college students at that time. If you were in college, you could be a Vista volunteer and get credit for the work you were doing. I ended up going to work for a year in a rural area south of Eugene. My task was to set up a youth employment program for kids in all of these little towns. I had no idea what I was doing. I was about twenty-three years old and had never done any job-placement work, but I learned more in that year than at any other time in my life. Probably a good chunk of what I still know today, I learned in that first year.

After that, I worked in a series of management jobs in job training programs, and by the late 1980s, I was tired of the treadmill. I still loved getting people jobs, but I hated the government funding process and the constant battle for money. I kept thinking, "There has got to be a better way than having your life tied to the vagaries of federal grant funding."

I needed to make a change, and what I wanted to do was find a not-for-profit organization that had an entrepreneurial approach, that was not dependent on direct government funding for everything. I got lucky, although it might not have seemed like that to my family.

I was just starting to look for another job, when a former colleague told me about an opening for the job of chief operating officer here at St. Vincent dePaul. It was exactly what I was looking for, except for the fact that I had a young family—a wife, a three-year old, and a brand new baby. When I started working here, I had to take a huge cut in pay and benefits, and there was no pension plan.

I took it anyway, and I finally started coming to work at a job I enjoyed. I'd hated the work I was doing before. I'd hated getting up and going to work in the morning. Now, I was charged up, because my success—both personal and professional—and my ability to pursue a mission were no longer tied to some bureaucrat in Washington, D.C. I became CEO in 1995.

A Double-Edge Mission

Becoming a CEO was very much a driver in my life. One of the reasons that I was willing to go from a fairly boring but stable job and jump into this uncertain situation was that the guy who hired me—who was then the CEO—said that he didn't intend on being here a whole lot longer. I was to be his successor, and that was great, because I started training from day one to be the CEO.

What I've discovered is that I grapple every day with the paradox of our business, the idea that we must not only find people jobs but make money as well. That is the most rewarding and the most difficult thing about this job.

For example, I recently had to handle a situation that raised that very issue. We have a group of about twenty severely disabled employees. Most are mentally retarded and developmentally disabled. These individuals formerly lived in institutions for the mentally retarded, and now they live in the community, and it's our job to employ them.

A decade ago, these people were doing basic assembly work, simple one- or two-step assembly work. That work is just disappearing left and right as more companies move their manufacturing off-shore. So it has become more and more difficult to find jobs for these people.

These twenty people had worked for the past five years at a big distribution center of a local business. When this business was bought out, these people lost their jobs. So suddenly we had twenty people to find jobs for, and placing a several of these folks at a time is very difficult.

An opportunity arose with a local electronics manufacturer to employ all twenty people to do very basic hand assembly jobs. The sales figures looked pretty good, about $300,000 a year. However, in order to get these jobs, we had to whack the price down to the point where we knew we were not going to make any money on it. A normal business would look at this as an opportunity to fill some capacity and pick up a little bit of overhead, but for us, we'd be lucky to pick up any overhead.

Though it is crucial that these people have jobs, the driving decision-makers for me are that these people have jobs and that I make money. It's not okay to fulfill just one objective. By agreeing to this contract, I would have to put pressure on other business units and other business contracts so that I would make money elsewhere. By losing it one place, I've got to make it up somewhere else.

The dilemma is measuring the social value versus the economic value. In this case, the reason we decided to do it is because of the tremendously high social value. I can employ twenty severely disabled folks on one contract that has huge social value for our organization. The economic value in this case, however, is not good, but I'm willing to eat it on the economic value, because the social value is so high.

Of course, if I made every decision this way, the traditional social worker approach, I'd be out of business. We would have been out of business years ago. Unfortunately, this kind of decision is the norm rather than the exception in social services.

After a lifetime of trying to balance the desire to do good things with the ability to earn a good living, I'm more convinced than ever about the value of the social entrepreneur concept. Everyone says schools, social services, and government agencies need to be more business-like. Fine, then pay us what we're worth. We have families to feed, and we have kids to put through college and rent to pay, just like everybody else. When did a vow of poverty get written into the mission of doing social good?

The truth is that the role of the social entrepreneur can be very conflicting. I have learned to live with it over the years, but the difficult thing for me is balancing the warring factions, the employees and the department managers who say, "You're giving me two messages." I always tell them "Yes, that's right. I'm giving you two messages. Live with both of them. That's the paradox of our existence."

The paradox affects me deeply on a personal level. It has had an impact on my family and my own balance in life. Not long ago, for example, I saw an opportunity to take over a struggling technical college in Seattle. It's a two-year community college that was founded by a fellow who is a quadriplegic. The goal was to give people with disabilities technical skills that would allow them to get real jobs and earn some real money.

The school was in trouble, ready to fold, and they asked us to take them over. It had been a dream of mine for years to get into higher-level training and education for the disabled. We did due diligence, and we thought we knew what we were getting into. But the school was in worse shape than we thought, and our investment has become a real nightmare.

My board was split on the issue. It became a very emotional thing, and it just appeared to be totally out of control. There were moments when I've thought, "What have I done here? Why did I do this?" I keep coming back to the fact that if I'm really an entrepreneur, then I've got to really be willing to take risks. It's the biggest risk I've ever taken. We've sunk a lot of money into it, and at this point, we're still not sure when it's going to turn around. I just have to keep reminding myself that the reason we did this is to make people's lives better.

This plus many other management issues started to produce deep stress and altered my focus. I have a strong belief in balance. My personal mission in life is to live a balanced life, but my ability to live that mission got lost.

I began working long hours, and my mind was focused on one thing all of the time. I was on the road constantly. My family was supportive; they realized that my job was on the line. But mostly I didn't like it. What crystallized it for me was one day my children came in as I was packing for yet another trip, and they said, "Daddy, you can't leave, you're gone all of the time now." I thought, "Boy, this is not good."

The other thing is I was not having fun. I don't mind working hard. I don't mind things being crazy, but I was not having fun. If I'm not having fun, then I don't need this. That has been my personal credo, and I tell people here all of the time, "Your work should be fun." For me, the fun had just disappeared.

I remember quite vividly how it all came together for me. For a week at Christmas, I took my family to our vacation home on the Oregon coast. It is the place where I seem to be at my calmest and most relaxed. My wife grew up on the coast there, and we really love it.

One day, I was gazing out the window watching a typical Oregon coast storm. The rain was driving down, as it does there in the winter. I realized that I had really let my personal life get out of whack and that I was not happy. It was the closest thing to a spiritual revelation that I have ever had. I realized I had been telling myself that it was okay to be miserable now, because in a few months, I'd be through all this. But that wasn't good enough. I didn't want to do that. What I needed to do was enjoy every day, because every day is precious.

It all just hit me so hard. It was clear that I needed a major attitude adjustment more than anything else. All of these issues still exist, but

I'm not miserable anymore. I'm back to having fun. I hired a good manager to run the college in Seattle and addressed some of these other issues. I've given more responsibility for day-to-day management to a broader array of managers. So I don't have so much day-to-day responsibility.

I think mostly it's been the attitude adjustment, just a realization that we don't have all that much time on earth. Being miserable every day at work is just no way to live. The reality was that being miserable was ridiculous, because what do I have to be miserable about? I'm paid a very good salary. I get to control much of what I do during the day. I'm not disabled. I have a very loving family. My wife and I have been together for more than twenty years. Why be miserable? I have a great job.

More than that, I think about the people I meet everyday who have jobs that we provided. I met one fellow who works in our wood-fabrication shop. He came in to see me, and he said, "I'm really glad I'm here. Before this, I was in a drug treatment center. Drugs and alcohol had taken over and ruined my life. I had my own business, and I lost that business and everything else I had in life. I ended up on skid row and was living on the streets. Now here I am. I've gotten my life back." On any given day there are a thousand people whose lives we're affecting, some more than others, but all in some positive way.

Every morning, I ask myself the same question: "How am I going to make a difference today?" Meeting these people always helps me answer that question.

Eleven
Learning How to Swim

Bill Kent
Horner Equipment of Florida, Inc.

Before Bill Kent got into the pool and spa business in south Florida in 1972, he worked for five years building rockets for General Electric's military unit in Cincinnati. Although Kent didn't see a future for himself in rocket science, he became a lifelong fan of G.E. and its commitment to employee education and training. When he decided to make a switch, the Ohio native realized that a career in pools would likely be more successful in Ft. Lauderdale than in Cincinnati, so he moved there, joined Horner Equipment, a three-year-old pool wholesale distribution business, and eventually bought out his partner to become CEO. At fifty-six years old, Kent has built Horner into a $50-million international company with more than 200 employees, steady profits, and a culture that thrives on Kent's personal passion: education.

In the mid-1980s, I had this intense desire to continue to learn, and I didn't find reading books and going to seminars and trade shows an effective way to do it. There's no continuity there. So with my M.B.A. degree as a background, I decided I'd try to get a Ph.D. at Stanford's graduate school of business. We had an office in Palo Alto, where Stanford is located, and I went to the school and said, "I've been fairly successful in business. I'm not a Silicon Valley guru, but I've been pretty successful. I'd like to get a Ph.D. and teach and continue my business career as well." The dean of the business school at Stanford said that being successful in business "wasn't relevant."

So I gave up on the Stanford idea, but I've never given up on learning. I think learning is a continuous process that you do throughout your entire lifetime, and I'm truly committed to that concept in my business. I think learning is one of the things that brings great joy to someone's life. I also believe that part of being a CEO is bringing the values you create for yourself and for your life to your company.

Normally, a CEO has a higher level of self-motivation and a stronger desire for excellence than most people have. I believe that's one of the things that sets us apart as a group. It's not necessarily greed. I've never been that motivated to maximize profits. I understand the rules of the business game: if your company is not successful, the boat sinks, and it is not a fun place to be. But for me personally, maximizing profits has never been the key focus of the business.

I always looked at things from a life cycle standpoint, and I know that there are just so many years on this earth for each one of us and that we need to make sure that our lives are lived in a constructive way. So my personal value system is built around the concept that I want to do the very best I can with all the talent that God has given me. If I do that, I'll be a success.

Seeing people grow and develop and become better human beings is more important to me than maximizing profits. If you think about it, the first twenty years of our lives are spent totally focused on personal improvement. Then, for the most part, people stop learning. Some phenomenal percentage of people, once they get out of school, never read a book again!

There is certainly a lot to be gained from what I told my kids is the "University of the Real World," the school of hard knocks and all that. But there's also a great deal to be gained from more a formal education, and I'm just a big believer in it, because I think it adds joy to your life to be continuously improving and having new ideas and fresh input. It keeps the barnacles off the hull.

At G.E., I also saw what education can do. I went through a one-year program at G.E. called Manufacturing Problems Analysis. We met for two afternoons a week for a year, and I remember thinking that some of the things I learned in that G.E. program were a lot more valuable than what I had learned in four years at college.

Based on that premise, I instituted a continuing education program here at our company that is taught exclusively by in-house teachers.

The program has twelve segments and is offered to employees and customers. Our employees are paid to come. There is a test after each segment, and if they pass it, they get a $50 bonus. If they pass all twelve segments and graduate, they get another $250. So, if a new employee comes in and attends all twelve segments and passes all twelve tests in the first year, the employee makes an extra $850. Some people go for the money, but ultimately they get something out of it beyond that, both from an educational and from a spiritual standpoint.

Half the courses are technical, related to the pool business. The other half are the basics of accounting, investing, personnel development, credit and collections, and other general business issues, such as marketing and advertising. Employees teach each of the segments, because I don't want them taught by someone outside the company. If you teach something, you learn it far more competently, and this way I have people continuing to learn at a more advanced level.

I've always tried to figure out ways of making continuous education a bottom up process, a process where everybody wins. Too many times, someone at the bottom of the ladder says, "That's not for me. That is for people higher up in the company." I try to eliminate any class differentiation. In this light, I remember looking at a book called *Turn Your Customers into Your Sales Force* by Ross R. Reck and thinking, "This is a fantastic book. I wish everybody in the company could read it." I knew for a fact that I wasn't going to get a lot of takers if I just said, "Hey, everybody, let's read this book." I've never minded people being motivated by money. Once they start learning, I figured, they will start to enjoy it from a nonfinancial standpoint.

So I set out to organize my mercenary plan. I offered people a dollar a page if they would read the book. We asked people to sign up to read the book, and we broke them up into groups. Then we broke the book into four to six different segments, maybe fifty pages per segment, and gave out the books. Since we have so many different companies, some in manufacturing, some in export, some in distribution, we had people from all the different companies come together for an hour discussion once every other week for twelve weeks.

They became internal book groups. There is a group leader for each section. We try to keep the groups to around twenty people, because group dynamics get in the way if you have a hundred people in the room. It really works. If you attend all the sessions and you've read the book, let's say a 225-page book, you will receive a bonus of $225 in your paycheck at the end of the program.

We can't monitor if they've actually read the whole book, but they must sign up for the meeting, and it's only an hour right after office hours. It's a discussion and absorption process, and the goal is to discuss ways to bring the ideas to the workplace. We've generally done one or two books a year for the past six years. We've read *The Leader in You* by Dale Carnegie, *The Magic of Teamwork* by Pat Williams, and another called *Samurai Selling* by Chuck Laughlin.

We've probably spent more than $150,000 on the program over the years, but so what? I don't think of it in terms of money. I think of it in terms of overall salaries for the company. If you can spend 5 percent more of your salary base on education, think of the tremendous benefits—not just to the people, but to the business.

Most people spend 95 percent of their time reacting to what comes at them. If you can instill in people a sense of continuous improvement and investment in their own lives, then they will be a lot happier with themselves and with their lives in the company.

I don't believe you can measure the value. It's qualitative and spiritual, not quantitative. I get great feedback from people, and I feel very responsible for trying to provide creative opportunities for everybody to grow and prosper in the company.

I also realize that I have to continue to grow as well. I'm not perfect. I'm just like everybody else. I make mistakes. When you are the boss, people have a high level of expectation and think that you know everything. They watch everything you do. I mean, how I walk down the hallway makes a difference. So, I make sure that I'm trying to provide leadership with every action that I take.

Most organization charts have a guy at the top, and there's a pyramid beneath him going down. Around ten or twelve years ago, I realized that the pyramid here had been inverted. Instead of me being on the top, I was on the bottom, and everyone else was on top. I now assume that I work for the employees. We grew as a business to the point where basically I'm working for them. I know they think they are working for me, but that's not how I see it.

Standing on top of the conference room table with a chain saw and some bullets hanging around your chest isn't exactly what I think of as the image of a good CEO. If I can provide capital, leadership, and a value system, and if the employees give it their best in terms of how to develop the business and how to satisfy the customers and exceed their expectations, then we will win. And that's really what life is all about.

The most important lesson to me is that I've come to see that money is not the key measurement of success in life. That may not be something a CEO should say, but money is not what makes a person's life a success.

I heard a CEO speak once. He had developed a big brokerage business, and his theory was that you built a company up and sold it. Then you went and built up another company and sold it. The process took from two to five years, and he was real fat and happy sitting on a ninety-foot yacht down in the San Diego harbor. But I thought, he doesn't have any relationships with any of those people from over the twenty to thirty years he has been in business, whereas I've got wonderful relationships with customers and employees and suppliers. I value that. While we still need to do business and collect on our bills and the rest of it, in the end, maintaining those relationships is what's important to me.

Twelve
Leaving the Tribe

Walt Sutton
W.G. Sutton International, Ltd.

Walt Sutton, fifty-five years old, started and built four companies during his twenty-three-year career as a CEO, each company more successful than the last. Well into his third company, however, Sutton developed a malady common to many entrepreneurs who ride the fast track to success—the "Midas Touch Syndrome." Believing he could do no wrong, he personally guaranteed $25 million in building leases. When several major contracts went south, so did his business, forcing him to declare personal bankruptcy. After a brief period to take stock of his life, Sutton started his fourth and most successful company, planning a management development and exit strategy before he even started the company. Several years later, he sold the business to his management team and embarked upon life post-CEO. Like a man released from indenture, Sutton now travels, writes, consults, and spends "shameless" amounts of time with his wife and grown children. His new mission is to educate the tribe of CEOs about life beyond the corporate walls.

I formed my first company in Seattle in 1972. Prior to setting out on my own, I had worked as a vice president of contract administration for a large mechanical/electrical contractor. Thinking I could write construction claims better than the folks I worked for, I left during a management shakeup and formed W. G. Sutton Construction Consulting. We wrote construction claims and analyzed projects on behalf of clients who needed to settle disputes about the costs of building stadiums, airports, hydroelectric dams, and other similar structures. After several years of steady growth, I sold the business to an international engineering firm.

My second business, Cipher Paralegal Services, spun out of the first one. In the process of figuring out these massive claims, I noticed that nobody did paralegal work as an outside contractor for law firms. So I started a paralegal outplacement firm that also helped paralegals form teams to support large construction lawsuits. We combined a novel idea with emerging computer technology to create an entirely new service, one that now forms an integral part of every big law firm in the country. To this day, I consider that one of my biggest accomplishments. However, I made the mistake of bringing a partner into the business, and we soon got bogged down in your typical partner disputes.

My third company came about after I bought out my partner. I tore apart Cipher Paralegal Services, started from scratch, and founded Cipher Inc. to provide computerized litigation support and help law firms manage paper and information in very large lawsuits. We worked on some of the biggest litigations in the nation at the time, including some huge antitrust and early toxic-waste cases. Cipher rapidly grew to $40 million in sales and 350 employees. As happens to so many entrepreneurs who taste only success on the way up, I began to overestimate my ability to control the events surrounding my business.

In the process of building Cipher, I signed a $25-million personal guarantee for some building leases. No sooner had the ink dried on the paper than we lost 40 percent of our business. Through no fault of our own, several very large cases got put on hold, and the resulting blow to our revenue stream proved too much to overcome. I let a lot of people go and drastically cut costs in many areas, but I could not get out of the lease. After two years of unsuccessful attempts to renegotiate the lease terms, I had to shut the company down and start all over.

It took me two years to wind down the business and pay off all my creditors. The experience absolutely devastated me, personally and professionally. Until that point, everything I touched had turned into gold. Plus, I had signed dozens of personal guarantees before, so it never occurred to me not to do it again. With an unbroken track record of success, I had no reason to suspect anything otherwise. Then I lost it all in a heartbeat. I went from living in a very exclusive Seattle neighborhood (with visions of my own private Lear Jet) to a bleak rental home in a Los Angeles suburb, with no assets, no job, and no prospects on the immediate horizon. Worse, I lost my sense of self, my sense of direction in life, and, I felt, the respect of my family and peers.

Prior to this debacle, I had enjoyed the lifestyle of a multimillionaire, with fancy cars, nice homes, and all the perks that come with being a CEO. Then it all melted away like ice cream in rain. I couldn't believe how hard I had worked for it and how quickly it went away. As the days passed, however, I began to realize that I didn't really care about all that "stuff." It caused me far greater pain knowing that I had disappointed my wife and children. I went a long time thinking I should just get a job as a postman and live the simple life, but after a month or two, I realized I only knew how to do one thing—start and build businesses.

I realized I had grown weary of the job of CEO. I had made ungodly sacrifices to get to my previous position, and I no longer felt the rewards justified those sacrifices. Yet my way out was to do again what I had done before, even though I didn't like to do it. Except this time I went into it with the intention of creating a company that would get me out of the job of being CEO. A close CEO friend of mine had convinced me that you could build a team to run the business so that you wouldn't have to do it day by day. She convinced me, not by talking but by showing me how to do it. Based on her experience, I became determined to build a management team that would run the company and allow me to focus on just a few key areas and not have to work so hard.

With that in mind, I formed Logan Pearsall Inc., which basically did the same thing as Cipher but on a different scale and in a different way. I intentionally limited the size of the company and took on only select lawsuits. I made a deal with the management team for building the company. I would collect a nice retirement pot and then sell them the business. In the meantime, I would step back as much as possible from the daily operations, and they would run the business. When we reached $16 million in sales in 1992, they bought the company. I permanently retired from the CEO battles and embarked on an entirely new way of life.

Despite the wonderful outcome from my last business, I left the CEO's life angry and resentful at all that it had taken from me. I rejected everything about it, and for a while I wandered about the country playing the charade of the affluent bum, sort of an American fop with paid-up credit cards. I briefly enjoyed this nomadic period, but the novelty soon wore off, and I found myself bereft of direction or purpose.

At that point I began to write as a means of processing my experience. In this process of gathering and analyzing my thoughts, feelings, and experiences, I began to suspect they might have value for others. Encouraged by feedback from several friends and colleagues, I wrote my first book, *The Secret*. Not only did the book help me understand who I was (and what I still had left to accomplish in life), but it also forced me to assess and eventually embrace the adventure of being a CEO. At that point, the real payoff began to emerge.

I realized that by having performed the CEO job long and well, I would now get to live a second life, one that would have been impossible without the first. In the ultimate irony, the first life that had almost crushed me now rained a torrent of dividends. It gave me the energy and standing to live a second life, one that includes everything the previous life precluded. I now have a completely free-form life, one that allows more time with my wife and grown children than I ever imagined possible. I can exercise as I should and work in a pattern that suits my own style, which usually involves six or seven consecutive hours of intense work and then spending the rest of the day as I please. So many things are available to me now that once existed far beyond my reach.

I discovered I have a tremendous passion for adventure and learning. Despite no longer being an active member, I stay hooked into the "tribe" of CEOs; and in my writing and speaking, I try to focus on my former colleagues. Having been a CEO gives me a very interesting platform in life. It gives me a credibility among people that is hard to come by. I can interview very high achievers, and they will tell me things they don't tell other people, because we share a common bond.

I enjoy meeting people and having long, windy arguments in Irish pubs in the dark of night. I love reading philosophy and traveling without ninety people back at the office tugging at my unconscious. Most of all, I cherish the freedom. Life as a CEO boxes you in. It forces you to give away too much of yourself. When I sat behind the desk, I couldn't disconnect from the job, no matter how hard I tried. Not until I pulled the plug did I realize how much of myself I had invested in the business and how much of it was invested in me.

Today, my job is to report back to the CEO tribe on this other world that only presents itself to people who aren't overly important, to people who travel coach and stay in small inns and pubs. This kind of life only appears when you walk places and get wet in the rain and have time to ask all the questions that job pressures and responsibilities rudely shove out of the way. My audience is my family, friends, CEO tribe members, little children, and anyone who has a need for this information. I have been given many wonderful gifts in this new life. I feel a sense of duty and obligation to give something back in return.

Thirteen

Sharing the Wealth

Debra Turpin
River City Studio

You can take the farm girl out of Kansas, but you can't take Kansas out of the farm girl. Debra Turpin, forty-six years old, is founder and president of River City Studio, a graphic design studio in Kansas City, with fifteen employees and nearly $3 million in annual sales. Fresh out of Pratt Institute in Brooklyn, she enjoyed life as a young, poor, bohemian art student. When she failed to land a job with a top New York ad agency, she decided to return to her roots. The move not only changed her life in ways she never imagined it could, it has changed others' lives and will continue to for generations to come. Unlike many who reach the top and never look back, Turpin hasn't forgotten the values she learned as a young girl growing up on the farm: tell the truth, treat your neighbors with respect, and help others in need.

My entrepreneurial career started out in a New York taxicab. In 1976, while struggling to earn a living as a freelance graphic designer, I often toiled into the wee hours of the morning. One night, while riding through Times Square at 3:00 A.M. on my way home from a freelance press check, I looked around at the asphalt jungle and all the crazies still out on the street and thought, "What the hell am I doing here? I don't belong here anymore." Shortly thereafter, I decided to move back home to Kansas, although not all the way back to the farm.

Until that point, I had wanted nothing more than to land a job with a top New York ad agency. In fact, I felt that if I returned home without achieving that goal, my whole life would be a failure. In that taxi that morning, however, in one of those little moments that don't

103

seem important at the time but that change your life forever, I had an insight. I realized that not getting a glamorous agency job had nothing to do with success or failure, that life was merely leading me down a different path. I thoroughly enjoyed my time in New York, but something inside told me the time had come to go home.

As I got on the plane to return to Kansas, I had no inkling that I would one day run my own business. Unlike many of my art school classmates that dreamed of running their own agencies, I just wanted to do design and nothing more. I loved the creative aspects of the business and didn't want any part of the aggravation, pressures, and turmoil that come with managing other people. I started my own business only because I couldn't find the kind of company I wanted to work for.

Shortly after returning to Kansas, I took a job as creative director at one of the area's larger agencies. I soon found out I didn't respect the owners, because they practiced what I considered to be questionable ethics. In particular, they didn't pay their bills on time, and I had a very hard time living with that. I grew up on the farm, and I was taught that if you owe money, you pay it—even if you have to sell the farm to pay it. In my early years at River City Studio, someone stole $250,000 from me, and I still paid the bills. So I don't buy that line about not being able to pay the bills—that goes against everything I believe in.

The longer I stayed at that agency, the more my discontent grew. The breaking point came one day when my boss chewed me out for no good reason. My staff and I had been working on a large project that involved a lot of evenings and weekends. Despite feeling overworked, tired, and stressed, I did my best to rally the troops and keep them focused on getting the job done. So when my boss called me into the office and said bluntly, "We have a problem with your attitude," my jaw hit the floor. I said, "Pardon me, but I have no clue as to what you are talking about. Could you please give me an example?" When he refused, I grew livid. Barely controlling my anger, I said, "I have a *lot* of deadlines today. When you figure out what you are trying to tell me, give me a call. Until then, I have work to do!" I then turned on my heel and stormed out of his office.

As I returned to my office to cool off, I knew I had to make a change. I tested the water with a few agencies, but the few I would have considered working for had no openings. At that point, I saw two options. I could sit around and wait for someone else to create my destiny, or I could do it myself. I put some numbers to paper, called one of the women who worked for me, and told her my plan. Without hesitation, she said, "Let's go for it!" and River City Studio became a reality. So, unlike many, my business did not come about after weeks and months of carefully crafting a business plan. I simply told myself, "I can't take this anymore," and I pursued what I saw as my only option. I bought out my partner in 1991 and have owned the company outright ever since.

Like everyone, we've had our share of good years and bad at River City Studio, but for the most part, this business has given me more success than I ever imagined. I make a very good living, and I get to work with a group of incredibly talented people. I've learned a lot about myself and have gotten very good at identifying my personal strengths and weaknesses.

More important, I've learned how to use those strengths to the company's best advantage and when to ask for help in those areas where I need it. The best part about owning my own company, however, is that it has allowed me to give back to the community in ways that I couldn't do on my own. As a devout Christian, I believe that those who have been blessed have an obligation to give back. Most of the time, I get involved in community activities by choice. Sometimes I feel compelled to do so.

In March 1998, a very well known and respected Kansas City illustrator and designer committed suicide. I remember sitting at the kitchen table one Sunday morning, drinking my coffee and reading the obituaries. (My husband gives me a hard time about that, but unfortunately I have reached the age where I occasionally see people I know.) I saw the obituary and said, "My God! That's Rick Richters." I assumed he'd had a heart attack; the article didn't specify the cause of death. On Monday morning, after phone calls from several colleagues, I learned the truth. A marvelous freehand illustrator, Rick apparently felt he could no longer compete with the new technologies in the industry. Feeling unwanted and displaced and deeply in debt, he took his own life.

The news stunned me. I didn't consider Rick a close friend, and we had never actually worked together, but we interacted frequently at the art directors club, and I knew him as a very well-respected figure in the industry. As you might expect, the funeral was a very somber occasion, even more so than if Rick had died of natural causes. He had a family, a wide circle of friends, and the respect and admiration of his peers. You just don't expect someone like that to throw it all away. As they lowered the casket into the ground, I kept thinking, "How could this happen? Why didn't we see it coming?"

Driving home in the pouring rain, I felt like somebody had to do something and that somebody would have to be me. The next day I began making phone calls to friends and colleagues in the industry. Six or seven of us decided to hold a fund-raiser and formed a foundation to make sure that what happened to Rick Richters never happened again.

The Rick Richters Foundation provides support services and emergency funds for advertising professionals at risk in the Kansas City community. So far, we have helped two families with financial aid. A partner in a noted Kansas City ad agency contracted multiple sclerosis. The foundation has been making his house payments for the past six months, and it put him together with community advocates and legal representatives who helped him get approval for government aid. We are also making the house payments for Rick's widow until she can get back on her feet. It's sad that it took a tragedy like this to get the foundation started, but it feels good knowing that we have played a part in easing their burdens and that as the foundation grows, we will have the resources available to help others in need.

Sometimes, owning the company allows me to give back on a more personal level. As a young art student in Brooklyn, I became a friend of an older African-American woman named Mary. We went to church together, and she regularly invited me over to dinner, especially during the holidays. I had never met anyone from the projects before, and I immediately felt drawn to Mary, not just because she treated me kindly but because she was a real survivor. Instead of complaining about the lousy hand life had dealt her, she always talked about her blessings. I quickly learned to admire her personal dignity and grace.

Before I moved back to Kansas, Mary asked if there was any way I could move her daughter Carolyn and Carolyn's family out of the projects. Upon returning to Kansas, I got involved in the church, and our Sunday school class took on Carolyn and her family as a project. We held a series of fundraisers and scraped together enough money to move them out to Kansas. Several years later, Mary called and asked if I could find a way to move her out as well. She missed her family terribly and longed to be close to them once again. My company had just had its best year ever, so I took some money, bought a modest home in a nice neighborhood, and moved Mary out to be with her family, telling her she could live in the house rent-free until the day she died. My husband and others cautioned me about getting involved on such a personal level, but Mary wasn't a cause, she was my friend. I felt compelled to help her.

As my husband warned, Mary and her family have proved to be more than I bargained for. Although they have escaped the projects, they sometimes have a hard time adjusting to their new surroundings and learning the skills necessary to survive in it. In many ways, they have become too dependent on me, whether for financial assistance or personal help. I have learned to set limits, but sometimes this dependency wears on me. I have also learned that if you truly want to help people on this level, you can't get involved halfway. You can write a check to the Red Cross or United Way and let them worry about everything else. Or you can get involved in a more personal way, which carries a lot more responsibility but also a lot more satisfaction. When I depart this life, I can look back and know that my church friends and I have really made a difference in people's lives, which isn't always easy to do. Carolyn has earned her two-year college degree and currently teaches at a daycare center while working on her four-year degree. Her oldest son just graduated from college with honors and intends to go on to graduate school. So the little help I have offered will have an impact on generations to come, and that makes me feel very good inside.

Sometimes I look back and wonder what might have transpired had I not had that moment of clarity in the taxi. Not only do I think about how different my life would have been, but I wonder about all those lives I have been able to touch through my company. I think the key to success in life, regardless of where you stand on the social and economic ladder, is being true to yourself and giving what you can. I don't do these things because I'm trying to become the next Mother Theresa. I do them because that's how I was raised, and because they make me feel good. I have been blessed with more than my share of good fortune, and I've never had to ask for anything I want from life. I feel I have an obligation to give something back in return.

Fourteen
Finding the Defining Moment

Robert Cutler
C3

Bob Cutler, forty-three, is president and owner of C3, a promotional marketing firm in Overland Park, Kansas, that provides promotional products and support to national and regional restaurant chains such as Olive Garden, Sonic Drive-Ins, Arby's, and Chic-fil-a. A firm believer in giving back to the community, Cutler regularly contributes a substantial amount of time and money to support the Kansas City Jewish Federation. His civic involvement reached a new level, however, when his daughter Alexis, "Lexi", was diagnosed as Pervasively Developmentally Delayed (PDD) at the age of two and a half. Cutler recently helped found the Midwest's only school for autistic children and is currently working hard to create a board of directors for the nonprofit school. Ultimately, he hopes to establish an endowment to fund the tuition for needy families with autistic children.

Someone once asked me to identify my defining moment as a CEO, and I thought long and hard before answering. I believe that for CEOs, defining moments happen every day, all the time. We are like the headlights on an oncoming locomotive. We lead the way in everything we do and say, and everyone in the company looks to us to set the example. Everything we do sets the tone for others, and every decision we make creates a defining moment. And it all comes back to us, one way or another.

Several years ago, we had contracted with a freight representative who messed up orders, lost shipments, and frequently made life miserable. We frequently butted heads over her mistakes, and from

109

time to time I would stop using her. But I always treated her honestly and with respect, even when I wanted to slam the door in her face, because those are the defining moments for CEOs. How I act in those moments sends a very powerful message to everyone else in my company. Eventually we got big enough to hire our own distribution person. But the freight representative and I parted on friendly terms, which set off a chain of events that have had a lasting impact on my personal life and the business.

On her way out, she recommended several people for the distribution position, one of whom we hired. She also introduced us to our current director of operations, Barbara, who brought in an operations assistant who introduced me to my second wife, Marida. Marida worked at an ad agency when we met, and since then several outstanding people from that agency have come to work for us.

My decision to do business with the freight representative led to many positive things for my business. Could I have known or even expected it at the time? Of course not. But my maintaining a good relationship with her represents the kind of definitive moment that I have to pay attention to all the time. Not just because these decisions might lead to something good, but because they represent who I am as a person. As a business leader, you face these situations all the time, and you don't do the right thing because bad things will happen if you don't. You do the right thing because it is a reflection of your character and values.

Like many entrepreneurs, I set out on my own because I felt like I could build a better mousetrap. After seven years at Hallmark Cards, I worked for a New York promotional agency that specialized in creating licensed character properties for national chains like Burger King and Pizza Hut. Looking to make my mark, I began calling on regional accounts that seemed to have real potential. I couldn't hit a home run with these accounts, but I knew I could score a solid single. Unfortunately, that wasn't good enough for them. When the company refused to support my sales efforts, I decided to relocate to the Midwest and start my own business.

I've enjoyed watching how the company has evolved over the past fouteen years. At first, the name of the game is survival, because you have no other income. But as the business grows, you evolve as a person and a leader. Our initial objective was simple—to provide regional restaurant chains with the level of service, quality, and creativity that national restaurant chains receive. Over time we have refined that strategy somewhat, but essentially it remains unchanged. My motivation for running the business, however, has evolved to a higher sense of purpose. Today, we strive to make a difference in the lives of our customers, our associates, and our customers' clients.

Over the years, the success of the business has allowed me to give back to the community in many ways. I aggressively support a number of charities in the Kansas City area, and I sit on the board of the Kansas Autism Foundation. Through my initiative, we started the only autistic school within 2,000 miles of Kansas City. My daughter, now five, was diagnosed with autism at the age of two and a half. My ex-wife and I were fortunate enough to stumble upon the applied behavioral analysis (ABA) approach for teaching autistic children, which had a good track record of success. But we had to apply it ourselves at home, because although several institutions teach the ABA approach on the East and West coasts, we couldn't find any such schools within 2,000 miles of Kansas City.

Through networking, we located a local therapist who used the ABA approach. She put me in touch with the director of the Kansas City Autism Foundation, and the two of them shared their dream with me of opening a school in Kansas City for autistic children. I immediately enlisted in the cause and helped them find a site for the school. I also coached them on prudent business practices, such as proper legal documentation, financial planning, cash flow, budgeting, insurance liability, and so on. The school opened its doors in October 1998 with four students. We currently have eight and can accommodate up to fifteen.

Although our daughter was taught at home using the ABA approach, the school has made a tremendous difference, because she receives daily attention from trained therapists. A very gregarious, outgoing little girl, Lexi is at the high end of the functioning scale. Her IQ has improved nearly twenty points since participating in the ABA protocol, and she constantly amazes me with her improving ability to respond to the world around her. One night we were playing a silly game, and I said to her jokingly, "You're a big hammerhead." She responded, "You mean a hammerhead shark?"—which amazed and delighted me. She now makes associations like that all the time and is constantly learning and picking up new things. For the parent of a PDD child, there is no greater joy than watching your child develop skills that previously seemed well out-of-reach.

Unfortunately, the school puts a tremendous financial burden on the families of the children who attend. Because of the one-to-one nature of the teaching, tuition costs $60,000 a year. I've been blessed with the financial resources to meet that demand, but other families are mortgaging their homes, cashing in their savings, and doing whatever it takes to get their children in the school, because for the first time, they have real hope. Once we get a quality board of directors in place for the school, we hope to create an endowment fund to aid families who can't afford the high tuition.

Unlike many of my entrepreneur friends and colleagues, I don't work seventy hours a week and have no intention of doing so. I learned early on that having balance in your life creates more opportunity. I also learned that the more I give, the more I get back, often in ways I don't expect or anticipate. Early in the life of C3, I got involved with the Jewish community here in Kansas City, giving both of my time and my money. The first few years, it wasn't easy to write the check for what, at the time, represented a substantial amount of money to me. Yet, every year that I extended myself, my business kept doing better and better. It's the old story of which came first—the chicken or the egg. I believe that if I hadn't committed first, I wouldn't have had the opportunity for my business to support that commitment.

My favorite expression is "givers gain and takers toil." Whenever I give of myself in the community, I *always* get something back that benefits me or my business. The fun part is I never know how or when it will come back. When I first came to Kansas City, I met a girl in a bar who invited me to attend a Jewish singles organization. Out of the blue, they called to ask if I would help make phone calls to support the community campaign. I agreed, and that started my involvement with the Jewish community. Through that organization, I met a wonderful older gentleman named Leonard Bettinger who befriended me. We had lunch several times, and one day, while driving back in his car, he asked me what I would do with my business if I had $100,000. Nonplussed, I stammered that I didn't know but would probably not have to use my credit cards or cash in my IRA every year in order to finance the business. He then offered to put some of his own bonds down as security so that I could establish a credit line at the bank. That took a tremendous financial burden off my shoulders, and we have self-funded the business ever since. Sadly, he died suddenly a few years ago, but I will never forget his kindness and generosity.

And my involvement in the Jewish community helped me rethink the structure of my business. Two years ago, the Jewish Federation went through a complete strategic planning process that resulted in a very forward-looking, collaborative model of community support. For example, when dealing with the aging issue, the Federation brings together all the stakeholders, such as the geriatric center, the B'nai B'rith, the representative from the Jewish Family and Children Services, and so on, and creates a collective community response to the identified needs. That sounds simple, but the model and the process you have to go through to get there are fairly complex.

That process, which I got to participate in, inspired C3's current business model. Instead of having separate account managers call on clients, we now have strategic teams that service four or five major clients. This collaborative approach allows us to do a much better job of servicing our clients. As an organization, we have become more responsive, more adept at change, more willing to take risks, and more in line with today's marketplace. So my charitable efforts with the Jewish Federation helped revamp and reposition my company for the future, an outcome I did *not* expect when I agreed to make a few phones calls one Sunday several years ago.

I love running my business and I spend a great deal of time at it. But as you might guess, my world revolves around my daughters. People often wonder what it's like to raise a child with special needs. In many ways, it's not that different from raising any other child. I have the same hopes, dreams, and aspirations for Lexi as any other parent has. I wish for her a life full of richness and meaning and a loving partner to share it with. I know what I have to do to give her that opportunity, so I focus on getting her whole by seeing that she gets great therapy, plenty of interaction with full-functioning children, and lots of love from her entire family.

Lexi has such a warm and sweet personality and is so cute that sometimes even her therapists fail to push her as much as she needs. Fortunately, her teachers at school have learned not to get taken in by her cute looks and sparkling smile. The older she gets, however, the more she risks being chastised and hurt by unknowing peers. I fear this more than anything, and it will break my heart if it ever happens. This has taught me that there are challenges out there that even the best CEOs cannot be sure how to handle until having to face them head on. How my child's life unfolds will undoubtedly lead me through an endless series of defining moments.

Fifteen
The Accidental CEO

Keith Swayne
Case Swayne Company

Keith Swayne, fifty-eight years old, is president and CEO of the Case Swayne Company, a specialty-food processor based in Corona, California. Founded by his father and a partner in 1943, the company currently does $150 million in sales, has processing plants in three states, and employs 600 people. An ardent supporter of multicultural diversity, Swayne works hard to break down the barriers that often exist between people of different backgrounds and cultures, both in his business and the community in which he lives. Fifty-five percent of Case Swayne's employees represent ethnic minorities, and the company regularly provides education and diversity training to promote tolerance and understanding among different cultural groups. In 1997, Swayne earned a regional Inc. Entrepreneur of the Year award, and the company won a training award from the American Society for Training and Development. For his efforts in the community, Swayne also received a Civil Rights Leadership award from the California Association of Human Relations Organizations.

I never intended to become a CEO. In fact, I didn't want to work in my father's company no matter what the position. I've always placed a high value on personal independence, and the idea of working for a family business contradicted everything I felt I should do with my life. But when my father took ill with lung cancer in 1969, I joined the company in order to help out. Although he recovered from his initial bout with the disease, I never seriously considered leaving the company, because I felt a strong sense of responsibility and obligation. Had things turned out differently, I probably would have pursued a career with a Fortune 500 company and had a great time doing it, but I ended up at Case Swayne, and it forever changed my life. Not once have I looked back and wondered what might have been.

One thing I didn't expect when I took this position is how much the CEO job dominates your life. The company is *always* foremost in your thinking, and on those rare occasions when something manages to displace it, it floats just beneath the surface, waiting to take over your consciousness. Sometimes I don't realize how much it controls me until we're out at a social event and my wife points out that I'm talking about strategic planning for the company. So the business never gets very far below the surface, no matter where you are or what you're doing.

The position also comes with a tremendous sense of responsibility for your employees, customers, and shareholders. Unless you have a heart of stone, you can't help but connect with those people, especially those who work for you year in and year out. When you own the company, you tend to take those burdens on at a very personal level. To a large extent, you hold these people's lives in your hands, so I'm not talking about some abstract concept of duty or loyalty. The responsibility is very real; it's there every day, and it never goes away. If you get fed up, you can't just take your golden parachute and gently float away. As the owner, you commit yourself for the long run, and that includes the bad and the good.

People who have never run a company have a hard time understanding that mind-set. If you work for someone else and hate your job, you can quit and find another one, without having much impact on the company. I don't have the luxury of that option. My first few years on the job I remember thinking, "My God, what have I gotten myself into?" Fortunately, I haven't felt that way for a long time. In reality, I was never really trapped. If I had wanted it badly enough, I could have figured a way to get out.

Those early years taught me something: you cannot wallow in the past or play the victim. I may have felt an obligation to help my father, but *I* made the choice to join the company and eventually run it. Nobody forced me. You have to take the cards life deals you and move on. Besides, you can't be a victim and run a company at the same time. You focus so intently on the business that you don't have time to think about how life is treating you. You simply don't have time to dwell on the past.

Another thing I didn't expect was the level of risk that comes with the territory. In the late 1980's, changing market conditions forced us to get out of the canning business and devote our full attention to specialty-food products. We had to cut the business almost in half and invest a huge amount of money in new equipment before we could grow again. We stretched our credit to the limit, and if it had snapped, I could have lost all my assets to the personal guarantees. Did I want to sign my life over to the bank? No. But when you see no other course of action, you do what you have to do to protect the business. Fortunately, my wife has been very supportive throughout my career, including my decision to remain at Case Swayne. She didn't like putting everything we owned on the line any more than I did, but she understood that we did it for the good of the company.

At the time, I felt like I had a clear picture of where the company needed to go and why we needed to do it. My real challenge was communicating the vision so that everyone else bought into it and felt good about the new direction for the business. That's tough to do when you're eliminating half your work force and changing just about everything you do. Plus, your own gut is constantly churning, because you're putting the entire company on the line. We had some rough moments when it looked like we might not make it, but there were others that made up for the tough times. One was a meeting that my staff asked to have with me. I still recall it very clearly. My staff asked to meet with me first thing on a Monday morning. I remember thinking they wanted my assurance that everything would turn out fine. We all gathered in one room, and I was prepared to give them a rousing pep talk. Instead, they told me in a rather emotional way that I didn't have to feel alone, and that they would support me to the end. I got so choked up I couldn't speak for several minutes. To this day, thinking about it almost brings tears to my eyes. When you make that kind of massive organizational change, people don't necessarily share your point of view. Knowing I had their unequivocal support took a tremendous load off my shoulders.

Our society promotes the perception that a business leader can't show any weakness, especially during tough times. Having served four

years as a Navy officer, including a tour in Vietnam, I could easily buy
into that, but I don't happen to agree with that perception. In fact, I've
learned that the best way to connect with people is by letting your
guard down, by sharing your concern for the situation and having
some compassion for the other person.

For example, a couple of years ago we acquired a company in
Kansas City. As much as I tried to pay attention to people's needs and
make them feel involved and empowered, we simply moved too fast.
In trying to implement our way of doing things, I failed to properly
acknowledge the value of the management team. In the process,
I bruised a lot of egos and caused some serious damage. Nobody
walked out the door, but many came close.

I ended up going back to the general manager with hat in hand
and apologizing for the way we handled the situation, which was a
very humbling experience. I asked the management team to spell out
in black and white all the things we had done wrong when we
acquired them. I wanted the feedback from a business standpoint,
because I didn't want to make the same mistakes in the future, but
I also wanted to show that we could acknowledge our mistakes and
try to correct them. That one small effort on my part went a long way
toward resolving the situation.

Despite my occasional blunders in the area of human relations, I
have a real passion for trying to help people get along with each
other. For the past fourteen years, I have worked with the Orange
County Human Relations Council, a nonprofit organization that
supports the Human Relations Commission. The O.C.H.R.C. helps set
up outreach programs by forming community partner groups
composed of business, academic, and community leaders. We serve as
advocates for human-relations programs in the county and help to
source funding for various programs.

Our most successful program to date, which has been chosen as a
model for other areas, is an intervention program aimed at
intermediate and high school kids. We obtain the funding, and the
Human Relations Commission goes into the schools to teach young
people that by understanding each other's differences, we can
generate tolerance rather than hatred and fear. The program seems to
be having a real affect on young people and their attitudes toward

people of different backgrounds. I'm proud to be a part of the program, and I intend to continue working with it when I retire from Case Swayne.

I've also become involved in a mentors group, a small collection of business leaders who get together to learn how to become more effective coaches and mentors. I joined because I thought it would help me deal more effectively with people, not just in business but in all walks of life. I also hope to help fledgling minority-owned businesses by sitting on boards and mentoring young entrepreneurs. So I went into the mentors group expecting to learn how to work better with others, which I have to some extent, but to my surprise, I have learned a lot more about myself.

In particular, the mentors group has taught me to become a lot more open to the way other people see the world. I've also learned that I become a much more effective leader when I facilitate helping people find the answer rather than just giving it to them. For example, about a year ago I hired a chief financial officer from a very large corporation. After a while, it became obvious that he had the potential to assume a position of real leadership in the company and perhaps even run the business after I leave. In the old days, I would have sat him down and told him, "Here's what you need to succeed, and here's how you are going to do it." Instead, I asked him to draw up a list of the traits he thinks successful leaders need to have. I made up my own list, and we sat down together to have a conversation about it. As a result, I now have a clearer picture of who this man is and what he is all about, and I can make a better decision about whether to begin grooming him for the CEO position.

Despite my personal growth on the inside, on the outside I remain very focused and goal-oriented. I doubt those characteristics will ever go away, but the most important lesson I've learned from sitting in the driver's seat is the unshakable goodness and value of people. By far the best part of this job is helping people succeed and being a party to their success. To have an organization of 600 employees and share in their energy, pride and commitment, and success really changes your outlook on life. I sure didn't set out on this path thirty years ago, but I have been blessed to travel down it with a group of outstanding people from all walks of life.

Section Three
Epiphanies

Sixteen
Fulfillment After Failure

Red Scott
Intermark Inc.

Charles "Red" Scott, seventy-one years old, epitomized Horatio Alger's American dream. Growing up on the "wrong side of the tracks" in Paris, Texas, Scott won a scholarship to the University of Texas, worked in journalism for two years, and then began a long and distinguished career as an entrepreneur and business leader. He ran a successful mutual fund firm in Dallas and later became CEO of Roberts, Scott & Co., a highly successful brokerage firm in San Diego, California. In 1970, he became chairman and CEO of Intermark, Inc., a billion-dollar conglomerate and holding company with such subsidiary corporations as Pier 1 Imports and Simplicity Pattern Co. under his leadership. During the 1970s and 80s, Scott helped create great wealth for his shareholders and himself. He became widely active in a host of charitable organizations, such as the Scripps Memorial Hospital Foundation and the Boy Scouts of America, and he was voted one of the top twenty-five CEOs of the 1980's in California. Fittingly, he won the 1984 Horatio Alger Award of Distinguished Americans. Then, in 1991, with retirement staring him in the face, Scott made a fateful business decision that changed his life.

I've been the chairman or CEO of eight companies, five of which would have qualified for the Fortune 500 at the time we owned them. While I was the head of Intermark, which we called an operating holding company, we owned twenty-five or thirty businesses, including Pier 1, Simplicity Pattern, and Munson Sporting Goods, with a total of 13,000 employees. Intermark was the parent and controlling

123

shareholder, and I served as the chairman of each of these subsidiaries. I was the CEO of Intermark for twenty-one years. For a period of sixteen of those years, Intermark had a compounded return to its shareholders of 47 percent a year. We made a lot of people very rich.

One of our major investments in the late 1980s was in a company called Fuqua Industries, based in Atlanta. We owned 26 percent of Fuqua, and in 1991, Fuqua was falling on its ear. In plain English, it was a mess. Being the largest shareholder of Intermark and the one who had put the Fuqua deal together, I said that my last business act would be to go to Atlanta and turn Fuqua around. I was sixty-three years old. What I thought would be my swan song, my final business triumph, turned into a nightmare.

When we first bought Fuqua, the idea was that I would be a non-employee chairman and it would simply be another Intermark investment. I wouldn't be active in the day-to-day management of the company. I'd fly in from California in my jet once a month, we'd have a board meeting, I'd pontificate a little bit, wave the magic wand, sprinkle a little holy water, and go back to California. And Fuqua would hum and sing and make lots of money for us.

But it became obvious in the late fall of 1990 that that was not going to happen, that Fuqua was auguring in and going south. Reports from Fuqua got worse and worse. While the problems were many, the most serious issue was that Fuqua's most profitable subsidiary, Snapper Lawnmower, was in serious trouble, because the market had shifted dramatically and caught Snapper unprepared.

Lawnmowers were now being sold as disposable commodities directly to consumers at discount mass merchants such as Home Depot and Wal-Mart. Customers took them home, assembled and used them for a year or two, and then simply bought new ones. Snapper was totally dependent on a two-step distribution system that included nearly 10,000 small neighborhood dealers, most of whom owed Snapper a substantial amount of money. It would have been suicide to go directly to the mass merchants and thus break most of Snapper's dealers who would, in turn, not be able to pay their bill. Beyond that, another subsidiary had overstated its operating earnings for several years and could not hope to duplicate those numbers moving forward. The problems seemed endless and there was no quick fix.

Finally, in January 1991 it became obvious to me that I was going to have to do something dramatic. I'd either have to sell the Fuqua investment at an enormous loss or find somebody to come in and take it over. Or I'd have to take it over myself and try to fix it.

I was like a little boy. I was so angry at myself that I had gotten us into this mess. I couldn't blame anybody else, though I looked around for someone to blame. But it was my doing that got us into it, and I was determined to fix it.

I flew to Atlanta in February 1991 for the regular monthly board meeting and, to my surprise, was elected CEO. I had just one change of clothes, because I'd thought I'd only be there a day or two. I'll never forget the phone call to my wife. I said, "Honey, we're moving to Atlanta." There was this long pause and she asked, "Who?" I said, "Well, you and me. We've been partners for thirty years now, and I'm going to take over Fuqua, and we're going to move from La Jolla, California, to Atlanta." She said, "You've had a lot of dumb ideas, but this is the dumbest one. I'm not coming." And she didn't for a while. But finally she did, and now she won't go back. She loves Atlanta. For me, Atlanta was a different story.

It turned out to be one of the darkest moments of my life and my business career. I had achieved so much success, had been such a toast of the town, and had had such phenomenal luck. I had been featured in a number of national magazines. I had been on some national TV programs, such as the "Pinnacles of Success." I had been the boy wonder. I'm sure my ego got too big. I made this enormous investment in Fuqua, essentially investing half of Intermark's assets, and it didn't do well. Here in the waning years of my life, I stubbed my toe and made a terrible investment.

In my mind, I felt like I had bought a salted mine. In the old days, when people tried to sell a gold mine, they would salt the mine ahead of time by sprinkling in some gold and then hope that someone would buy it. What I bought was not what I had been led to believe it was. I did a lousy job of due diligence. It was my own fault. I learned a quick lesson. When you're on the way up, the world loves to help you and boost you higher. When you trip and start down, however, the world is happy to help you slide. So I went from being a hero to being a goat almost overnight because of the bad investment in Fuqua.

When I arrived in Atlanta, the local press and some of the local business community didn't exactly greet me with open arms. Atlanta did not throw open its doors and welcome a "carpetbagger" from California to come in and take over one of its premier old companies. I didn't show a lot of patience with the local press, and my picture and story appeared in the paper several times in the first few weeks. The articles were mostly uncomplimentary. In the meantime, J.B. Fuqua and some of his key people left the company. There were some hard feelings on my part, because I thought, quite frankly, that they had not treated me fairly.

There was some bloodletting. Fuqua had a big, fat, corporate office that was burning money like there was no tomorrow. The corporate office had 104 employees. We cut that quickly down to 52. Over a three-year period, we cut that number down to 13.

I'm sure those folks thought that I was being too brash, too harsh, and was acting with too heavy of a hand. I don't want to take anything away from their viewpoint. But I felt like I had been badly abused. I was publicly chastised in national publications, such as *Business Week, Forbes,* and *Fortune*. Everyone took a shot at me. How could I have screwed up this badly?

Of course, it gets extremely lonely at that point of the game, because by then, I was not willing or capable of admitting that I had made a mistake. I was still trying to be the boy wonder, which was sad, because I was sixty-three.

I simply wasn't dealing with myself honestly. I was still trying to decide if I could save Fuqua myself or if I should hire somebody else to do it. I thought, maybe I was too old and ought to just take retirement and call it quits. I was really thrashing around.

I remember in the middle of all this, I got a call from a man named Ross Johnson, who had been the CEO of RJR Nabisco. The book *Barbarians at the Gate* was written about RJR. It was not very flattering, to say the least.

I'd never met Ross Johnson. I didn't know him from a barrel of grapefruit. But he had moved RJR to Atlanta, and one day my phone rang. I'd been in town for three or four weeks with this mess swirling around. My secretary came in and said, "There's a Ross Johnson on the phone." I said, "I don't know any Ross Johnson other than the guy that runs RJR. Why would he be calling me?" So I picked up the phone and said, "Is this the great barbarian?" And he said, "None other." He said, "You're about as welcome in this town as I was. You need a friendly face. Why don't we go have lunch?" I said, "Boy, you're right." So he took me to lunch that day, and we became wonderful friends, and I will never forget that.

Other than Ross Johnson, who became my friend, and my California TEC group, I felt very much isolated. I didn't deal with the Fuqua board well, although many of them were nice people. They were strangers to me. I did not feel I was in a position to just fess up and say, "Hey, guys, I really messed this up. Help me work my way out of it." I was still trying to bravely stand on the bridge and act like we had not hit an iceberg.

But it was an iceberg, a big one. Intermark's cost basis in that block of Fuqua stock was about $32 a share. At one point, Fuqua stock had evaporated down to about $6 or $7 a share. So it had lost 75 percent of its value. It was ultimately sold for $16, about half its cost. We had invested $140 million, and when it dropped to the bottom, it was worth about $35 million.

Those were especially difficult times, because I just didn't know which role to play. I would have been a lot better off if I had been able to deal with it very candidly and say, "Hey, I made a mistake. I've done it, and it's terrible, and I ought to be taken to the woodshed and whipped." But it's hard for a leader to publicly stand up and say, "I need a whipping." As I look back, that would have probably been the most efficient, economic, and therapeutic thing I could have done, but I kept trying to defend my territory.

Finally, father time simply ran out on me. I passed age sixty-five, which was when I'd planned to retire. I didn't retire until I was almost sixty-seven. I finally said, "Okay, this is going to take longer, and it's a bigger job than I thought, so I need to step aside and let some younger guy come in here and wrestle this giant to the ground." In 1995, the board went out and picked a new CEO, who came in and took over Fuqua; and I completely stepped out of the picture.

This whole mess was a very humbling experience. I am able to make speeches about it now, and they serve as good, therapeutic treatment. I titled the speech "Doing a Pratfall at Center Court,

Wimbledon." Assume it is the final day of Wimbledon, with the Queen in her box, and you come dancing out to center court to play, and the first thing you do is slip and fall right on your ass in front of the whole world. That could be pretty embarrassing.

Referring to an NFL player name Hollywood Henderson, Bum Phillips, the former NFL football coach, once said, "Hollywood didn't know that a ladder had splinters until he started slipping down it." Well, I now know firsthand that you get a lot of splinters when you slip down that ladder.

My colleagues in TEC (a group I've belonged to for more than twenty-five years), were the biggest help to me. They made me talk about Fuqua at length, and it was like going to a psychiatrist's couch. I talked about my experience and got some of it out. They said, "Why don't you go make a speech about this? There would be a lot of people who would like to hear it." So I did. And once I started talking about Fuqua publicly, I began to be able to work with it and live with it and deal with it.

In the speech, I admit that I messed up. I tell people that I had a vision of being a $4-billion company instead of a $2-billion company and that I started worshipping the wrong goal.

Basically, what caused my problem was that I was ego-driven. I got focused on the wrong thing. I loved the limelight. I loved all the media attention. I liked having a big staff, a limo, a jet airplane, and all of that. I just started chasing graven images. It's not a religious speech. I just say that I started chasing the wrong thing and paid a dear price for that folly.

Almost inevitably, every time I make the speech, people come up and say, "You ought to see how I blew one, but I never did admit it to anybody. I can't believe you get up here and admit your mistake publicly."

There is an upside to such an experience. You really get a great education and begin to understand who you are and how God deals with you. I've always been a person who tries to look forward. I don't spend much time looking backward. Once something is done, I'm over it, and I don't usually dwell on it very long.

By the grace of God, I won a scholarship to the University of Texas. Otherwise, I might still be in Paris, Texas, pumping gas. As such, I have a great need to put things back into the system, to try to make it a better world. I have spent a lot of time on charity and civic work, because I care about those things. I'm seventy-one now. I don't think of that as being old, so I still try to go 900 miles an hour. I only know one speed, and that's full speed.

What I see out there is that most young executives think they are bulletproof. I did. If they hear me talk, they think I'm some old fart who doesn't understand the business world today. A small percentage will listen and believe; most don't. That's why I start my speech off by saying that the more something succeeds, the more something works right for you, the more likely you are to fail. If you do something six times in a row and it works, you begin to think you have the bulletproof answer. That was my mind-set.

We bought and sold many companies, with great success. We would buy a company that was well and make it even better, or we'd buy a company that was sick and make it well or grow. With such a record of success, I began to think I was bulletproof.

I got way too big for my britches. I needed to be a lot more conservative and a lot more humble. When I finally retired and sold my stock and went to Palm Springs, I said, "I'm going to play golf, and to hell with the past." I was still mad and in denial. After a few weeks, I realized this wasn't doing me any good. I needed to get back to doing something. Like an old farmer who needs a garden patch, I needed something to plant and tend and grow.

None of us want others to see our own dark underside. A public flogging is not a lot of fun, but once you say, "I'm human. I made a mistake. I need help," people rush to help you.

I ended up buying a small business, the TEC license for the state of Florida. I've gone back to work, and I'm having the time of my life now. I can joke about things. Instead of a staff of people, I lick my own stamps and mail my own letters. I work at it two or three hours a day, and then I go play golf or do something civic or charitable. My life has now come back full circle, to where I'm a happy, meaningful, useful person. I have proved to my own satisfaction that I can run a business successfully, and it doesn't really matter whether anyone else knows.

Seventeen

The Sound (Management) of Music

Ron Rowe
J.W. Pepper & Son, Inc.

Ron Rowe is the CEO of the 126-year old J.W. Pepper, the world's largest retailer of printed sheet music. The $45-million company, located in Valley Forge, Pennsylvania, targets schools, colleges and churches—anyplace where amateur musicians sing and play music—as its core customers. The company has 185 employees in twelve locations, and it buys sheet music from music publishers and retails the music to high school bands, orchestras, choruses, and church choirs. Rowe, sixty-years-old, graduated from college in Michigan with a degree in music and taught high school band. He realized that a teacher's salary was not going to suffice for raising a family, so in 1966, he joined J.W. Pepper. He has been with the company ever since, rising from sales manager to CEO in 1986. As CEO, he orchestrated a dramatic makeover of the company's organizational structure, essentially redefining the way everybody works.

In the world of sheet music, we do 70 percent of our business during four months of the year: September, October, January, and February. The reason is that most of our business is geared around schools and the teachers' schedules. In September and October, teachers buy music like crazy—they buy all the sheet music they need for the marching band at the football games, for Christmas concerts, and for music classes in the school. Then they spend November and December rehearsing and performing it. Everything shuts down for the Christmas holiday, and when they return after Christmas, they buy music for spring concerts, graduation ceremonies, and more classes. So business booms again during January and February, but then drops off because teachers stop buying when they're rehearsing and performing again.

I spent twenty years with the company, trying to find a way to smooth out that curve. Our problem was simple. We didn't have enough people to handle the peak seasons, when business was the most critical for us. During the valleys we had what we call "bore outs," people standing around watching the clock all day with nothing to do. We couldn't do cyclical hiring, because we're not the kind of company that hires and lays off, hires and lays off.

The stress is unbelievable. During the peaks, you're beating dead horses. Well, we don't actually beat the horses. But what happens is that you must say to the employee, "Come on Frank, come on in and help us work Sunday to get caught up. I know you've worked sixty hours already this week, but we'll give you free pizza and overtime." And after a while, that gets to be pretty old.

It sure got old for me. I grew tired of working twelve-hour days, seven days a week. I approached my job like the general. "I'm going to take the hill gang, follow me!" I thought that if I worked hard, everybody would follow me up the hill.

That's the reason there had to be a change. Every time we came into the fall season, I went crazy. Nobody could live with me. Nobody could talk to me. There had to be a change.

I got so tired of this routine after twenty years that in 1988, a couple of years after I became CEO, I decided that I had to do something—anything—to change it, or I would have to leave the company. I just couldn't face the cycles anymore. I couldn't do this for another fall. I came up a with a plan, and I wish I could say that I knew it was going to work, but in truth, there was no way that I could know what was going to happen.

I'd studied that business curve over and over. I thought, "We're not sending rockets to the moon." We were picking and packing and shipping. Our average order was $80. The average piece of sheet music that we sold was $10. We had 65,000 accounts, and we sent about 3,000 orders a day.

The answer lay in the idea of shifting people around to where the action was during the workday. If we could do that and move away from the conventional focus on job specialty, we might be on to something.

We're in the mail-order business, and we want all the orders to be filled at the end of the day. So when we come in at 8:30 in the morning, the most important thing to do is to open the mail. Everything else is unimportant. It is not important at 8:30 in the morning to be posting to general ledger or to be wrapping packages. The most important thing, more than anything else, at 8:30 in the morning is to open the mail.

What we had was a *department* to open the mail. Not surprisingly, it took them all day to open the mail. We humans stretch out our jobs to fill the time that we have available to do it. We had five or six people in our shipping department, and at 8:30 in the morning, there is nothing for them to ship. We haven't opened the mail. We haven't started answering the phone. There are no orders on the floor.

Yet management stands around making sure that those shippers aren't late for work. If they are, they get docked. At 3:00 in the afternoon, however, the six guys in the shipping department are screaming bloody murder about working too hard.

So my idea was to shift people throughout the day from job, to job, to job. Wherever we needed a function served, we would put the resources there and do that function. I had heard a management guru named Peter Schutz, the former CEO of Porsche, espouse an interesting concept. Management really screws up, because we tend to make decisions autocratically, and we tend to implement democratically. We sit back and decide what strategic thing it is we are going to do, and then we go out and we try to talk the staff into supporting this decision that we just made because it's so wonderful.

Schutz says you should turn that around. In order to make decisions, you should get everybody in the whole place involved in the decision-making process. Then when the decision is made, people have some degree of ownership, and implementation becomes a much easier task.

Based on that, I decided to bypass the first level of management. I knew they would resist it, because they would lose their power. Of course, I couldn't just ignore the supervisors and not tell them what was happening. I went to the CFO, the sales manager, and other executives, and I said, "This is going to be really far out, and you've got to give me your word that you're going to support me on this for a year. No matter what happens, if at the end of the year you don't agree that it has been the right thing to do, then I'll can it. But you've got to support me. You're going to go sweep the floors, and you're going to wrap packages, and you're going to go do what everybody else does. Just support me on it."

I got their commitments. Then I went out and gathered eight employees, and for a full year, we met weekly for a brown bag lunch to discuss the concept of shifting people around to where the action was.

We eventually named the concept: the Company Enrichment Organization, or CEO. CEO is now the employee team that is responsible for the daily mechanics of running this company. CEO consists of employees who serve on a rotating basis, and it includes everyone in the company. Everyone in the company has served on CEO at least once. Many of them have served twice.

They are responsible for who does what when. They have developed an extensive computer program that creates work schedules and assignments. We all give two hours of our day to be shifted to where the action is. We don't take as many phone calls in November as we do in September. We need twice as many people taking phone calls in September and October as we do in November and December. So in those months, everyone answers phones. We had a secret ballot of our employees, and they said that 30 percent of their time was wasted over the course of the year. Here was a plan to change that.

If you have the right atmosphere, if you have the right culture, you don't need supervisors at all. What we needed were super teachers. What we needed were resource specialists. These are the people who do the job the best. Their job is to teach their specialties to everyone in the company. They are responsible for qualifying people to do these specialties. We don't have job descriptions anymore. I don't like them. What we have are the most detailed work descriptions imaginable.

I became an evangelist for this idea. A general's approach to management became an internal quest to find better ways to do things. The carrot was that if we could increase our efficiency and change the scenario from boredom to shipping more packages faster to the customer, we could all take a day off a week with pay during our slower times of the year. So now, twenty-three weeks a year, we all take one day off with pay in addition to our regular vacation.

We didn't start with twenty-three weeks. We used the concept as an internal motivation to make everything as efficient as possible and to pick up as much time as possible. It started out at fourteen weeks, and then it went to eighteen and then twenty. And then it went to twenty-three, and it has been holding at twenty-three. But here is the best part: in the first six years, we doubled the sales of the company, and we held the number of employees exactly the same.

I can't say the sales increase is only because of this concept, but I guarantee it's contributed a great deal to the attitude in the company. There is a passion now for answering the phone, for dealing with customers. Our customers can buy anything that we're selling far cheaper at a lot of different places. The only reason they're coming to us is because it's easy to place an order, they get exactly what they order and quickly, and they enjoy talking and doing business with us.

The key lesson for me has been that all people need in order to become really involved is for them to be part of something. They can't be convinced to be part of something. They have to be the inventors.

Of course, this all sounds wonderful, but there was a personal aspect that I had to deal with. I had to give up a tremendous amount of control. It felt terrible. I was extremely nervous, because I had to change my whole pattern of being and my whole way of thinking. I am not at all sure that I would have crossed the river twenty years earlier. I was much smarter twenty years ago. Like everyone else when they are young, I thought I knew everything there was to know.

That's the mistake that so many people make. You get to be the boss, and you think immediately that the way to be the boss is to be responsible for everything, keep your eye on everything, make sure that you've got every *i* dotted and every *t* crossed. We forget that that will totally limit the growth of a company and the growth of the people, because one person can only do so much.

The main thing I've learned is that a CEO's role should be to develop and create an atmosphere that promotes personal growth within the company. If the CEO just concentrates on that, wonderful things will happen.

Eighteen
Scaling Seven Summits

Lee Nobmann
Golden State Lumber, Inc.

Few, if any, CEOs have scaled the heights reached by Lee Nobmann. Though he has achieved more than his share of success with his family-owned lumber company, Nobmann's peaks are literal. In 1996, he completed his quest and became the twenty-seventh American to summit the highest mountain on each of the seven continents. Upon completing that Olympian quest, Nobmann purchased an airplane, learned to fly, and now spends much of his free time at mountaintop altitudes, only without any ground beneath his feet. When he's not trekking or soaring above the clouds, Nobmann manages to find time to run Golden State Lumber, a $150-million contractor-based lumber company outside San Francisco that has grown 25 to 30 percent a year for the past several years. A second-generation business owner and CEO, Nobmann believes and demonstrates that hard work and quality of life can go hand in hand.

First, let me say that I do not consider myself a mountaineer, although Mount Everest has always intrigued me. My seven-summit quest started out as an excuse to recharge my batteries after the 1990-91 recession nearly buried my business. Like it did for most Californians, that recession took us by surprise, and it hit with the force of an avalanche. Sales plummeted 50 percent, and I had to lay off half our workforce. I came *that* close to signing the business over to the bank. Thanks to a tremendous effort on everyone's part, we managed to hold on and get back on track in 1992.

By midsummer of '92, I desperately needed a break, so I scheduled a long vacation for September. As we walked out the door, my wife handed me a book entitled *The Seven Summits*, a story of two men who had scaled the highest peaks on each continent. I read the book during our vacation and said to my wife, "This is something I need to do." I don't know if she took me seriously at first. But six weeks later I stood on top of my first summit, Mount Kosciusko, in Australia.

In rapid succession, I climbed Mount Aconcagua in Argentina, Mount McKinley in Alaska, Mount Elbrus in Russia, and Mount Everest in the Himalayas. I originally planned to summit all seven peaks in one year, but after trekking foreign slopes for six months in 1993, I decided to take a rest and get reacquainted with my family and my business. In December 1995, I topped Mount Vincent in Antarctica, and I completed my world summit tour in February 1996 by ascending Mount Kilimanjaro in Africa.

Although each mountain proved difficult in its own right, Mount Everest, far and away, presented the toughest challenge. Any time you get over 20,000 feet, it's hard work. It took eleven long, grueling weeks to summit Everest, and I lost thirty-five pounds in the process.

Climbing Everest is *not* like taking a vacation. You don't eat or sleep much, and once on top, you don't feel any particular sense of euphoria from having conquered the mountain. You just grind it out one step at a time. You set up several camps along the way and wait for the right weather conditions. When you finally reach the summit, all you want to do is take the pictures and start the descent. Once safely back to base camp, you give thanks that no one got injured or killed. On our way up, the Lohtse Face, a particularly dangerous section of the mountain, gave way, and an avalanche completely wiped out Camp III. We lost 30 percent of our oxygen and all our tents. Fortunately, no one was in the camp at the time; they surely would have died. We never saw a trace of the camp again, as if Mount Everest had wiped it clean from the face of the earth.

Although we had our share of close calls, I never felt any real fear on the slopes. In fact, the recession scared me a lot more than anything I faced on the mountains. I had never experienced such a precipitous plunge in the business, and it really shook me. One day you're humming along nicely, and the next day the bottom drops out, and half your sales go away. Worse, you have no control over it. You can cut costs and lay off people, but when the building industry stops building, I can't sell any lumber, and I can't do much about it. Fortunately we managed to hang tough, and today I run my company a lot "leaner and meaner" as a result of those painful lessons. Over the past five years, we have grown from $50 million to $150 million in annual sales, and I expect to reach $250 million within two or three years.

Despite the company's success, I've had a hard time becoming this "CEO guy," because when I took over Golden State Lumber from my father, I clearly didn't have the tools to get the job done. Although I had worked in the business for many years, I didn't have a Harvard M.B.A. or any formal management training or experience. In fact, I flunked out of college during my sophomore year. I didn't understand balance sheets, financial statements, inventory control, or any of those management things a CEO has to know in order to run a business.

That lack of experience created a real credibility gap when I went to borrow money. The lenders knew I lacked the knowledge and tools, and the only way I could get them to work with me was by plowing ahead and proving I could do it. When you do what you say you're going to do and you make money year in and year out, eventually you build some credibility, but it didn't come easy for me. I had to earn their respect and confidence an inch at a time.

To this day, working with bankers continues to be a source of frustration for me. I like to take risks, and bankers don't. Combine that with our very aggressive growth track, and the lenders still get antsy, no matter how much credibility we have. I've learned how to do some things to make them less nervous, like hiring a strong CFO and laying out our financial projections each year, but I doubt we will ever see eye-to-eye.

Given my lack of formal education, the one factor that has contributed the most to my development as a CEO is that I'm not a quitter. When faced with a challenge, I simply refuse to back down. During the recession, for example, I could easily have thrown in the towel and given up on the business, but that's not in my nature. For one thing, I felt a responsibility to all the people who worked for the company, and I didn't want to let them down, but more important, I didn't want to let *me* down. I didn't want to have to look at myself in the mirror every morning knowing that I'd given up. The few times in life when I have quit have absolutely devastated me.

For example, a few years ago I attempted to scale Mount Hunter in Alaska, which tops out at about 14,000 feet but has some unbelievably steep faces and requires a lot of very technical climbing. After three days on the mountain, I realized the summit lay beyond my skills. Feeling the risk factor had reached unacceptable limits, we turned around and came down. That experience crushed me. Here I had climbed the tallest peaks on every continent in the world, and yet I couldn't conquer a mountain half the size of Everest. Despite the high risk to life and limb, coming down off that mountain was one of the toughest decisions of my life, harder even than laying off people in my business, because it was personal. You never like to lay off workers, but you do it for the sake of the business. On Mount Hunter, I let myself down, and it took me a long time to get over it.

That said, I don't consider climbing mountains to be my greatest accomplishment. I take a lot more pride in the way I've grown into the role of CEO, particularly in learning to delegate and hire people far more talented than myself who can get the job done. Like many young entrepreneurs, when I first took over the company, I tended to use the "command-and-control" style of leadership. You can get results that way, but it doesn't do much for your own personal growth or for those around you. Today, my greatest satisfaction comes from watching people come into the company, grow and develop, and take on increasing levels of responsibility. That really turns me on. To me, that's what being a CEO is all about—not just building the company, but building the people in it as you grow.

At forty-eight years old, I'm the oldest guy on our team. I'm having a lot of fun, and as long as it stays that way, I'll keep putting Golden State Lumber through its paces. As soon as it gets boring, I'll find something else to do. In the meantime, I plan to continue working on my flying skills. I also enjoy competing in water skiing competitions, and I intend to spend more time on the tennis court with my son. People wonder how I can take so much time away from the business, but you get to do that when you have a great management team. I can trust them to do the right things, while I'm away adding quality to my life.

I've also been getting the urge to strap on the mountain boots again. I don't feel like I have anything left to prove in that respect, but there's something about mountaineering that keeps calling you back. A few years ago, Mount Hunter defeated me a second time. For some reason, it bothered me a lot less the second time around. Perhaps I'm developing a new sense of my limitations and accepting that I can't win all the time. Either way, I'm thinking the time has come to take another shot at that peak. In a way, it's like seeing how far I can take Golden State Lumber—I just can't resist a challenge.

Nineteen

A Time to Reap, A Time to Sow

Paul Mariani
Angas Park Fruit Company

Angaston, South Australia, is in the heart of continent's richly fertile fruit-growing belt, an hour's drive from Adelaide. That is where fifty-four-year-old Paul Mariani, a transplanted Californian, runs the Angas Park Fruit Company, a $70-million worldwide supplier of dried fruits. Mariani's family is in the fruit business in California, and in the 1960s, they bought Angas Park Fruit in Australia and sent Mariani back and forth to keep an eye on the family's investment. In the late 1960s, at age twenty-five, Mariani emigrated to Australia and eventually married a young Australian woman. Mariani spent ten years manufacturing beef jerky, and then in 1987, along with his father-in-law, Colin Hayes, he bought Angas Park Fruit from his family in California and took over the business. As managing director (Australian parlance for CEO), Mariani acquired a thriving $35-million company along with a frustrating management dilemma that lasted more than a decade.

Going into business with my father-in-law certainly set up some pressures. He was the preeminent trainer and breeder of thoroughbreds in Australia. He has since retired, but he has a very high profile and has been extremely successful. He is also very demanding, and I tend to have a similar personality, so my wife worried that we would have trouble in a partnership. She thought we'd be like two bulls in a paddock.

As it turns out, my father-in-law has been a superb partner. He trusts our relationship, and he told me from the outset, "You know that business. I know my business. You run that one and keep me informed as to how we're doing."

So it's the best of all partnerships. Plus, I'm aware that one of the reasons he invested in Angas Park was to get this damn Yankee, who'd moved his daughter 2,000 kilometers away, to move his daughter and his grandchildren back to be near him.

Despite his great trust, the pressure is always there. I want to make sure the bottom line stays healthy. I don't want to give him reason to worry about his investment and thus lose the autonomy I've established, and I don't want to negatively affect our personal relationship, which is an excellent one. I work better under pressure, and had I gone into this alone, I wouldn't have felt as much pressure to keep the company growing as fast as it has. I've no doubt that because I have had two reasons to perform, the company has achieved more.

The greatest challenge didn't come from my father-in-law but from Graham (not his real name), the person who had been Managing Director of Angas Fruit when we bought the company. Graham had been a young manager with the company in the late 1960s when my family first bought it. He became the boss in the early 1970s and had overseen the company's success in the 1970s and early 1980s. He had a very good relationship with my family over the years, but when I bought the company from my family in 1987, everything changed.

Perhaps the worst part was that when my family put the company up for sale, Graham had headed up a team of managers who tried to buy the company, but my father-in-law and I outbid them. So here was a guy who'd been with the company for more than thirty years, thinking he was going to be an owner, and he got beat out by the owner's son. You wouldn't call it a real sweet start; it never got too much better.

I remember when I got there, he asked, "What do you plan to do, since I do all the work around here?" I had different ideas about how to run the business than he did, and it quickly became an unpleasant situation for me. In fact, I struggled with this situation for eleven years before finally asking him to resign.

For the first five years, I felt that he was simply too important to the business to let go. Graham had a tremendous amount of experience and knowledge about the organization and the market. We have seven locations and we deal with over 1,500 growers. He had been in the industry thirty-one years. He had a tremendous influence on our source of supply as well as our operations. He had relation-ships with the growers and everybody else I needed to work with. I needed his vast depth of experience and knowledge. My first commitment was to get the best results we could from the company, and there were areas of the business that I wasn't up to speed on— like raisins, for example. I needed to learn that side of the business before I made any major decisions. It was only prudent management to try to effect change in a piece-by-piece way and hope that he would accept our changes.

So I tried to manage jointly with him, but I couldn't get him to cooperate. After several years of that, I finally realized that Graham wasn't going to change on his own. I then had to build a management team and change the structure to a team-based organization. I tapped four or five people who had the experience and expertise to move us forward and allow us to grow. Each year, I made attempts to fit Graham into the team structure, but to no avail.

My frustrations grew, because despite our personality differences, Graham's ability and experience and his knowledge in certain areas of this business were probably the best in the world. Any transition was going to risk the company's bottom line. I probably put up with the frustrations more because of the responsibility I felt to my partner, my father-in-law, than for any other reason. I wanted to make those changes and still get the same excellent results out of the company operations, but because I felt this was too risky, I waited until the appropriate time when the change wouldn't have a negative impact on the company.

Needless to say, the atmosphere at work for me was not very pleasant a good deal of the time. Attempts at change always unraveled, and during the unraveling, you could cut the tension with a knife. I had no one to bounce ideas off of. I couldn't talk to my father-in-law. He'd have said, "Just fire him." It was no fun to go to work, and somewhere around the four- or five-year mark, the years of frustration I had felt in trying to manage my responsibilities for the company's performance despite my ongoing troubles with Graham caught up with me. I ended up with a bad asthmatic condition. I felt lousy and couldn't get out of bed. I just couldn't move; there was so much emotional baggage, and I just couldn't perform.

I tried to keep all this under wraps at home with my wife and four children, but it undoubtedly took its toll there too. I wasn't a very happy person and was probably a bit sharper-tempered and less patient and understanding. I didn't talk about it. My two older children were away at boarding school for much of the worst of it, but I know I missed out. My wife, of course, knew I was unhappy. We have a great relationship, and we can talk about those things.

In fact, during this period, when I felt so sick, my wife and I went away to a health resort, the Golden Door Health Resort in Queensland, in eastern Australia. We had nothing but vegetarian food. There was no alcohol, no cigarettes, not even tea or coffee. Your body gets a good flushing and continual exercise. I remember vividly that on the fourth day, I woke up and felt great. I didn't have any symptoms of asthma. It wasn't because of the food or the exercise; it was just the realization that there was nothing wrong with me besides what was in my head. The time away gave me a chance to refocus. That break helped me see more clearly what was going on. I said, "I'm going back, and we're going to make some changes." I never looked back from that day.

I made the decision in February of 1998 that by the end of the year, a change would be made. Rather than confronting Graham with it, I set this before my senior management group, and they said, "We have to make a change." The team said that Graham had to move into a non-operational capacity, and I offered him a position as a coach and mentor, as well a chance to continue as a director of the company. He didn't refuse, but he didn't accept, and when enough time had passed with no response, I finally said, "Graham, we haven't been able to work together for nearly eleven years. Changing your responsibilities isn't going to make it work any better for you or me. I think it's time that you move on and we move on." I offered him the maximum severance package that could be justified, and that's how we finished.

It was a rough couple of months, but when his last day came, to his credit, he accepted his departure gracefully. He now has a nice payout package and a little vineyard, and he is moving on with his life.

As you can imagine, there was fallout inside the company. We have 400 employees, and head count swells to 900 during fruit season. Some people inside the company, especially in the production area where his influence was the greatest, didn't understand why Graham left. Some, who had worked with him for twenty to twenty-five years, were very uneasy. If Graham could be sent packing, they thought, anybody could be. I quickly reassured everyone that their jobs were safe. We lost only two people, and neither left because of Graham. Most of the other employees saw this as a very positive step forward. The word "change" is no longer a dirty word around here.

Not surprisingly, since we did this, people have asked me again and again why we didn't do this sooner. The reality was that the situation was a lot more gray than black and white; despite our differences, Graham was a damn good operator who made me a lot of money. Because of that fact, timing was everything, and safeguarding the bottom line might not have been so easily achieved if Graham had departed sooner. In hindsight, I believe that the transition, no matter how long it took, was worth the frustration.

Twenty

A Taxing Journey to the Top

Gerald Golub
American Express Tax and Business Services

Gerald L. Golub, chairman of American Express Tax and Business Services, arrives at his Manhattan office at 5:30 every morning. He not only opens the door and turns on the lights, but he brews up the coffee—regular and decaffeinated. A certified public accountant, Golub, sixty-years-old, began his career in 1961 with a New York accounting firm and early on had the itch to run his own show. In 1968, at age twenty-nine, he started Gerald L. Golub & Co. He built it quickly into a profitable firm and merged with a bigger company in 1971 to form Goldstein, Golub Kessler & Co. Taking over as managing partner and chairman in 1981, Golub steered the firm through three mergers and tremendous growth, up to 465 accountants and $50 million in revenues. In 1998, Golub led the firm into an industry-shaking merger with American Express. Golub (no relation to Harvey Golub, the chairman and CEO of American Express) became chairman of the business unit. It now has 2,000 employees in sixty cities and, he says, is on the way to being the most dominant accounting firm in the country serving the small- to middle-market business communities.

When I was a young accountant, I handled a couple of tax examinations for some prominent people. The first one took me a half a day to prepare, and I went in to the boss and asked him what I should bill. He said to me, "What did you do? How much time did you spend? How effective were you?" I related what I had done and how I had saved the client several hundreds of thousands of dollars. He said, "Bill them $7,500." I said, "Wow, that's terrific." A few months later, I did another audit, and this one only took me an hour and had the same result; I saved the client a lot of money.

And this time my boss said, "Bill them $10,000."

I was in my mid-twenties at the time, and I learned a valuable lesson. The lesson was that when you are your own boss, you have an opportunity to achieve significant success from value provided. When you are an employee, unless you are appreciated beyond expectation, you may never be the person who is enriched by the organization.

So I decided then that I wanted to be my own boss. I started my own shop in 1968 and got my first client for $3,000 a year. The same week, I hired my first employee, a senior-staff certified public accountant at $16,000 a year. My wife said, "If your only client is $3,000, and you have to pay $16,000 in salary, how are you going to survive?" I said, "Look, it is August. If by the start of January I can't build the business, we'll run out of money, and then I'll go get a job. Since I am one of the best tax guys in New York, I'll have no problem getting a job January 1, and I'll put away my dream."

By October, I had $40,000 in clients. By April 30, I had $125,000. By the next summer, I had about $180,000. Then I merged with Stan Goldstein and Stu Kessler. That was in January 1971. We were twenty people.

I became managing partner—essentially the CEO—of our firm in 1981. When we merged with American Express in 1998, I had the choice of either continuing to simply run our New York operation and play a lot of golf or taking on the national chairmanship of this new Tax & Business Services operation. I thought it would be much more productive and more fun to have that new role.

In fact, these are the kinds of choices that make the job of CEO what it is. Periodically, there are opportunities in the business world to make a decision for your company to take either the left road or the right road. You never know what would have happened had you made the other decision. You are only able to deal with what you choose.

How you measure your company's success and progress against your goals is done by the choices you make. If you've chosen the left road, and that proceeds along with modest growth or whatever suits your goal, that is outstanding. You've hit the ball just the way you wanted to. Had you chosen the right-hand route, you might have even exceeded those other objectives or missed them completely. That is the interesting part about making the yea or nay decision. At some point, you get facts and information and input from advisors and other executives. When all the faces turn down the long conference table toward you, you ultimately make that choice. You do so with a lot of data that you try to convert into information, and you hope for a little bit of good fortune. At the end of the day, it's your decision, good or bad.

In fact, when you see CEOs of major companies jumping from opportunity to opportunity, it's not simply because they are looking for more enrichment, a bigger company, or a more challenging role. They jump around, because they get to choose the right road this time instead of the left road. They simply don't want to do it the same way over and over again. They want to test their own prowess to enhance their sense of accomplishment. In essence, moving around gives them a second chance.

Look at what someone like Lou Gerstner has done coming out of American Express. He moved to RJR, a different kind of company, and then, more impressive, he made the giant leap to IBM. He was not a computer person, and he didn't know that industry; but he understood leadership, he understood people, and he understood how to make a company prosper like it never had before. He threw out the old rule book—even down to the dress code, and brought in an innovative style that made that company highly successful, more successful than anyone probably ever thought it could be. That doesn't mean the principles weren't right before. That doesn't mean the machine wasn't well oiled. It just means that someone had to understand when to shift out of second gear and get into third. That's a CEO getting a chance to turn right instead of left.

I've had several of those chances myself. Deciding to merge my own company back in 1971 was, for me, an important event in my business career. I was able to get new business. I was able to meet people. Some would say I was able to do it all. It's not that I wanted to do it all. I only wanted to surround myself with other smart people. When I met Stan Goldstein, Stu Kessler, and the other partners at the firm, I felt they were a team of five or six guys who were smarter than I was.

I felt that if I could balance with that team and let them do the administration and technical side of the business, I could continue to do what I loved: the negotiation, the business advising, the people-intensive kind of work. I'm a person who loves to solve client problems, who loves to be in a client meeting, negotiating or coming up with a marketing strategy for growth. I've always enjoyed that part of my professional career. So I thought, "I can really have more fun, and maybe I won't have to work so hard." At that time, I was getting in at seven o'clock in the morning and working until seven o'clock at night. Maybe I could work less. My concept of joining another group was outstanding. We were able to build the firm. I continued to bring in new business, so I was well received by my new partners. Everything was great, except I started working even *longer* hours. I started getting in at 6:30 in the morning and leaving late at night. In fact, our firm grew to be so good and so strong that I'm now working longer hours than ever. Now that I'm successful, I get in at 5:30 in the morning, but I have more fun today than I have ever had before, and the firm has more recognition.

What was interesting is that I set out to be my own boss, and I did that. But in the end, what was more important was that I understood the kind of firm I wanted to build. I wanted to build the best firm in New York, not the biggest. Although we did become the largest independent firm, that was not the goal. The goal was to be the highest-quality, most recognized firm, a firm where you could be proud to say, "I'm a partner in this firm." I wanted a place where people wouldn't feel the need to leave, where they'd rather help us build the firm to even greater heights.

Building the best means you must give back a lot. That means you spend a lot of time training. That means you spend a lot of time putting seeds out in the field to grow later. That means you do things for people that don't get you a dollar today but hopefully will build you a firm tomorrow. That's what we did.

The decision to merge with American Express was simple after we did our research. Most traditional professional-services firms would have rejected the deal, because the conventional wisdom is that big corporations shouldn't be involved in the professional-service world. Other firms may have understood that this deal could be good for the profession but, frankly, were afraid to venture in, because they didn't understand what their role could be or what they could bring to the table to become recognized in an organization.

We reviewed the list of large, strong firms from twenty-five years ago that are no longer around today. We searched for the reasons for their disappearances and their reasons for merging or going out of business. What were the characteristics of longevity? What keeps a firm not only around but visible and thriving? Frankly, the American Express relationship was a growth strategy, not an exit strategy. It was actually a way of firming up and strengthening an organization and having it live forever.

The one thing that doesn't exist in the professional practices today is capital formation, especially in the accounting profession. There is such pressure in the area of compensation today that firms squeeze every nickel they can to distribute to partners, which means firms are typically left dry. That was fine when all you had to do to stay technologically advanced was go out and buy a new box of pencils, but that doesn't work anymore. Firms are spending millions of dollars every few years to stay competitive. The technology used to last five years, then three years. Now people have an eighteen-month to two-year window on state-of-the-art technology changes.

You can't make it for long by taking on debt, because the economy won't grow forever, and there are going to be setbacks and squeezes. There are going to be firms that get in trouble. In order to create longevity for an organization, capital infusion from outside third-parties is a smart thing.

Obviously there was the question of what we would have to give up in order to be part of a bigger organization. My belief was that we wouldn't give up anything because of the way the transaction was structured and the way American Express took the time to learn about the culture. American Express didn't focus on how much the company was worth. Rather, it focused on learning why our professionals felt such pride in this organization.

I had five meetings with the American Express representatives in which we talked about the vision, the culture, our organization, and theirs. It wasn't until the fifth meeting that we even talked about compensation and the transaction itself. I'm not sure where this merger will lead, but I believe it will do nothing less than change the industry. If a CEO's career is a sum of his or her choices, this is a choice I'm proud of.

Of course, everything has its price. Working as many hours as I have over my career, I have missed some afternoon basketball games with the kids. But my wife made it her business to be there, so we were represented. She worked on the weekends, and when the baseball and football games were taking place on the weekends, I was the one standing on the sideline. I also had two season tickets to the New York Jets football team. I used to take my children, one-on-one, to the games for about ten years. Sitting out in the cold one-on-one with a child and having the hour trip in the car to and from the game was terrific for building relationships. I share different interests with each of my children, and that has created a unique bond with each of them. My children would say that we have wonderful relationships with each other. There is no gap there.

I think all children could say that their parents worked too many hours. There has to be balance in everyone's life, and the question is how much is enough? I did play the Little League coach, and I did participate in other events, but the criteria were different in those days for a businessperson. I know it is very important today for parents to run home for an afternoon basketball game, to be there for their kids. I don't take anything away from that, but frankly, I do think there has to be a balance to all this. I think some people actually overdo it today.

We've got jobs to do, and the focus of our jobs has to be to accomplish what we set out to do. If we are hunters, we go out to hunt. If we are observers, then we go out to observe. Having always been a hunter, I like to get out in the woods looking for prey rather than sitting in the lodge.

I was very focused on building the business. I recognized that it would have been nice if I'd come home before midnight. But I gave up a lot of that during the early years, because I was driven to be successful. I came from a very poor background. There's always a relative in every family who has more money and gives you a taste of the good lifestyle. You understand that there is another way. I had an uncle like that. I used to say that if I worked hard enough and was lucky enough, maybe I could be successful too.

I don't think of myself as driven by money, but coming from my era, the 1940's and 1950's, are a lot of people from poor backgrounds. People in my era worried about putting food on the table. They took one-bedroom apartments and raised two kids there, because that's the way you did things. That was acceptable at the time. When I got out of school, I got married and had a child twelve months later. My job was to go out and earn money, because I had to pay rent. I guess somewhere inside me I still need that motivation. I need to get up, go to work, earn my living, and provide value for the income I generate.

Profits were never the bottom line for me once I got started. Profits in my mind are really only a means to the end. You need money to pay salaries, but to me, gross volume was always the answer. Unless you had gross volume, higher revenues, you didn't get a chance to make profits. Unless you had gross volume, you didn't get a chance to help people expand their capabilities and technical prowess. Unless you have gross volume, you don't get a chance to build a business, and for the CEO that is about leadership. I think leadership carries with it a burden. That burden is the risk to succeed or fail. If you are made CEO and you plan to simply maintain your firm, you are the wrong person for the chair. People like Jack Welch, at General Electric, and Lou Gerstner are people who have taken leadership positions and have transformed their firms. They have set new courses and new paces to make their firms into special vehicles, and they are willing to take the personal risk of being deemed failures in steering the boat in a new direction.

I am willing to do that. I like the spotlight. I want to be applauded. I want to be personally gratified. I am willing to take a chance on being a success or a failure, and I have a sense of balance about myself that allows me to discern the left road from the right road.

I believe there are two parts to success. There is financial success, and then there is success in achievement and reputation. "Who are you?" is the key question. Maybe CEOs question themselves the most, because there is always that doubt. "Am I really that good? Can I really do the job? Do I really have the wherewithal?"

Every CEO, when that important yea or nay decision comes at them, takes a deep breath, because he or she is charged with a responsibility. A lot of people today don't like the idea of accountability and responsibility. But CEOs have it. They have it all the time. What they do with it determines the legacy they leave behind.

Twenty-One
"I Can" Always Beats IQ

Clark Johnson
Pier 1 Imports

When Clark Johnson, sixty-seven years old, stepped down as CEO of Pier 1 Imports in 1999, he left behind a remarkable legacy of accomplishment. During his thirteen-year tenure, the renowned international retailer grew from $170 million to more than $1 billion in annual sales, with 13,000 employees in 800 stores worldwide. Before taking Pier 1 into orbit, Johnson co-owned the very successful McGregor Golf Company with the golden bear, Jack Nicklaus. Prior to that, he served the Wickes Corporation in a variety of capacities, including as president of Wickes Lumber and of Wickes Furniture and executive vice president in charge of thirteen divisions. Happily retired from the day-to-day corporate wars, Johnson now sits on the boards of a number of large companies. A frequent public speaker, he regularly shares his management philosophy with a new generation of CEOs.

The turning point in my business career and my life came in 1978 while working for the Wickes Corporation as a senior vice president and group executive. I had just taken one of their poorest performing divisions from a $6-million loss to a $15-million profit in only three years. As a reward, Wickes decided to send me to the prestigious Harvard Business School's Advanced Management Program (AMP).

The class I attended consisted of 161 CEOs and senior executives from around the world, most of whom had much more experience and education than I had. I felt like a triple-A baseball player getting called up to the big leagues. I *thought* I had the talent, but when I actually stepped up to the plate, could I hit a major-league curve ball?

To my surprise, this impressive group of business leaders elected me class president. And after interacting closely with them over the course of three months, I concluded that I had the skills and ability equal to or better than many of them. Now I *knew* I could play with the big boys.

When I returned to Wickes and the corporate world, I elevated my goals and set my sights on becoming a CEO. Had I not gone to Harvard, who knows what would have happened. I had the motivation, proper work habits, and integrity. I had credibility with my associates, because I always did what I said I would do. Now I also had the certain knowledge that I could match up with other very successful executives and do what they did. More than anything, that experience gave me the confidence that launched the rest of my career.

How I made my way into the class probably tells more about me than anything else does. The class started on February 4, but I didn't learn until late December that Wickes had given me the green light to attend. When I called to enroll, the director informed me that the class was full but that I could sign up for the following year. I immediately jumped on a plane and flew to Boston. Upon arriving, I rented a car, drove to Harvard, and knocked upon the director's door. I told him that getting into the class was *the* most important thing in my life. I implored him, "If you give me a seat, I promise to be the best AMP student you've ever had. I will work the hardest and contribute to the knowledge of others." He let me in, and I followed through on my promise. At the end of the class, he shook my hand and said, "I guess you were right."

Several times since then I've gone after opportunities in a very aggressive fashion, and it has always paid off. I hate to waste opportunities, because I've always found it a lot harder to get up to bat in the ninth inning at Yankee stadium than to hit the ball over the fence. So whenever I see a chance to step up to the plate, I don't let it slide by. The other side of the coin is that I've often paid a heavy price for my turn at bat. I have moved fourteen times in my career. Whenever the chairman of Wickes said, "I have a problem," I asked, "When do you want me to be there?" My wife and children hated being torn away from their friends and school, but it never occurred to me to do anything else.

I grew up in a very different era than today. My father was profoundly shaped by the Depression, when good jobs did not come easily. He instilled in me the attitude that you don't question your superiors, for fear of losing your position in the company. In addition, most of the managers I worked for early in my career had served in World War II. They learned to salute smartly and march up the hill, and once back in the business world, they incorporated that attitude into their management style. So when my superiors needed me to relocate, we packed up and moved without the slightest hesitation. I didn't see it as good or bad; that's just the way it was.

Throughout my career, my biggest challenge has been building the management teams—bringing together the right kind of personalities, aspirations, and motivations in game-breaking positions and creating the right culture to accomplish corporate strategy. Corporate culture is nothing more than a set of shared beliefs about what the company can be and how the people in it should work together. The hard part is putting together a team that fits your culture.

You overcome that challenge by staying cognizant of your organization's bench strength and being willing to take risks in your selection and promotion of people. When building teams, I've always operated on the philosophy that "I can" always beats "IQ." When you get highly motivated people who share your commitment to the company's goals and strategies and you turn them loose, they usually produce outstanding results.

Over the years, I've developed a decent talent for judging people, but I don't always hit a home run. I learned the hard way that when you put your chips on the wrong person, you can pay a steep price. In 1986, I hired a CFO who seemed to have the right mix of experience, professional skills, and personal character. He held positions of importance in his church and community, and I had no second thoughts about offering him the job. Toward the end of his career, however, he supervised some unauthorized investments that cost the company $19 million. We recovered most of the money through various means, but I had to dismiss him from the company. I learned that when somebody at a very high level wants to beat the system, that person will find a way, even with adequate financial controls in place.

As a manager and a friend, I felt betrayed and disappointed by his actions, but I didn't take it too personally. You think you have a handle on someone, but you never know for sure. This man had good morals and ethics, but somewhere deep in his heart and mind he decided to take a side trip. Although I cared for him as a person, he left me no choice in terms of my course of action. He made the decision for me with his own actions. All I did was respond to the decision he had already made. On the whole, though, I've had a pretty good track record of selecting winners. I attribute most of my success to surrounding myself with top-notch people.

Another key to my success—I've never backed away from making the tough decisions, even when it's meant going against the grain. Several years ago at Pier 1, we needed to install new cash registers throughout the system, which represented an investment of $22 million. You always take a deep breath before spending that kind of money, so I gathered a task force of the best and brightest minds in the company. After exhaustive research, they recommended an emerging vendor that offered a state-of-the-art system. Despite the task force's impassioned presentation, I overrode their recommendation and went with IBM. The chairman of the task force, a man whom we had identified as someone with the potential to go far in the company, resigned in protest.

I hated to lose a good man, but I stood by my decision. The system he recommended had a lot of bells and whistles, but I questioned its reliability. Before I spend $22 million on cash registers, I have to be sure they will work. I had worked with IBM before, and I found their systems were backed up with the best service in the industry. So to me, it seemed like the safest choice. It turned out that I made the right decision. A colleague purchased the other system for his company and ended up incurring several million dollars in additional maintenance costs.

A decision that didn't turn out so well occurred early in my career. In 1974, as head of Wickes Lumber, I authorized the CFO of a subsidiary to participate in the futures market in lumber and plywood. We gave him a limit but failed to establish adequate controls to enforce that limit. He ended up losing $3 million, which represented a fair amount of money back then. I took a lot of heat and deservedly so. I don't think I erred in authorizing the investments, but there's no question I should have done a better job of monitoring the situation.

Perhaps the biggest lesson I've learned over the years—and one that has guided my management philosophy for a long time now—is to clearly define a strategy and then stick with it.

As a young man, I started out selling lumber and plywood in South Dakota. I had a fair amount of success, but I discovered that selling is a somewhat random process. I succeeded, because I made more calls and asked for more orders than anyone else, not because I had an understanding of the big picture. As time went by, I learned to think more strategically. When I began running organizations, I found that you succeed by defining the strategy, goals, and objectives in clear, understandable terms. More important, you succeed by making sure that everyone in game-breaker positions signs off on the goals and accepts them as their own. Without that, you don't have a snowball's chance in hell.

In particular, my tenure at Pier 1 Imports taught me about the importance of consistency, of grinding away day after day and resisting the temptation to change tactics and goals every time you suffer a minor setback. People in organizations yearn for clarity. They ask, "What are we trying to accomplish around here?" If you truly believe in your strategy and know you have the right people to execute it, you have to hang in there and stick with it.

In the early '90s, we opened our first Pier 1 stores in the United Kingdom. Right off the bat we lost money. We then opened a distribution center and lost money there too. This happened concurrently with the CFO's $19-million investment debacle. Not surprisingly, my standing with the board of directors was strained. They constantly questioned my strategy and urged me to shut the stores, to take a $6-million write-off and move on. I hung in there despite their constant negative pressure. I met individually with each director to review our five-year plan and ultimately convinced each director to give us the time to let the strategy unfold. Three years later, five stores had grown to seventeen, and a river of red ink had turned into a tidy $2-million profit—mainly because I believed in our strategy and refused to deviate from it.

Did I ever doubt that we would succeed? Of course I did. Any time you delegate responsibility to others and give them the freedom and authority to move ahead, you have some doubt. Plus, with our headquarters in Texas, I didn't have the ability to personally supervise things on a daily, weekly, or even monthly basis. But I didn't lose any sleep over it, because I knew we had a good man in the game-breaker position, and I believed in our strategy. You always have to entertain the notion that your plan might fail; otherwise, it won't be based in reality. On the other hand, when the time comes to move forward, you have to put your doubts to rest and focus on doing what needs to be done.

Often, that means making some very hard decisions. Many people reach a certain level on the chain of command and don't want to go any higher, because they can't face the necessary hard things that happen when you run a business. Declining sales and profits, personnel problems, and difficulties with the board are just part and parcel of running a business. Successful CEOs hang in there, continue to sell critics on the soundness of their projects and make sure people are properly motivated and working hard to make their strategies come to life.

Sometimes the hard decisions get very personal. When I ran Wickes Lumber, I had to fire a man who had six children and a sick wife. From a humanistic point of view, it seemed like a brutal thing to do. But from an organizational point of view, I had no choice. He wasn't cutting the mustard and had become disruptive to others who were.

I've always operated with the philosophy that it's okay to be tough-minded, but you shouldn't be tough-hearted. This decision had a little of both. The man has since become second-in-command at one of the nation's largest personal-services firms and regularly earns more than $2 million a year. He recently told me the best thing that ever happened to him was when I clearly stated that he did not fit in the rough and tumble corporate environment and would probably have better success in a more individualistic career path. He took my advice and has gone on to enjoy a very successful career.

Most of the time, people can't or won't make these kinds of decisions for themselves. So you help them out by forcing the decision. As long as you do it with a good heart and treat the person fairly and equitably, it will work out in the long run. You have to separate your feelings for them as people from your feelings about their performances. You have to believe in your heart that people who can't cut it in your enterprise will find situations better suited to their skills and abilities. But it doesn't feel good for them at the time, and you don't like doing it. I've known some people who take pleasure in it, like pulling the wings off of flies, but I never have. It's just a distasteful byproduct of being a CEO. You have to do hard things and make tough decisions, and that's one reason you get paid a lot of money.

By retiring from Pier 1, I may have stepped back from the front lines, but I haven't withdrawn from the war. I feel like I still have plenty left to contribute to the business world, particularly in the area of helping companies devise clear strategies for profitable growth.

I hope people will remember me as someone who built outstanding management teams and accomplished his personal objectives, as a leader who stood up for the organization and made the people who worked for him better at what they did. I also like to think that the companies I led were better at the end of my tenure than at the beginning, that they operated with integrity, had good reputations for quality products and customer service, and that all the associates felt like part of a winning team.

For me, business has always been about more than just having a healthy bottom line. That's just a byproduct of doing things right. The real fun comes from pulling together as a team and knowing that, no matter who sinks the winning basket, everyone had a hand in the victory.

Twenty-Two
A Danish Difference

Hannah Kain
Alom Technologies, Inc.

Few CEOs have followed Hannah Kain's path to the executive suite. Kain, who was born in the same Danish town as Hans Christian Andersen, ran for Parliament at age twenty-one and narrowly lost the election. Twelve years later, however, she got a chance to serve. Her political career was brief, and she ended up getting her M.B.A. and later teaching at Copenhagen Business School. A textbook she wrote on market analysis, now in its fourth edition, is still used at the school. Kain held several marketing positions at Danish companies before emigrating with her husband, a computer scientist, to America in 1990. She served as chief operating officer at a Silicon Valley computer peripherals company before starting her own company, Alom Technologies, in Fremont, California, in 1997. In short order, the software company has reached close to $10 million in sales and has thirty-five employees. Kain, now forty-two-years-old, has needed to use all her management skills acquired in the United States and Denmark to keep her fairy tale career on track.

There's an old joke in Europe about how it is in heaven and hell. The Danes are the managers. I understand how that joke originated.

In Denmark, it is important to be straight and fair with everybody. That is why I feel such a great responsibility for my staff as well as for our vendors and customers. That is my key stress factor as CEO. One of my visions has been to create a company that treats everybody fairly and where people like to come and do business. That is the Danish management style in me. There are really good, strong values in Danish management, and I've tried to bring those values to the table here.

Of course, in a startup, it can be a bit of a bumpy ride. Right now I'm happy to say we pay everybody within thirty days, but we've had periods where we just couldn't. That, of course, makes everybody, especially me, feel very bad.

We had a situation about eight months after we started where our cash resources were spread really thin. I tried not to go by the "squeaky wheel" theory and pay those who made the most noise first but be fair to the people who were fair with me.

I was very anxious about getting that situation over with. I sat at my desk for an extra hour every evening after everybody had gone home, just looking at the situation and trying to concentrate on when we would be out of it. I needed, for my own psychological well-being, to be able to visualize ahead and see that after a couple of months we would be fine, that there was light at the end of the tunnel.

To do that, I tried to create a sense of achievement inside myself. I asked myself, "What is the most important contribution I can make to get us through this situation?" I wanted to be sure that I had not overlooked anything simply because I hadn't asked myself that question.

After I decided that I'd done everything I could do, I tried to keep everybody informed. Who needs to know? How might it affect them? It's a very difficult, deciding who needs to know what and how rosy a picture you want to paint if it's not rosy at all. I once worked for a guy who was terrible about that. He would paint rosy pictures, and the company would virtually be in bankruptcy. You can do that for a couple of weeks, but after half a year it gets tired. So I don't try to deceive anybody. On the other hand, I don't want people to carry around anxiety that they don't need to carry.

I share the information employees need to know in order to do their jobs. Then, of course, if I had to make nasty decisions, such as laying-off people (which I haven't), I would have to do it swiftly and get it over with. I don't want my staff members to go home in the evening feeling like they might not have a job the next day. Uncertainty is terribly demoralizing.

Uncertainty is also an aspect of being a CEO that has hit me harder than I thought it would. In order to go into business, you have to sign personal guarantees with the bank. More than just the business is riding on its success. It's one thing to lose your job, which is bad enough, but if you lose your home and your savings and if your spouse has got to work off the debt for the next ten years, that can be devastating. This possibility certainly ratchets up the pressure to succeed and you makes me more keenly aware of my role as CEO.

I'm extra sensitive to the differences in management styles between here and Denmark. People here are more afraid of their bosses, much more into covering their behinds and not contradicting their bosses. It's very hard for people from hierarchical environments to come to work at our company. The mentality in the United States tends to be, "If you want to do something, you'd better get two signatures." It's especially difficult trying to get employees to contradict the managers and think of new ideas. We expect our staff to think on its feet and ask, "Why not do it this way?" Creativity and innovative thinking are more suppressed in companies here than in Denmark.

To me, it feels like there is an overall fear in United States companies, a sense that people believe their jobs are in jeopardy. Some smaller companies are trigger-happy and fire people quickly. I would never think of firing somebody for making an error, unless it was very gross negligence. People are human. People get afraid and try to cover up. Perhaps the most important tool I use is my sense of humor. I try to laugh and deflect tension from situations.

Like other CEOs, I find that people hesitate to tell me things. This creates a definite need for an outside, impartial point of view. Because I own all the shares, I don't have a board of directors. I am the board, so we have very short board meetings. And though it's very easy to solve other people's problems, you don't have enough distance from your own problems.

Occasionally, it feels like everybody knows about something going on here but me. The CEO is always the last one to hear the rumors floating around. A friend who runs her own company hired an outside consultant to come in and interview staff members. She was really surprised at what she learned. Sometimes, things are going on that you simply don't know about.

But my philosophy is to trust people. I believe people show up for work with the intention of doing great work. If the CEO has that belief, she'll get taken for a ride once in a while. Someone will abuse it. But I'm willing to risk that, because the pluses are enormous. You create a culture based on trust, and the alternative is not acceptable. If you don't trust people, you end up with a culture where two signatures are required.

I see my staff members as huge stakeholders. Building a loyal staff who really buys into the company culture is extremely important. For that reason, I do a lot of team building with the staff members. We don't go out and do rope courses or Outward Bound, but we do projects together. For instance, last fall we applied for ISO9002 certification, a key quality stamp of approval for high-tech companies. It was a huge project, and everybody needed to buy in and do a lot of work on top of the usual workload. We did it and got the certification. It was a great team-building experience. I believe that by doing things like that you really can create a culture.

My ambition is to make this company grow to a very large size, so I need to grow at the same time. Of course, that means I work a lot of hours. During the week, I work twelve hours each day. On Saturdays, I put in six to eight hours, and I try to keep Sunday for myself and my husband. He travels a lot, and we have periods where we don't see each other very much. We usually don't see each other in the morning. If I don't have an evening meeting, we try to have dinner together. We spend Sundays together. But this is nothing new. We lived together for four years before we got married, and we were always both very active in our careers. We've made a choice not to have children. Neither of us is fascinated by the idea of having kids. We simply don't think it was for us. It is a conscious choice on my behalf. Of course, that choice is a bigger deal for women than for men. Every once in a while, I feel it would be nice to have a child. Three minutes later, I hear some screaming kid, and I'm glad I don't have to deal with that. I get satisfaction in dealing with adults. The company is my child.

Being a woman CEO evokes different responses from people. It's an advantage in some places; not so at other times. I'd been looking for a new building for the company, for example, and some prospective landlords asked me, "So what does your husband say about this?" One wanted me to sign a personal guarantee that as a married woman, my personal property was pledged as part of the guarantee.

On the other hand, there have been fewer negative reactions to my being a woman than I anticipated when I started the company. Sometimes I have advantages. A lot of buyers and decision-makers are female. Some prefer to give business to another woman. I also think that some of my staff members prefer to work for a woman. We have a disproportionate number of women in higher roles.

In the long run, running a business is not about gender. I have respect for all individuals. I like the differences in people. When I build a team, I like to have different points of view. I work daily here to get people to respect each other and not make fun of the guy who sits in the corner and doesn't say a lot.

My great reward, other than the thanks from our customers, is seeing our people grow internally. I have a staff member who has been working on my team for three years. She worked with me at a previous company before joining me here. She recommended a former supervisor of hers for a job here. It's been clear that in the three years she has been on my staff, she has grown, not just to be the equal of her former supervisor but far surpassing her. In the he way she handles things and reacts to other people—on all levels—she has grown to be far better in a business environment than the person who used to supervise her. That brings me great satisfaction.

Twenty-Three

When David Swallows Goliath

Tony Shipley
Entek IRD International Corp.

Tony Shipley, fifty-two years old, is president and CEO of Entek IRD International, which develops and markets integrated-condition-monitoring systems for rotating production machinery. Entek IRD delivers its products worldwide, with distribution points in ninety countries. It employs nearly 400 people and racks up annual sales of $55 million. Unlike many companies that enjoy a steady growth rate, Entek IRD attained its current status as a global market leader by acquiring a company three times its size. The Herculean task of integrating two very diverse companies and cultures forced Shipley to grow as a business leader and as a human being.

My background is in industrial engineering, but the entrepreneurial spirit has been in my blood as long as I can remember. As a young boy I always had some kind of job. I mowed lawns, delivered papers, raised produce that was sold throughout the community—anything to earn a few bucks. After college, I worked for a couple of different companies and attended night school to obtain my M.B.A. When the opportunity came along to start a business, I had no second thoughts. We were young, with no children and no debt, and my wife traveled a lot in her job. So I had nothing to hold me back.

In 1977, I founded, along with two partners, the Anatrol Corporation, which did noise and vibration consulting work. The company did reasonably well for a few years, but in 1981 my partners and I reached a parting of the ways over the future of the company. I left to found my own company, Entek Scientific, which initially developed off-the-shelf mechanical engineering software packages, mainly for vibration and acoustic analysis. That market never materialized like we'd expected, and by the mid-1980's we had transitioned into a company that focused on machinery condition monitoring. Just as a doctor performs tests on your body to determine various ailments, our software analyzed rotating machines and reported back on their conditions.

Entek Scientific grew slowly but steadily until 1996, when we reached about $13 million in sales and 100 employees. At that point, an opportunity presented itself to purchase the oldest company in our industry, IRD Mechanalysis, which just happened to be three times our size.

Founded in 1952, IRD had originated the concept of machinery condition monitoring, and for a long time reigned supreme as the unchallenged industry leader. Over the years, however, its market share shrank from more than 80 percent to less than 20 percent. We had tossed around the idea of making such an acquisition for several years, so when IRD came on the market, we jumped at the chance. We bought IRD, which had $36 million in sales and nearly 300 employees, because its strong hardware and systems integration focus seemed like a perfect fit with our software focus. The only question was whether the snake could swallow the elephant and come out of it alive.

The merger changed Entek Scientific in every way you can imagine. We went from being a close-knit, 100-person company where you knew everyone on a first-name basis to being a 400-employee behemoth that required a lot more organization and structure, particularly on the senior- and middle-management teams.

All our processes and systems, such as order processing, customer support, and sales and service, had to change. We went from a narrow focus on software development to having a large, in-house manufacturing group that produced $30-million worth of electronics a year. We had to come to grips with what products to manufacture, how to manufacture them, and how to get them to market. We had to do it quickly.

As the CEO, I had to significantly alter my focus and leadership style. With Entek Scientific, I basically ran the whole show. Now I had to hire the right senior managers, delegate responsibility, and trust the managers to get the job done. I also had to become more involved in

172

the planning of the business and rely on people to execute those plans. For many entrepreneurs, letting go of the day-to-day stuff can create a lot of fear, but I actually looked forward to it and saw it as the next step in my growth as a leader.

Despite all our rigorous planning and preparation, merging two such diverse cultures proved an immense undertaking, harder than I think any of us imagined. IRD had been around for nearly half a century, and some of its people had worked there for more than thirty years. Plus, at one time IRD literally ruled the industry. In many ways the IRD people saw IRD as Goliath and Entek Scientific as the upstart David. Had I fully understood what the merger entailed, I might have had second thoughts about moving forward with it. At the least, I would have gotten a much larger sling!

Resolving our cultural differences tested the limits of both companies. It also tested my own personal resolve. I spent many a sleepless night trying to quiet the incessant questions whirling around my head. Had we bitten off more than we could chew? What would happen if we brought the wrong products to market? What would people think of me if the company crashed and burned?

In particular, I agonized over key personnel decisions, particularly when they involved letting long-term employees go because they just couldn't fit into the new culture. Fortunately, I had a few trusted mentors to turn to in times of need. When the internal voices of doom grew too loud, the wisdom and counsel of those mentors kept me from getting overwhelmed by the enormity of the task at hand.

I take great pride in the fact that we came through the merger in good shape, but there have been several other instances in my career that I found more personally rewarding. Several times I've had to rescue the company from a desperate situation, and pulling us back from the brink of extinction has given me a great deal of satisfaction.

For example, in the early 1980s, we developed eleven software packages and prepared to roll them out to the marketplace. Just prior to the rollout, our operating-systems provider decided to dump our operating system, rendering all those products obsolete. In 1994, our biggest customer stopped selling our software. Just like that, 50 percent of our revenue stream vanished into thin air.

In each instance, we pulled together as a team and fought our way through. In 1994, when we lost that customer, we received the news in morning, and by that afternoon we had convened a crisis team. In no time at all we had a plan in place that not only replaced the lost revenue but allowed us to surpass it.

Nevertheless, it's a sickening feeling to realize that if you don't change things quickly, you'll go out of business. When you're sitting there with everything you own on the line, including personal guarantees on all the bank loans, it scares you to death. It's not so much the thought of personal bankruptcy, although certainly no one looks forward to that ignoble outcome. More, it's a fear of letting down all your employees, suppliers, and customers, and losing everything we've worked so hard to build.

At the same time, there's something exhilarating about having your back to the wall and hunkering down to do what you absolutely have to do. I'm not sure why, but I seem to thrive on that kind of challenge. Perhaps it's built into my chemistry or DNA. Like Michael Jordan taking the last shot with two seconds left, I want the ball in my hands when the game is on the line. In business, you either have the desire to take the reigns in times of crisis or you don't. Most people don't.

Maybe part of it stems from my upbringing. When I was a kid, my parents always drummed into me not to give up. Plus, hearing someone say, "You can't do that" sets off a trigger in me. Something inside me says, "To hell with you!" and then I go out and do what needs to be done. When the chips are down, you can't sit there and dwell on why the world is treating you badly. You have to come up with solutions and then engage your people in a conversation around those solutions.

I firmly believe that a group decision will work better than my individual decision. As CEO, I have to set the direction and say, "This is where we're going." But then I have to involve the team in mapping out how we will get there, then get out of their way, and let the whole team move forward.

One thing I've learned over the years—and I think this holds true for any business or industry—is that the toughest decisions always involve people. Product lines, bank accounts, inventory, and equipment come and go, but at its most fundamental core, business is all about personal relationships.

The hardest thing I've ever had to do was fire a partner, a guy who helped me start the business in 1981. After we opened the doors, it soon became apparent that his lifestyle wouldn't accommodate the requirements of an entrepreneurial company. As the entrepreneur, you can't go home at 5:00 P.M. when everyone else is staying till all hours of the night. You have to set the pace. If you're not willing to step up to the plate and get the job done, you can't expect anyone else to do it.

At the same time, I wanted to respect his lifestyle. I believe in giving people every opportunity to turn things around, especially those who are taking risks with you. You may not like someone's behavior at the time, but you can't cut that person off too quickly, even when everyone else says you should. So I wrestled with that decision for years before finally deciding he had to go. Once I committed to doing it, it took another nine months to actually complete the process. Fortunately, those kinds of things don't happen too often. Those nine months definitely qualify as one of the worst periods of my life.

What I enjoy most in business is building a good team of people and having the faith and confidence that they can get the job done. That's one area where I feel I have grown as a person and a business leader. Most young entrepreneurs have a need to show people that they know a lot, and I was no exception.

In my early years as CEO, I tended to be too instructive and autocratic, telling people what, when, where, and how to do it. I had to eat humble pie on several occasions before finally realizing that I don't always have the best answer. More important, I learned that people don't want to be told how to do something. They want to be told, "We're going in this direction," and then be given the opportunity to show their own energy and creativity and make things happen. That was a tough lesson to learn, but I finally realized that when I get out of the way and let people do what I've hired them to do, they will work very hard for the company and me.

In many ways I feel lucky, because if I had to do it over, I wouldn't make many changes. Sure, I would try to avoid some of the dumb mistakes that I made (and continue to make). I would have given my people more responsibility a lot sooner than I did. But in the grand scheme of things, I wouldn't change much of it. If I were not running

Entek IRD, I would probably be running another company, because this is what I love to do. I've geared my whole life toward running a business, and I hope to keep doing it for a long time. I've had a lot of fun, and I've been blessed with more than my share of success. We're not looking to acquire another Goliath any time soon, but in today's business world, you never know what will happen.

Section Four
All in the Family

Twenty-Four

In the Name of the Father

Stuart Booth
Roma Color

Stuart Booth, sixty years old, is the president and CEO of Roma Color, a $21-million manufacturer of organic pigments based in Fall River, Massachussets. A former Navy pilot with an M.B.A., Booth began his career in the pigment business with the Kerr-McGee Corporation in 1968 and later joined his father, John, to start a family business making and selling pigments. Four years later, the Booths sold their company in order to purchase Roma Color, which sells pigments to the printing ink industry. The company was in worse financial condition than the Booths had been lead to believe, and after struggling for several years, they were just turning the corner when the banking crisis of the early 1990s struck in New England. Facing bankruptcy, the younger Booth was forced to make the toughest decisions of his life.

Prior to the spring of 1991, the banking environment for small companies was loose and casual. You asked for a loan and the lenders pretty much gave you what you needed. You had to make the interest payments, but they were pretty lax about all the covenants of the agreement. It was just a very comfortable, casual, easy-going kind of atmosphere.

All that changed in the early 1990s when the banks, particularly in New England, got into a lot of trouble with their loan portfolios because of a lot of overbuilding of condominiums and shopping centers. As a result, there were too many vacancies, and the banks started foreclosing. Things got so bad that the banks started closing on demand notes, even for companies that were not in any real trouble,

179

so they could cash out quickly on their loans. One of the companies the bank decided to go after was Roma Color.

We were not delinquent on our loan payments, and the company was making money, but we were slightly low on our profitability covenant, which was $150,000. We were profitable but not as profitable as we should have been.

Part of the reason we were in this condition is that during the period from 1984 until this happened, my sister, who was the majority stockholder and who had invested a lot of money into the business, simply did not hold our feet to the fire. She was an absentee kind of stockholder and an absentee member of the board of directors. Rather than pushing us hard, she was too lenient. When we needed money, for whatever reason, we could call in the morning, and the money would be there by the afternoon.

My sister and her husband started a highly successful computer technology company about twenty-five years ago. She had quite a bit of money and became our lead investor. So frankly, we got a little fat and happy and complacent. We did not do the job we should have been doing in terms of financial management and stewardship of assets. So the bank crisis became quite a wake-up call. In fact, it was the loudest wake-up call I've ever had.

The bank officers came in for their usual quarterly meeting where we'd sit down and review how things were going and where the company was heading. This time, there was a new bank officer present, and as I was starting to give my presentation, she stopped me and said, "Let me interrupt. Let's get to the heart of the matter. I'm giving you notice today that you have thirty days to pay off your $3.5-million bank loan." Then she got up and left. It was that abrupt.

I remember exactly how I felt. I compare it with the feelings you go through when somebody very close to you dies. I felt anger, despair, confusion, and a sense of "Why me? Why not somebody else?" I quickly ran through a whole gamut of emotions. I was simply dumbfounded and, initially, probably more angry than anything else.

I went home and ruminated, just mulled over what had happened and tried to figure out where to go. My natural reaction was, "What's going to happen to me? What's going to happen to my family?" The focus was initially very personal, because here I was, fifty-two years old, and I thought, "What am going to do for a job? I have kids in college and I have all these expenses. My God, what's going to happen?" It was terrifying on a personal level. After that first week or so, I calmed down, and things improved. But it was a real nightmare at first.

It is important to note that at this time, 1991, my dad was still quite active in the business. Essentially, I was serving as president and he was CEO, although we didn't have formal titles. He, my sister, and I were the three board members. My father's reaction was one of disbelief. He said that the bank would never do this, that it was a bluff. He came from the old school. Among the people in the business world that he most despised were the insurance man, the banker, and the tax man, because he felt they were totally unproductive and wasted your time. So when the bank called in the loan, my father, having never believed a bank would ever do that, took a very arrogant, resistant attitude toward the whole situation.

After thinking it over for several hours, I concluded that we had a crisis on our hands and we had to figure what to do. A couple of days later, I called the bank officer back and asked her for a meeting to talk through the situation. We set up an appointment, and I went over to her office. When I was shown into the conference room, I saw that in addition to her, there were five other people from the bank, including a credit officer and an attorney. I quickly realized I was being sandbagged, big time.

Rather than having the meeting I'd anticipated with the bank officer, I was being called on the carpet in front of their so-called "workout" group. I tried to be honest and forthright and explain where we were and where we were going. I told them that I couldn't understand why the note was being called. The more I explained, the more clear it was that everything I was saying was being used against me. I left there totally distraught. It was just awful.

The following Monday, I got a phone call from the bank officer, and she said, "The bank strongly recommends that you hire a turnaround consultant," which I did. The next day, I had four different consultants in for interviews and hired one of them.

Meanwhile, my father was still resisting the entire process. To him, the last thing we needed was a turnaround consultant. His view was, "They don't know the business. They haven't been here all these years, and they don't know it like we know it." So he resisted very strongly. Add to that the fact that my sister had put a substantial investment into the company, and my dad firmly believed that she, as the senior investor in the business, should simply add more money to the pot and take the bank out of the picture. He thought, "If the bank has the problem and the bank doesn't want to invest, fine. The senior investor has the responsibility and, indeed, should step forward with the money to take the bank out."

I didn't agree with my father on this at all, and two weeks later, before we could hash that out, the bank officer called and said, "We want both you and your father to reconfirm that your personal guarantees are alive and well. So we want you to resign the personal guarantees and give them back to us." Our personal guarantees, which put all of our private, personal property at risk if we couldn't repay the loan, were already signed and legal, but the bank just wanted to grind it into our guts. So I signed mine and gave it to the bank.

Dad, however, decided that he was not going to sign it. Now telling a bank—when you're in the work-out section—that you're not going sign a personal guarantee is tantamount to saying, "I challenge you, baby!" Our lawyers advised us to sign, but Dad said, "Do what you've got to do, but I'm not going to sign it." He didn't sign it.

Our turnaround consultant came to me and said, "You have a problem. If you, as the president of the company and chairman of the board of directors, don't take action against your father, who is taking an action that threatens the survival of the company, then you're derelict, and you should be taken off the board." So I ended up in a position of having to remove my father as CEO.

I'll never forget that day. I walked into his office, and Dad was sitting at the desk I now sit at. I said, "Dad, I have to relieve you. You're threatening what chance we have of surviving this thing. I have to relieve you of office."

He was quiet. He didn't start yelling or anything like that. He understood it on a business level. He certainly understood my position, but he felt very strongly about his principles and wouldn't budge. I also think that at seventy-four years old, he was ready to get out anyway. But he was someone who always went out with a boom of thunder.

He said, "Do what you've got to do."

I felt awful. From the day he graduated from Princeton until then, he had been a leader in the industry. He worked for nearly every major pigment manufacturer in the country, in different management and sales roles. He was certainly seen as a leader. More than that, he was my mentor, both in business and in life. I loved him and admired him deeply. And here I was, his son, challenging him on the basis of what he felt very strongly about: his business principles. It was one of the more difficult things I've ever had to do, no doubt about it.

Afterwards, I went back to my office. At the time, I was working in an office that was two doors down from where Dad was. I closed the door and sat behind the desk not moving for probably two or three hours. I was just paralyzed. By the next day, however, I had to get back to the job of staving off the bank.

Dad stayed with the company. It wasn't like I told him to clean out his desk and leave. I simply relieved him of his title. He did stay around that day, but then he took some time off. When he came back three weeks later, he came back in a research position. He and I agreed that would be a good thing for him to do, because he had a lot of experience, understanding, and, frankly, an inquisitiveness to do development work. That's what he did for the next three or four years. He kept his nose out of what I was doing and went on and did his own thing.

He did, however, write some harsh memos to Susie, my sister, implying that she should simply cover the debt. I would get caught in the middle and felt that asking her wasn't right. I tried to walk a tightrope between Dad and Susie's positions. It was very difficult.

Despite what was going on, I had an underlying confidence in our business. I believed that if we could convince the bank not to pressure us quite so much, we could work our way out of this thing. So within three or four days after this crisis had started, we had a turnaround consultant in who was a real tough guy, and that's what we needed.

So I began to go through the turnaround process. The very first step was to create a team of seven people, not necessarily all managers, who were influential in the company, in whatever positions they held. I brought them together, and we called them the management team. That was the first time we'd ever had a management team. Prior to that, Dad and I ran things pretty much, from the top down.

At that time, we had about fifty-five employees, and we were a $12-million company. With the help of the management team and the driving support of the turnaround consultant, we worked very hard to put together a business plan. The first business plan was a six-week business plan. It was designed to respond to the turnaround section of the bank's demands and the need to preserve capital. They wanted to make sure that the cash was not depleted any further and that we weren't going out of business.

We gave them a six-week cash flow projection within about ten days. That convinced them to give us another thirty days to operate before they finally called the note. I believed we could make it. After all, we weren't in trouble. We were making money. We weren't bleeding.

Nonetheless, we put together the business plan, showed them the cash-flow projection, and then substantially exceeded that number. Then we proceeded to clean up the balance sheet and write down anything that was even remotely questionable. For example, we had $50,000 or $60,000 in patent costs on the balance sheet. They were really patents that should have been expensed rather than put on the balance sheet. So we wrote them off.

Originally, we started out that last six-month period with a $400,000 loss because of all those write-downs. We went to the bank with a business plan and said, "Here's our plan for the next six months. We planned on taking this $400,000 loss, but after cleaning up the balance sheet, we're going to take it up to a $200,000 loss by year-end. In other words, we'll make $200,000 during the last six months."

We worked like crazy from that point on and actually ended up breaking even for the year. So instead of a $200,000 profit in the second six months, we ended up with a $400,000 profit. We had weekly meetings with the bank representatives, and we had to prove ourselves every time. They were not fun people to work with. It was enormous pressure. It left me unable to carry out other responsibilities that I should have been carrying out with my family and children, such as kids' sports and all those kind of things.

I can remember working day and night, being here until three o'clock in the morning, along with several members of the management team, as we were preparing those business plans. I never knew you could work for weeks on end, for eighteen to twenty hours a day, and still be alive. It was an incredible amount of effort. Everything else simply became non-existent.

I have a good family and a very supportive wife, which is extremely important, and she was behind me the whole way. If anything, she became defensive if anybody criticized me for anything I did. It was unconditional support. That's the kind of support you need when you're going through something like this. You need a place you can go where you feel like you're doing the right thing no matter what. That's the kind of family I have, and that's the kind of support they gave me.

Just to make this whole thing a little bit more complicated, the controller of the company at the time was my oldest son, Barry. As a small company, there were a lot of family members working here. One of the members of the management team was my brother, Mike. So it wasn't just the family ties between Dad, my sister, and me. There were other family members, as well and their families, who were dependent on what we did. They were affected by all of this.

On a broader level, I consider Roma to be a family, and we have a lot of people who've worked here for thirty-five, forty, or forty-five years, and they're certainly family as well. So from my perspective, it wasn't just the blood family to worry about but the larger family. Feeling the weight on my shoulders of having to make this thing work so that their living, their source of bread on the table and a bed to sleep in, was provided was just overwhelming.

Though I had friends and my religious faith, the support really came from within the organization itself. The management team grew very quickly. It's amazing what happens when you're under pressure. A group can homogenize and come together very quickly.

We had our common enemy: the bank. But that anger diminished pretty quickly. Rather than doing what the bank was telling us to do for the bank's sake, we started to do it for the company's sake. We thought, "Roma has tremendous resources, opportunities, and abilities. Let's focus on building this company into the company we all know that it is." We did that. We did it more on a positive thrust than on a negative, reactionary thrust.

I feel proud to take responsibility for that positive attitude. I believe in that kind of thinking. It's the kind of thinking I hoped would prevail, and people responded. It wasn't just me. I can only do so much. I can show people the way, but it takes buy-in and acknowledgment on everyone's part to make it happen.

It has been a steady climb since that crisis. We got involved in strategic planning for the first time, and that has made a huge and positive difference. We even did a joint venture in China, which we never would have done had the crisis not happened. It has positioned us in a market where the opportunities are staggering.

I've also worked out a more equitable stock arrangement with my sister, which took years and much debate. Most amazing, our relationship with the bank, the very same bank, is terrific. I've managed to get back all my sister's collateral, which is usually unheard of, and I've convinced the bank that we are strong enough as a company that they no longer needed my personal guarantee. I've been released from that guarantee, and for a CEO, that guarantee creates enormous pressure. It is amazing to finally have it lifted.

I've learned a lot from the whole process. I think it is absolutely crucial that family businesses properly plan, as they're being formed, exactly what's going to happen to the family members under all kinds of circumstances. That's something we did not do. We never had a stock purchase agreement. We never had an understanding about what would happen if one of us wanted to get out. None of that stuff was ever talked about, let alone defined from a legal point of view. I had nowhere to go. I couldn't have left if I'd wanted to. Not that I wanted to, but certainly I was well aware that I couldn't. These things can lead to a lot of heartaches if they are not planned properly.

My dad passed away in August, 1998, but we remained very close even in his later years. He never dwelled on what happened with the business, and he was my mentor until he died.

I can remember, for example, he was always tough, and you really had to do a good selling job to convince him of something. When I was trying to get approval to spend a large sum of money to do the China joint venture, my sister said that if I could convince Dad to agree that going into China made sense, then I could go ahead and do it. She knew my dad was vehemently opposed to the idea. So I put together my business plan and presented it to him. I knew it would be a very tough sell.

I went up there and made a two-hour presentation to him about

why it made sense. I really poured it on, and at the end, he got very
emotional and said, "That sounds like a real winner. You should go do
it." I felt that he was very proud of me, after all of this. I was very
proud of him too, no doubt about that. He certainly shaped the
principles that I try to follow as well as I can: to only do those things
you have to do, but do them well; always step back and re-examine
them, because what you have to do today, you may not have to do
tomorrow; stop the unnecessary things, or they go on forever. That's
the kind of guy he was. He was just a unique individual.

Twenty-Five
Accepting the Winds of Change

Cindy Minon
JC's Glass, Inc.

*Few people have assumed the position of chief executive at a
more inopportune time than Cindy Minon, president and CEO of
JC's Glass in Phoenix. Immediately upon taking control of the
company from her father, the auto glass industry underwent major
upheaval in which independent family-owned glass companies were
driven out of business all across the country. Determined to stay the
course, Minon hunkered down and guided JC's Glass through the
turmoil, but at tremendous cost to the company and her own peace
of mind. In 1996, just as she was about to give up and declare
bankruptcy, a freak windstorm swept through Phoenix, causing a
major catharsis in the business and in Minon's management style
and approach to life. Today, a calmer, wiser, and more balanced
forty-year old Minon runs a healthy and growing company based
on her new philosophy of "Let go and let God."*

My father founded JC's Glass in 1969. I joined the company in
1980 as a sales rep and worked my way up through the sales and
marketing side. I became president in 1991, and my father retired the
following year. Little did I know that the company and the industry
would soon get swept up in a maelstrom of change that would turn
the next three years into a living nightmare.

At that time, the glass industry in the United States consisted
mainly of small, independent, family-owned and -operated companies.
In the early '80s, one of the larger independents went to the insurance
industry—which provided the bulk of our business—and asked, "If we
could do one thing to make things easier for you, what would that
be?" The insurance industry replied, "Give us one price and one phone

number to call anywhere in the United States." In 1991, that company instituted a one-price, one–phone-number program for its insurance customers and forever changed our industry.

Our largest insurance customer immediately stopped doing business with us, mandating that all their agents use our competitor, with no exceptions. Overnight, we lost $1 million in sales. Soon after, the other large insurance companies told all the independent glass companies, "If you don't want us to do the same thing, reduce your prices by 25 percent." So even though our margins had already been squeezed to the breaking point, we had to drastically cut prices. Many good companies were knocked out of business by this one-two punch.

In early 1992, while still getting my feet wet in my new role, JC's Glass began taking on water faster than the Titanic. Instead of focusing on "big-picture" CEO-type issues, I had to direct all my energy and attention on bailing water, but no matter how quickly I bailed, the water level continued to rise. As a company, we worked so hard to stay afloat that we didn't have time to fix the holes in the boat. After a while, it seemed like we forgot how to fix them. So the water kept rising, and we kept sinking.

I have to admit that much of the problem stemmed from my lack of experience as chief executive. Having lost our largest customer, I should have hit the streets trying to find new ones. Instead, I let myself get stuck dealing with operational problems, soothing upset customers and struggling to maintain a positive cash flow.

To make matters worse, my father hadn't completely left the business. Whenever I made a decision, everyone would gather around him and ask, "What do you think, Joe?" He wasn't deliberately trying to undermine my authority, but because he'd been the company's leader for so many years, people naturally looked to him first. So in addition to the industry turning upside down, we were also caught in the transition between my father's exit and my taking over, which didn't help matters at all.

Feeling more stressed than at any time in my life, I began to have second thoughts about what I had taken on. I remember feeling angry at and resentful of my father, even though I knew the situation wasn't his fault. I often wondered, "If you were going to give this business to me, why did you do it *now*?"

On top of that, I absolutely dreaded the idea of failure. My father had created a successful business and provided good jobs for a lot of people, and—thanks to my inexperience—it was going full-speed down the tubes. To add to the pressure, my parents had invested their full retirement in JC's Glass. If I failed, I not only lost the company, I lost their retirement as well. Many times, I fantasized about walking away and getting a job with another company. I had plenty of offers and could have easily earned six figures, but that wouldn't have been enough to support my parents and me in the lifestyle we desired. I also didn't think I could live with the failure.

You learn a lot about yourself in those kinds of high-pressure situations. I learned that I handle stress by becoming more authoritarian, which didn't score a lot of points with my employees. It also put further strain on my relationship with my father, but I wasn't going to let anyone or anything get in my way. Like the NASA chief in the movie *Apollo 13*, I adopted the motto, "Not on *my* watch." That bull-headed determination kept me going when I wanted to throw in the towel, but it also made me dictatorial. I micro-managed *everything*, which totally destroyed company morale. I became nearly impossible to work with, and we lost a lot of good people. Out of fifty employees from that period, only three still work for JC's Glass.

I realize now that those people had every right to leave, because I was a poor manager and a lousy CEO. I failed to create any sense of vision or mission that might have rallied the troops and pulled us together as a team. Worse, I never told my employees the full truth about the situation. They eventually found out when I had to lay off nearly half my staff, and rest assured, that is *not* the preferred method for finding out the company has hit rock bottom. By putting my needs above theirs, I did them a terrible disservice.

By 1995, we finally began to see some light at the end of the tunnel. I hired a wonderful general manager, the industry began to settle down, and we learned how to play the game and work around the glass networks. I brought in some highly motivated sales people who helped the company start moving forward again. Exhausted and burnt out, I felt a strong need to bring more balance into my life, which I had put on hold for four long years.

In particular, I hungered for a renewed sense of spirit and personal purpose, so I started going back to church and became involved in its program for teens. There, I found a wonderful community and a purpose in life beyond the business. Most important, I learned to "let go and let God," meaning I no longer took responsibility for everything that happened in the world.

Once I started letting go and letting God, I became a new person at work. I still worked as hard as ever, but I began to work a lot smarter. I began to see God in every person, meaning I could finally recognize that everyone had unique talents and abilities. If I let people express those talents, they could take a lot of the load off my shoulders. When I finally let go and let God, I allowed people's talents to come forth. I learned to focus more on my employees and less on the business itself. My new philosophy became, "I'm not a good CEO unless I'm helping you become a better person." I let go of all the micro-managing and began to use my talents as a visionary and motivator. I felt like a "born-again CEO."

In 1995, we showed a profit for the first time in three years. Employee morale zoomed back up, and I had great plans for 1996. But just as the old excitement began to come back, the cancerous morale of 1991 started to take hold again. I felt like I was doing all the right things, but my employees began turning on me once again. I discovered later that a few bad apples—people I had previously looked upon as leaders—were actually ruining the morale. Consequently, my stress level soared, and I despaired of ever getting the company back to where I wanted it to be. I had fought and fought to turn the company around, and now I saw it slipping away once again.

After watching morale spin out of control during our busiest month of the year, I threw up my hands in surrender. I sought refuge in a tiny chapel on the outskirts of Phoenix and spent the afternoon praying, meditating, and asking God for guidance. In the end, I completely and absolutely surrendered. I said, "OK, God. It's all yours. If you want me to file for bankruptcy, that's what I'll do. I will live with the pressure of failure, and I'll work things out with my parents. But I just can't do this anymore."

When I left the chapel, I felt a deep sense of inner peace, like the weight of the world had been taken off my shoulders. I placed the outcome entirely in God's hand, but more importantly, I knew that I could live with the outcome, whatever it might be. If I had to close down the company, so be it. But I would not let this cancer ruin my life again.

Two weeks later, on August 14, 1996, a freak storm with 125-mph winds ripped through the west side of town. To this day, meteorologists can not explain where the storm came from or why. The winds caused tremendous damage, hurling massive objects through windows. Amazingly, nobody was hurt or killed. You'd had to have seen the damage to fully realize the extent of that miracle.

No sooner had the winds died down than our phone began to ring off the hook. We immediately shifted into overdrive, working around the clock for weeks on end, but something had changed. Now we had a vision and a cause, and we all pulled together as a team to get things done. It was like God had said, "O.K. Cindy. I'm going to put you back on track and boost the morale." I honestly believe that windstorm was His way of answering my prayers, because it started a momentum in JC's Glass that hasn't let up since. Morale has skyrocketed and we have grown at 35 percent a year for the past three years. I finally feel like we have the company back on track.

Aside from saving the business, the most important outcome of the crisis is my spiritual renewal as a person and a business leader. I now realize that the success of JC's Glass depends not on me but on how I manage my people and allow them to use their God-given talents. I still have my impatient, type-A personality, and I still suffer the occasional lapse where I want to micro-manage everything, but fortunately those moments of weakness come fewer and farther between. When I catch myself in dictator mode, I remind myself of my commitment to be more visionary and less hands-on. My job today is to worry about what will happen with JC's Glass in 2005 or 2010, not what will happen next Tuesday.

I'm very proud of the fact that JC's Glass survived all the turmoil. I take even more pride in the fact that I realized that I can't run the company as a one-woman show. I have no doubt whatsoever that if I had kept trying to force things my way, I would have taken the company down and had to file for bankruptcy. I learned the hard way, but now I feel like I have earned the titles of president and CEO.

Today, I actually have a life outside the company. I'm forty-years old, have no children, and have never been married—but who knows what the future holds? My involvement with the teen group at church is very fulfilling and enriching (it even led to me meeting the Pope in Rome), and I have a sense of inner peace that I never dreamed possible. All because I let go and let God.

Twenty-Six
A Father's Daughter as CEO

Peggy Andrews
Andrews Distributing Co., Inc.

Peggy Andrews is the forty-seven-year-old president and CEO of Andrews Distributing, a $43-million heating and air conditioning distributor in Nashville, Tennessee. The company, with just under 100 employees, supplies dealers and contractors with Carrier products. A decade ago, Andrews took the reigns of the family-owned business, which was established by her father and grandfather in 1957. Her father remains chairman of the board. Despite the company's success, the difficulties of merging family and business have been evident throughout Andrews's tenure.

I started working at the company when I was in high school. I worked full-time during the summers doing clerical work. People would save up things for me to do all year. I really hated the job, to be honest. In fact, I couldn't have hated it more.

I went off to college in south Florida and graduated with a degree in psychology. I felt then that I wanted to be in some kind of business, perhaps retail. I worked for a year in a specialty furniture store in Ft. Lauderdale and really enjoyed it. I did some sales, some office work, even some employee relations. It was very educational, and I liked it, but I wasn't sure where I was going to go from there.

My dad called me and made me an offer: I could stay in Florida, and he would buy me a condominium, or I could come back to Nashville and work for the company. It took me a month to decide. The condo was enticing, but it was very short term.

When I was growing up, I thought I'd go to college and graduate. But I was pretty sure that afterwards, I would get married, and I wouldn't work. I'd have a family and a really nice life, as my mother had. But at some point in college, I realized that wasn't what I wanted, and it probably wasn't going to happen. I'd seen a lot of friends, especially women, not thinking very much about their futures. They were just trying to get the most out of the moment. They had no money, and they were not going to have any money. They spent every dime that they had and were probably not going to have careers. That was not at all what I wanted for myself.

My father really loved his business, and my sister, my brother, and I had grown up around it. He talked about the business at home, and so we knew all about manufacturing, distribution, and retail. We knew and understood what he did.

He'd never made a whole lot of money from the business, until I'd gone off to college, which is when things really started to take off. But I don't believe his reason for asking me to join was to keep the business in the family. I think he saw that I was a bright person and that I really was willing to make an investment in myself. I was a little bit different from most of the younger people that he saw at that time, which was the mid-1970s. I believe that he thought I would be a welcome addition to the company.

I don't know how far ahead he was thinking, but I decided to take the position with one thought in my mind: someday I'll take over the company. If I'd thought of it as just a job, I never would have accepted it.

Strangely, as soon as my father made me the offer, I felt that he was afraid that he had made a mistake and that he would end up having to fire me. I don't know why he thought that, perhaps it was because he didn't know if a twenty-four-year-old was capable of running a company. He really didn't know what I was capable of.

When I started my first job, as head of the order department, I was met with a great deal of resentment. My job was to handle all orders from sales people and directly from customers. It was a very difficult and demanding job, a real challenge.

A few people treated me well and with respect, but many didn't. The sales people were respectful, because they saw that I could fill their orders and solve problems for them. But many others, not in the sales area, felt that I had been handed the job. I wasn't even getting paid very much to do it, but because I was the boss's daughter, they thought I'd been given a gift.

Even though I was earning every penny I made, I was not fully accepted—especially among the clerical staff. I had to fire one person who continually sabotaged me. It was nothing but pure resentment. I know this is not unusual in a family business, but it's very painful. It's difficult to get used to people hating you for no fault of your own. This continued for a long time, until nearly ten years ago when I took the CEO job.

There were more than a few times when I felt like leaving, especially when this resentment came from people higher up in the organization. My dad didn't always see my side. Often he would take somebody else's side. It made me somewhat cynical. When I came to work here, I was a very nice person with an open mind, but all these experiences have made me a little quick to judge in a negative way.

I stayed, because I knew it would be worth it emotionally, financially, and for pure professional satisfaction. It's hard to put into words. It's very frustrating, but it's very satisfying at the same time. I knew it would be satisfying and tough. I feel I've accomplished something, even though I've had a lot of help along the way from my dad and family. Also, I simply never thought that the people who caused me the problems were worth quitting over. If I'd quit, they would have won, and that was not acceptable to me.

Despite these issues, I began taking over the business about a decade ago. I felt ready for the role. My dad was never very hands-on. He wasn't the type to come in at 8:00 A.M. and leave at 6:00 P.M. He played golf several days a week and spent a lot of time in Florida. And gradually, he backed away, more and more. He's seventy years old now and still involved, even when he's in Florida. He has a fax machine, so he can get his daily dose of business stuff. He's still very interested in the business, but he isn't very familiar with how we operate on a day-to-day basis.

Basically, I was handed a very nice business. It wasn't struggling, and it was very profitable. My goal was to keep it that way. But unfortunately, things have never been very easy. My dad and I have had intense periods where we weren't getting along. It was lonely and frustrating, because I just didn't have many people I could talk to about it.

Eventually, I realized that I had to change my approach with him and become less confrontational. He was the way he was, and he wasn't going to change. He was going to do things the way he wanted to do them and handle things the way he wanted to, and there was nothing I could actually do about it. I recognized that if I wanted to continue working with him, I was the one who was going to have to change. I think I did.

What triggered these changes was not only my dad, but a confrontation with my employees. At one point, a lot of the employees weren't very happy with me, either for real or imagined reasons. They called a meeting in our Nashville office and told me their feelings. It was extremely emotional and, at times, extremely personal. It was, to be honest, pretty horrible. I thought a lot of their complaints were imagined, but often things that are imagined might as well be real. Perception is reality in many cases.

Of course, that caught my attention. At the same time, I saw that my dad didn't believe me and wasn't going to take my side. So I realized that I was going to have to do some changing in order to be accepted.

After that meeting, I went home and sat in my house for hours, just sitting and thinking. I was devastated. I had one person, a friend, who helped me sort through it. But I was basically alone. It was certainly a low point in my life, but I used it as a springboard.

Eventually, I decided that the employees were partly right, that I was mostly right, and that I just needed to make them think I was right, whether I was or not. So I went back to them.

First, I admitted that I was guilty, which went over very well. After that, I tried to behave in a more compassionate way. As always, much of it was a personality issue. Over the years, I had built up a lot of resentment because of the way people treated me, and my resentment became a shell that I put around myself.

Making matters worse, though, were a couple of people high up in the company who were very resentful of me, very chauvinistic, and they really wanted me out of here. They had gone to my father, and he'd taken their side. He actually asked me to leave. I told him that wasn't at all what I wanted to do, that I was willing to do whatever it took not to leave. He indulged me.

It's hard to make changes. I still have some difficulties with people. I'm not at all convinced that some of the problems that I have would exist if I weren't a woman. For example, I don't think that I'm as nice as people expect a woman to be.

A long time ago, I made a conscious decision to be a *person,* not a woman. That decision changed my life in some not-so-positive ways. I had to become hardened to business realities and embrace a certain toughness. After so many years of being in business, it's hard to get back to a softer side of yourself.

With that said, I'm not at all lonely. I have a very busy life and a very full life. I'm very happy the way I am, but I do know I'm missing a big part of life. I'm single. I'm never going to have any kids. But I have my horses. They are my personal life.

I enter riding competitions. I ride Hunter Jumpers, and I'm pretty active in that. It takes a lot of time on the road and at home; it gives me an escape and a focus. It is quite fulfilling. I get to see how people treat each other in another world. I've learned how to treat people in the horse world. It's ironic. At work, not everyone thinks I'm a wonderful, warm person, but at the horse shows, I'm one of the nicest people there. It's a rejuvenating feeling.

Lately, my father and I have begun to agree on things more and argue less. We don't really talk about it. That's not his style. I've just tried to do what I want to do in a way that's acceptable to him. Most of the time, he's actually right. Most of the time, I know he's right. I'd like to believe that he is proud of me and of the job I have done. He might be, but he doesn't say so. Hearing that from him would mean a lot.

Twenty-Seven

Lessons from the Straits of Alaska

Dick West
Alaska Sightseeing Cruise West

At the tender age of thirteen, Dick West began work as a bellhop in Skagway, Alaska, at a hotel operated by his father's tour company. That summer job turned into a lifelong passion, and thirty-three years later, West owns and operates the largest small-ship cruise company in the United States: Alaska Sightseeing Cruise West. A tiny player in a multibillion dollar industry controlled by huge multinational corporations, the Seattle-based company operates six 80- to 100-passenger vessels, primarily in Alaskan waters. A second-generation business owner, West knows first-hand the trials and tribulations of running a family-owned business. Although sibling rivalries nearly sank the business during the ownership transition to the next generation, the familial squabbles vanish amidst the pristine beauty of the wild Alaskan coastline.

I suppose you could consider me a classic second-generation family business owner. I grew up in the business, and except for summer jobs during high school and college, I've never worked anywhere else. Even those summer jobs involved driving tour buses and working in hotels or on boats, so I never strayed very far from the tour and cruise-ship industry. All my life, I have lived in the Pacific Northwest, one of the most spectacular areas on Earth. There's nothing I enjoy more than sharing these wonders with people from all over the world, and I consider myself fortunate to be able to make a very good living at something I love so much.

My father started the business way back in the 1940s. He built Westours into a fairly large company and then sold it to Holland America in 1971. We immediately started our tour company and bus line, the predecessor to Cruise West, and I have been president since 1989 and CEO since 1991. We just reached $50 million a year in sales, and we currently employ more than 450 people during the peak season and 150 during the off-season. All our ships are United States–flag registered, which presents some very interesting, competitive challenges for us.

The vast majority of cruise ships we compete against are owned and operated by foreign companies. These ships have a tremendous competitive advantage because they don't have to comply with United States labor laws or pay United States taxes. We compete by sticking to a market niche where we don't fight the big boys head-on. In Alaska, which is our primary market, the huge foreign-flagged boats can't venture far from the middle of the channels for fear of running aground. We use much smaller boats that allow us to explore all the little nooks and crannies along the coastline. We get up close and personal with the whales, the waterfalls, and the magnificent onshore wilderness, and our passengers regularly spot bear, caribou, and other wildlife roaming the woods or foraging on the beach. Our guests get a much more hands-on experience than what the Carnivals and Princess Cruises of the world can provide.

Despite my love of the outdoors, I spend way too much time behind a desk and in meeting rooms. The highlight of my job comes on those rare occasions when I get out on one of our ships for a "quality check." Sure, I'm keeping an eye on the quality of the experience we provide our passengers, but I'm also adding to the quality of my own life. When I'm standing on the captain's bridge, cruising down the straits of Alaska and drinking in nature's splendor on all sides, I feel like I'm on top of the world. The grandeur and awesome scope of the landscape help to recharge my batteries and remind me that maybe—in the grand scheme of things—I'm not so important after all. There's nothing like a little ego deflation to put things back in perspective and help a CEO make better decisions.

No matter how rewarding, standing at the helm of Cruise West still has its share of aggravations. Without question, my biggest challenge —my biggest source of frustration, as well as what I consider my greatest accomplishment—was the struggle to convince my family to do the succession and estate planning necessary to ensure the business would survive the transition to the next generation.

It all began shortly after I took over as president in 1988, when I read several horror stories about what can happen when family businesses fail to plan for the succession of ownership and leadership. I learned that only 30 percent of family businesses actually make it to the second generation and, in the majority of cases, the lack of succession and/or estate planning proves to be the ultimate downfall.

At the time, my parents still owned the majority of the corporate stock and assets in their estate. They had done no estate planning—merely a basic will that divided the company equally among us children. After talking to several attorneys and accountants and reviewing the state of affairs, I came to the chilling conclusion that, as things stood, when my parents passed away, we'd have to sell the company to pay the estate taxes. Although it took the wind out of my sails at the time, I thank God that I looked into the matter when I did. One only has to look at probate-court files anywhere in the country to see the wreckage of once-successful family companies that couldn't pay the founder's estate taxes.

I immediately set out to correct our deficiencies in these areas, but I soon discovered that the rest of the family did not share my enthusiasm for succession planning. I broached the subject as delicately as possible, saying to my parents, "If anything should ever happen to you, the estate taxes could cause us to lose the business." At first, my father resisted. He didn't want to offend his attorney, a general counsel who had worked for him for forty years and had created the will. Plus, as he kept reminding me, my father had no plans to leave the planet anytime soon.

I had recently been through a divorce, which had opened my eyes to the many complexities involved in valuing and protecting stock and assets in a family business. I also realized that I didn't want to devote my whole life to building the company and then lose it all because we had failed to do the right thing. Not wanting to leave the business in the hands of fate, I kept chipping away at my father's resolve. I showed him the books and articles I had read and introduced him to some outside attorneys and accountants who managed to convince him that I wasn't making up a doom-and-gloom scenario just to get my own way. Eventually, he agreed to meet with an estate-planning specialist, but even then it took another two years to get that process underway.

Despite my fear of losing the business, the worst part was dealing with my sisters. Though we had not been a particularly close-knit family, I felt like an outcast and a pariah. My sisters seemed to think I was trying to steal their inheritance. When I tried to convince them that I only wanted what was best for the business and the family, they asked why I had to be so greedy. It took many years and a great deal of effort to educate family members and reach the point where progress could be made.

The first thing we did was restructure the corporation with two classes of stock, Class A, voting stock, and Class B, nonvoting stock. We also elected to organize as an "S" corporation for tax purposes, and we structured the company accordingly. My parents then made gifts of stock to the children, utilizing minority share discounts and their lifetime-gift exemptions. The folks kept 51 percent of the voting stock, which gave them control but represented less than 3 percent of the value of the company. This solved the estate-planning piece.

The next step was more difficult. It involved bringing on an outside board of directors to help make the company more business-oriented than it was with a family board. To ensure that the succession from my dad to me would be smooth, I would eventually need to have voting control of the company. We accomplished this by establishing a trust that would transfer additional Class A stock and voting control to me on January 1, 2000.

In the end, these decisions came down to mom and dad, and they eventually sided with me. I think the outside experts, who had no stake in the outcome, finally convinced them to come around to my way of thinking. Even the estate-planning attorney, among others, told my father point blank, "You can do whatever you want, but Dick will have a very hard time operating the business if he has to run every decision by a committee." Bringing in an outside board of directors helped to calm the family's fears, because it forced me to report to an experienced group of advisors; they knew I wouldn't be running the business on my own whim.

Today, my three sisters each own 20 percent of the business, but they don't get involved in the daily operations. I'm sad to say, however, that our relationships have still not improved. Even though the company is doing better than ever, they still harbor some ill feeling toward me. Many times, in the middle of the fighting and acrimony, I questioned whether the business was worth it. I often thought, "Why not just sell it and move on, so we can quit fighting and go our own ways?" But I realized that I loved the business too much, and it meant too much to my family for me to give it up.

One thing that intrigues me—and I would like to know whether other family businesses have the same experience—is the difference in attitude between generations. In 1993, we held a family meeting to talk about what the business meant to the family. My parents thought the business brought and kept the family together, whereas we children felt like it was driving a wedge between the family members. The first generation sees the business as a way for the family to come together and find common ground, while for the second generation, it breeds envy and jealousy. That contrast puzzles and saddens me. On one level, the business provides a wonderful life for all of us, better than if we were each taking care of our own material needs. At the same time, it extracts a terrible toll on what should be loving, nurturing relationships.

The hardest part is that I still get stuck on the hot seat. While everyone else can worry about what's best for themselves or the family, I have to focus on the needs of the company. Sometimes that means making some very unpopular decisions, such as replacing a brother-in-law in a key executive position. Everyone in the family came out against me. They all said, "How could you *do* this?" Their hearts were in the right place, but they couldn't understand that I had to do it for the good of the company. We gave my brother-in-law two year's severance, but that didn't make it any easier. Fortunately, he has gone on to establish a successful career in real estate, but years later the hard feelings still linger.

I learned two very important lessons from that experience. One, I should have done it sooner. Once you know in your gut that a certain decision is the right thing to do, you just have to go ahead and do it. Otherwise, you drag it out and make the situation worse. Two, I discovered that I *can* make those tough decisions, even in the face of considerable opposition from those close to me. There's an old saying that it's lonely at the top. Believe me, I know how that feels, but when you have bottom-line accountability, tough decisions come with the territory. If you're not prepared to make them, perhaps you ought to find something else to do.

Family squabbles aside, I truly love what I do. At Cruise West, we don't just provide high-end tours, we create memories that last a lifetime. Many businesses can make widgets or provide a useful product or service to the community, but I don't know too many others that give people a world they have never seen before, and that provide a life-enriching experience they will remember for the rest of their lives. That means a lot to me. I feel very lucky to be able to do that, and I intend to keep on doing it until the time comes to sail off into the sunset.

Twenty-Eight
A Price to Pay for Success

Bob Dabic
Dabico Inc.

Bob Dabic, forty-four years old, is president and CEO of Dabico Inc., a thirty-three-year-old, family-owned business that makes the in-ground utility dispensing boxes that provide aircraft with the various utilities they need while on the ground. He also runs Integrated AeroSystems, L.L.C., which custom designs and produces thrust-measurement equipment for jet and rocket engines. Both companies are privately held and have combined annual sales of nearly $20 million. Early on in his role as CEO, Dabic decided to undertake a major cultural change in his company. The transformation of his company had such a profound impact on Dabic that it led to the development of a personal mission statement and his involvement in a number of mentoring activities outside the business. Not all has been smooth sailing. The success of his business destroyed one of his most cherished relationships—an outcome that still haunts him to this day.

When my father first asked me to work for him at Dabico, I initially resisted. I wanted to prove that I could make it on my own, which I did, holding down two very successful sales positions. I also wanted to come to the company with some tangible, real-world experience, so I could earn my position and responsibility, rather than having it handed to me on a silver platter because I was Michael Dabic's son.

After several unsuccessful attempts to recruit me, Dad finally made an offer I couldn't refuse. I joined Dabico in 1978, moved into a technical sales role, and began working my way up the ranks. I became president in 1984 and have served as president and CEO since 1993.

Our first seven years together, my father and I made a great team. Dad taught me everything he knew about the business, and I brought some sales and marketing expertise to our growing enterprise. Unfortunately, as time went by, our relationship deteriorated. We butted heads on more and more issues and increasingly found ourselves engaged in a power struggle for control over the direction of the company. When my father finally decided to exit the business, the transition tore us apart. I know that most family businesses struggle with succession issues, but that knowledge hasn't made it any easier. To this day, our parting remains the low point of my business career.

Aside from the ongoing struggle to work things out with my father, my biggest challenge has been changing the culture of the company, which has taken years to accomplish. Like most major organizational change in a family business, it started with a new leader—me.

I can't pinpoint the exact date, but I remember coming to work one day and realizing I wasn't having a lot of fun. When I looked around, I didn't see anyone else having fun either. To outsiders, Dabico looked like a successful, profitable company, which it was. We made good products, had good relationships with our customers, and enjoyed what I considered a good working environment. Nevertheless, I realized that our culture did not lead to people feeling professionally satisfied or personally fulfilled.

I had always thought of myself as a humorous, fun-loving person, but when I looked in the mirror, I saw someone who had become too caught up in the old top-down, authoritarian, dictatorial management style. I made decisions with little or no input from my staff and expected them to hop at my command. Worse, that style had permeated our entire senior management group. We got things done, but the way we got things done put everyone on edge and took all the fun out of the workday. After some intense, personal introspection and much thought about the kind of company I felt we should have, I realized that we needed a cultural revolution.

Over the course of the next several years, we implemented a tremendous number of cultural changes, all of them based on the concept of "Values-Based Leadership," which I passionately believe in. The essence of Values-Based Leadership consists of a core of "Vision Values"—a statement on what you want the company to be in three to five years, the top four or five areas that senior management holds nearest and dearest to its collective heart. When you strive for perfection (but settle for continuous improvement) in those key areas, the culture transforms into an improvement-oriented work environment in which people are empowered to make decisions and use their full talents and abilities. As an automatic byproduct, you get long-term, net-profit growth—an outcome near and dear to the heart of every CEO I know.

While we haven't completely achieved our vision yet, we have dramatically changed the culture. We treat each other as real people, at all levels of the organization, and we try to address the needs of the whole person. We encourage involvement in the community, both as a company and as individuals. We focus on growing and developing our Team Members (employees), both personally and professionally. I'm having a lot more fun now, and I think our Team Members are too. Of the people who have voluntarily left the company in the last few years, I'd say nearly 50 percent have called to see if they could have their old jobs back or take another position in the company. So we must be doing something right.

Why did I undertake such a massive cultural transformation? Quite frankly, because I thought we could make more money as a company by getting everyone involved. Just as important, I also believe that a company should nurture people, enhance their self-esteem, and help them fulfill their personal goals and ambitions. In other words, people should enjoy their work.

My dream is to have all Dabico Team Members feel so fulfilled in their work that they actually dread the weekends. I realize that may be asking a bit much. I'll settle for seeing them look forward to coming in to work on Monday. I'll keep pushing for the ultimate goal, though, because I believe that one of my jobs as CEO is to provide the people who work for the company with more than just a paycheck.

As those who have attempted it know, cultural transformation, no matter how positive, comes with its costs. Whenever you move on to something new, something gets left behind. In the case of organizational change, it's usually people.

We saw from the beginning that certain people—mostly old-timers who grew up in the "John Wayne" management style of the previous generation—couldn't function in a team-based environment. Others didn't want to buy into the new values. So we suffered some casualties; some left voluntarily, others had to be asked to leave. Let me tell you, when you've shared blood, sweat, and tears with someone, and then have to look that person in the eye and ask that person to leave, it hurts. You feel devastated, frustrated, angry, and helpless—every negative emotion you can think of.

I remember one manager I felt particularly close to. We went way back together. I coached and coached and worked with him, and he just never got it. Asking him to leave the company tore my guts out. It took me weeks to get over.

Our cultural revolution also caused me to toughen up on the inside. When you regularly invite people to give you feedback and criticism (and don't punish them for doing so), by golly, they will give it to you! You had better be able to take it. When you're used to giving orders, shifting to a culture where everyone tells you what they think about your ideas doesn't come easy. On the other hand, I'm a much better manager and person because of it. I have a much thicker skin than I used to, as well as a much thinner skin that has allowed me to be more sensitive to people's feelings.

Perhaps the most important outgrowth of all this for me has been the development of a personal purpose statement. As we began coaching and encouraging our people to unleash their full talents, I gained a whole new outlook on what I could accomplish with and through others. My purpose in life now is to significantly enhance the lives of others through humor, through music (via my classic rock and country band), and by providing access to fulfillment.

I'm on a mission to help as many people as possible grow and develop themselves, set goals, and learn to laugh and enjoy life along the way. I've learned that goals come and go, and you have to enjoy the journey, or it just isn't worth it.

In pursuit of my mission, I recently began mentoring high school students, teaching them what I've learned about business and life. So far, I can't point to any dramatic breakthroughs, but I look at it as planting seeds. Five to seven years from now, when these kids get out of college and start into their careers, I hope some will say, "Bob Dabic made a difference in my life." I would find that very rewarding.

What's the high point of my career? There have been many, but I would have to say that increasing the company's profits while turning it into a more fun, productive, and nourishing place to work has given me the most satisfaction. Without question, the low point has been the damage to my relationship with my father.

My father is a truly gifted inventor. In fact, he is as close to a genius in the engineering field as anyone I know. He loves to invent things and then sell people on them, and he had a very successful career doing that. When it came time to let go and move on, he didn't know how, and it cost us dearly. I still love him and have the utmost respect for what he taught me about life and business. I learned more working with him than I could have in ten M.B.A. programs. The sad fact is, though, that we barely speak to each other anymore; he hardly knows his grandkids, and it just tears my heart out.

I have two pictures of my kids hanging on the office wall. The one of my daughter bears the caption, "Future President." My son's picture says, "Future COO." My wife had those made up many years ago, but I look at them now and realize I don't ever want my children coming into the business, because I don't want to risk my relationships with them. The romance of working with your kids may sound nice, but the harsh reality is very different. You start becoming business partners rather than family members, and everything changes. I've been through that once. I'm not about to do it again.

For now, my main focus with Dabico is to keep building the business, to continue to improve on our values-based culture, and to keep having fun. Do Dabico Team Members dread the weekend yet? I don't know about that. But I guarantee you that Monday mornings are a lot more fun than they used to be.

Section Five
Personal Sacrifice

Twenty-Nine

A Woman Fighting a Man's Disease

M. Christine Jacobs
Theragenics Corporation

*In the summer of 1998, forty-seven-year-old Christine Jacobs
became the first woman CEO to lead a transfer of a company's stock
from NASDAQ to the New York Stock Exchange. Surrounded by her
parents and eight siblings, she rang the bell to open trading that day. It
was also a first for a woman chairman and CEO in the Exchange's
207-year history. Just a dozen years earlier, her company—the
Theragenics Corporation—existed more on paper than in reality.
Jacobs joined in 1987 as director of marketing and sales and rose
through several executive levels to her current position as chairman,
president, and chief executive officer. Based in Norcross, Georgia,
Theragenics makes and markets a unique implant device for treating
prostate cancer. The Theraseed is a grain-sized device that is implanted
in tumors and kills cancer cells by emitting localized radiation over
several months. More than 30,000 men with the disease have already
benefited from the Theraseed. During Jacobs's tenure, Theragenics' sales
have reached $40 million annually, the stock has soared by more than
700 percent, and manufacturing facilities have quadrupled in capacity.
In the marketing realm, Jacobs negotiated an agreement with Johnson
& Johnson to sell Theragenics products around the world. For her
achievements, Ernst & Young named Jacobs "Entrepreneur of the Year"
in the health care turnaround category in 1997.*

In 1987, the company was hardly more than a bunch of ideas from
scientists at Georgia Tech. We had no sales, no doctors, no clinical
studies, and no real connection to the medical community. We did
have one product that had been approved by the Food and Drug

Administration, and it showed tremendous promise in treating prostate cancer. That product became the basis of the company.

I left a job as regional sales manager in Ohio to come here, and it seemed like a crazy thing to do at the time, even to me. I had been hoping to work in the medical division at the General Electric Company, but during an interview I asked how many women managers worked there, and the answer was none. It was that bit of information that made me think GE wasn't the place for me.

In the meantime, I received a call from a former colleague about a nearly bankrupt medical startup in Georgia. He said he could use me there for twelve months. He was honest: he said he didn't think they'd make it, but I thought, what the heck. I love medicine, and the good treatment of patients is a proposition that will always draw me. They asked me how much I'd need to live on, and I said $37,500. They agreed, and I headed to Georgia.

My father was astonished. I had a good, secure job, and here I was leaving for an unknown, unstable situation. I was used to tougher situations than that. As the oldest of nine children, I had helped raise the younger siblings in my family. When we turned twelve years old, my father expected each of us to get a job, or else he'd get one for us. He and a neighbor bought an old community swimming pool, just so my brothers and sisters and cousins would have jobs in the summer. I remember cleaning a lot of bathrooms. I'd say my father is responsible for my work ethic.

After graduating from college as a medical technician, I worked in a trauma unit in Columbus, Ohio. It was like the television show "ER," only real. I oversaw two shifts and thirty-seven medical technicians. I taught people how to put needles in veins. I often found myself at the bedside of an automobile-accident victim or gunshot victim with a wound to the chest.

In 1984, after thirteen years in the trauma unit, I decided to try something dramatically different. I went into sales at Amersham, a Chicago-based company that sold radioactive chemicals for tumor therapy. It was an entry-level job, but it taught me how to sell products and how to run a business.

I thought business was a wonderful place, compared with where I'd just left. Missing a quarterly number is nothing compared to giving fifty units of blood to a gunshot victim in the middle of the night.

I also figured I could always go back to the E.R. if business didn't work out for me. Nobody can take away the letters of accreditation—a Bachelor of Science in Medical Technology and an M.B.A. from Georgia State University—so I'm always employable. They are rainbows in my pocket.

Of course, my dad was devastated. To give up such noble work to go into sales at Amersham. He couldn't understand that at all, but I did well, and in less than ten months, I was promoted to regional manager. My territory expanded to include the whole area between Nebraska and Puerto Rico, and I was given eighteen months to rebuild under a new strategy. I did it and loved it. But when the company changed management, the focus and directives changed, and I decided it was time to leave.

My move to Georgia was certainly eye-opening. The company had thirty scientists at the time and very little space. I started along with a new controller. Our office was in a lab with nude mice. Here we sat, the future CFO and CEO of the company, in a rat room, sharing a telephone, while experiments were being performed. It was certainly humbling.

The atmosphere was also stressful and challenging. We needed to persuade doctors to recommend our product. We quickly realized that when a doctor has a treatment for cancer of any kind, especially prostate cancer, it's the doctor who will draw attention to an alternative such as ours. Patients faced with nasty treatments will try anything to avoid surgery. So our alternative treatment made for a strong pitch to doctors.

We built the company, doctor by doctor and patient by patient. Our first-year sales of $37,000 grew to $1 million by the third year. I became chief operating officer in 1992 and realized that for us to survive and control our own destiny, we had to change our manufacturing capability, and stop using outside vendors who had become unreliable. So the first thing I did as COO was build a plant in Georgia. We brought in proprietary machines that converted our own raw materials from electricity into isotopes, essentially converting an inert metal into a radioactive metal. We were the only company in the world manufacturing this isotope.

But the machines were expensive—at least $5 million to buy and install. Our first really tough decision was whether to buy that first cyclotron from Belgium. We had only raised $12 million in equity at the start of the company, and by 1991, $9 million was gone. With only $2 million in annual revenue, we decided to take on this new $5-million machine. The banks weren't coming forward with loans, so we were betting the company. It was pretty scary at the time. Everybody understood the risk, but we had to roll the dice.

I became CEO in August 1993, and I learned quickly that cash-management and expense-control is the real story of management—especially if you're making such large capital expenditures as we were. In retrospect, buying that first machine turned out to be easy. We had no choice if we were going to be in this business. Buying the second one was a different story. That took guts. We were already in the business, but we needed to grow. By 1994, we needed money very badly, and lenders were reluctant to get involved. Our assets were radioactive, after all. We went through incredible hoops to try to get a loan. The banks set incredibly tough terms. In essence, they wanted control of the company. So I threw them out.

That was difficult from an emotional as well as a financial point of view, but I just could not let them run this company. I took a long walk in the park alone to think about the potential I saw in Theragenics—potential that the bankers didn't see. They wanted to limit our growth, and I said no. It was a lonely time. Eventually, the bank saw it my way and came back with the loan. They decided to bet on the therapy, along with the CEO and our team. Was it frightening? You bet. We've been close to bankruptcy four times since I came here. The path isn't always clear. You have a vision, you want to make sure the product is in the right doctors' hands, and you make quality the parameter. Then you just have to hope the rest falls in place.

Along the way are people who want to block you. I stopped listening to them a long time ago. Everybody wants to tell you what you can't do, but you can't be diverted. You can't take no for an answer. After a while, you just smile—the Japanese are great at this—you just nod and smile and go do what you should do. When you know that what you are doing makes a difference for a dad, a brother, a husband, an uncle, a business associate—you don't mind taking the risk. You say, "By God, it sounds right. Let's go do it." You can second-guess yourself on a Saturday night, but on Monday morning you get shot out of a cannon all over again.

When you are curing cancer, you travel to the beat of a different drummer. I've been extremely lucky. I don't have too many diversions to draw me off track. I had a boyfriend in Ohio, but he didn't make the trip to Georgia with me. I'm single, so it's not hard to work an extra hour on a Saturday morning to make something happen. For example, I answered our cancer information hot line one such morning, and a man called from South Carolina. He said, "Please, I have prostate cancer, and I don't want surgery." I said, "There's a doctor here you can talk to. What stage are you in?" We connected him to the doctor, and the man received our treatment. That was eight years ago, and he is still free of the disease. He also went back to South Carolina and started a non-profit organization that screens men for prostate cancer for free. That all started with answering a phone call.

It is odd, I suppose, for a woman to run a company that makes a treatment for a disease that strikes only men. It is disconcerting to some people to see a woman walk in the room to talk about prostate cancer, impotence, and things that are wholly male. People say, "Why don't you work on breast cancer?" Well, this disease kills as many as breast cancer. Prostate cancer is more obscure. When I started in 1987, for example, there was less than $30 million in research funds for prostate cancer and $380 million for breast cancer.

Being female has, in fact, been a bit of an advantage. People are surprised at what I'm doing. It is unique to be a woman in this field. But that is not as important as what I do. I want to be known for my medical achievements, not for being female. I'd rather be known as a CEO who changed medicine.

My job does become overwhelming at times, but I keep it in perspective. Some of my heroes are women raising children and still working as many hours as I do. I don't know how they do that. I focus on making a contribution to people's health. I'm not worried about what they'll write on my tombstone.

Thirty

Success and Sacrifice, Joy and Regret

Karla Hertzog
Tops Payrolling Service, Inc.

Karla Hertzog is president and CEO of Tops Payrolling Service in San Diego. She started out as a part-time receptionist in her father's temporary staffing company, Tops Staffing Services, and within three years was running a branch office in San Diego. Hertzog became president of the entire company in 1985 and sole owner in 1991 when her father retired. The company grew to a peak of $50 million in annual sales. In 1998, Hertzog sold the temporary staffing part of the business and retained the payrolling business, which now does about $41 million a year in annual sales. Hertzog is a former winner of the Inc. Magazine Entrepreneur of the Year award, and in 1993 served as president of the National Association of Temporary and Staffing Services. Although Hertzog enjoys her lifestyle and thrives on the constant challenges facing a top decision-maker, being a single mother of two has forced her to make sacrifices beyond those most CEOs endure. At forty-eight years old, she has learned to tell the difference between the urgent and the truly important.

I never set out to run a temporary staffing company. My background is in social work, which I dabbled in for a few years. When I quit school to get married, my father gave me a temporary job as a receptionist in his company, Tops Staffing Services. I planned on a two- or three-week assignment at the most. While I was there, one of his key players got sick, and I began to fill orders. I never left.

One thing led to another, I grew in the company, and three years later I ventured out to San Diego to start this branch. We sold the

Denver branch in 1985 and moved our headquarters to San Diego.
As the business world began to change and outsourcing of staffing
gained greater acceptance throughout corporate America, the
company began to grow.

At Tops, we differentiated ourselves from the competition by being
locally owned and managed. While our competitors had to go back to
their corporate office to make important decisions, we could make
and implement decisions on the spot, which gave us a significant
edge. We also got very involved with the community, and we had a
great staff that displayed tremendous pride and a sense of ownership
in the company. Those three things combined to make the last two
decades very successful for us.

Very soon after opening the San Diego office, my husband and I
divorced. We remarried later but ended up getting divorced a second
time. We tried to make it work, especially for the sake of our two
daughters, but sometimes the best option is to live apart. My
daughters were ages six and twelve when we split up for good, and
there's no question that my running a business has had an impact on
their upbringing. The interesting part is how differently each has
reacted to the situation.

My older daughter admires and respects what I have done. She
often tells me that I represent a positive role-model for her. If
anything, I sometimes feel my accomplishments put undue pressure
on her to do the same, which I don't like. I don't want her to feel she
has to follow in my footsteps. I want her to follow her own path in
life, whether that means working as a retail clerk, running a company,
or staying at home with her children.

My younger daughter, however, does *not* look up to me as a
positive role-model, and she frequently reminds me of that. She was
much younger when her father left, and she always wanted—and felt
she should have—a "stay-at-home" mother. I know she has always
loved me, but there have been plenty of times when she didn't like
me, because I couldn't stay home with her. I always had a house
keeper, so she never was carted off to child care centers, but that
didn't change her feelings about the situation. She certainly enjoys the
money and the lifestyle that come with my position, but I don't think
she fully understands yet that if I didn't work, we wouldn't have the
money. Perhaps it boils down to the fact that she resents not having

been my first priority throughout the years.

Looking back, I have to say that, to a certain extent, I resent it too. I missed a lot of things that many mothers take for granted, and I can never get those back. I managed to squeeze in the big moments—Christmases, birthdays, the first school dance, and those major events—because when you own the company, you at least get the benefit of setting your own schedule. But I missed the little moments. I didn't get to share those times when they came home from school and said, "Guess what happened today?" And I never had time to just sit around and play games with them. I did all the urgent things, the have-to-be-done things, but I never got to do the little things. Now that my daughters are almost grown, I feel a deep sadness for that loss.

On the one hand, this has taught me a very valuable lesson: you don't get any second opportunities with your family. You get second chances in the business, but you don't realize it while you're in the middle of putting out all the fires. You think, "I *must* do this, or I *have* to do that." Most of the time, the same old problems keep coming around again and again. If you don't fix them the first time, believe me, you will get more chances. With your children, you don't get second chances.

When you run a company, a lot of people depend on you for their jobs, their careers, and their livelihood, but I don't know if most children understand or care about that. They just want you to be there for them. In a way, I feel sadder for me than for my daughters. I look at what I lost, and it far outweighs the fact that I gave thousands of people jobs over the past fifteen years. Maybe that's a woman thing. I don't know. But I struggle with it all the time.

What would I do differently? That's hard to say for sure. I know I would pay a lot more attention to what's important instead of what's urgent. In high school, my classmates voted me most likely to get married and have kids, and that's all I ever wanted to do. I was initially forced into this, because I quit school. But once I start something, I do it full force. I kept building the business because I just didn't know any other way.

Don't get me wrong, there have been plenty of rewards along the way. It is enriching to know that we provide a good service. I believe in our industry, and I know we help a lot of people find jobs and get through financial crunches. I get a lot of satisfaction from working with my staff. I seem to have a talent for helping people develop, and they have rewarded me with loyalty and dedication to the company.

It also feels good to get recognized in the community for all the different things I've done. Everyone likes to be recognized, especially when you're making a lot of sacrifices to do what you're doing. But when I was in the middle of it, I didn't see the sacrifice involved. Only afterward, when the damage had been done, could I see it.

I also like the money. Bill Gates doesn't have to worry about me knocking him off the top of the charts, but I make more money than I ever dreamed of. I started out earning $300 a month as a social worker, so I have it pretty good these days. Even so, I don't take that much money out of the company; I prefer to leave it in the business. My salary pales in comparison with those of many people in my situation, but it all depends what you want. I grade myself on the bottom line, and when that looks good, I feel good about myself.

In some ways, I feel that being a woman has helped me excel. Women put their hearts into their businesses, because that's how we are raised. If I can't put my heart into my home by baking cookies, cheering at soccer games, and so on, then I put it into my business. I think that kind of passion, caring, and attention to relationships has had a lot to do with wanting to keep my employees loyal, happy, and motivated.

I've learned how to prioritize. Trying to juggle everything that needs to get done in a family as well as a growing business presents a formidable challenge. No matter who you are, you don't have enough time, so you have to learn to make good choices. In particular, I've learned to narrow the circle of important people in my life.

As a business owner, *everybody* wants your time and attention. It's very easy to get sucked into boards of directors, trade associations, and those kinds of relationships. I don't mean to imply that those activities aren't important, because they are, but when I try to do too much, I can't do anything well. When I try to be all things to all people, the ones I really care about suffer the most.

Throughout my career, I've tried to avoid making decisions that I didn't believe in my gut were the right thing to do—morally, financially, emotionally, or whatever. I've walked away from business that I felt wasn't right or might hurt me financially and severed relationships that had the potential for more harm than good. To a large extent, I think my ability to trust my gut, to instinctively know what is right and good and true, has helped me get to where I am today.

I grew up in a very a different time than my girls. I learned early on that men succeed and women support them, and I still struggle with the notion that I can't or won't achieve as much as a man. In meetings, I often find myself automatically deferring to the men in the room, thinking they know more than I do, when in many cases they probably don't. I don't *ever* want my girls to feel like that. I want them to think they are just as capable as anyone else. If they grow up feeling that way about themselves, then I will feel that my sacrifices have been worth it.

Thirty-One
Doing It All

Cynthia Fricke Wollman
Sun Printing House

Thirty-six-year-old Cynthia Fricke Wollman had her first child, Ethan, in 1997. The following year, Wollman gave birth to twin boys, Sam and Max. Each time, she took ten weeks off and returned to work as president of Sun Printing House, a $5-million, 119-year-old, critical-information printing business in Philadelphia. Sun Printing was founded in 1880 by Wollman's great-grandfather. Wollman's father Heberton Fricke, though still holding the title of CEO, had handed the day-to-day running of the business to Wollman in 1992. She spent the six months prior to her children's births planning for her ten week absences and setting up child care for after she returned. Wollman came back to work both times with grand ambitions and pent up enthusiasm. Her goal is to double the size of the company by 2002, and she predicts growth rates up from 10 percent to 33 percent in just two years. Running a growing business while you are the mother of a toddler and infant twins is a formidable task most CEOs will never face.

Ethan was born on January 13, 1997. One wonderful thing about maternity is that you can plan for the event. So I had a good six months to plan what my needs would be, both personal and professional. I contacted ten women who had run their own companies and had had babies at the same time, and I found out how they did it.

The inclination might be to put one person in charge while you're gone. That is what I'd been planning to do, but one CEO told me that such a move could be a real problem, because that person wouldn't want to relinquish control when I returned. I'm very glad I didn't do it that way, because I didn't have to undo that authority later.

Doing It All

I had a general outline for what I was going to do. Of course, babies are no more predictable than business cycles. Ethan was born a week early. I worked on the Friday before he was born. He was born on a Monday at 3:00 A.M. after about five hours of labor. Obviously, I didn't make it to work that week.

I was in contact with the company a couple of times a week. There were six managers that I left in charge, running things by committee. I stayed home with Ethan for ten weeks, although I was in once a week for a couple of hours. Things were in place for my key executives to give me weekly reports about what was happening. We discussed the critical things that I needed to know. The company had a few minor crises, but I got lucky, and no major disasters came up.

My husband Mark and I had discussed all this for months. He is an attorney in Philadelphia, and we've been married for eight years. Before Ethan was born, Mark was hoping that I would have a change of heart and stay home for the first six months with the baby. As the time grew closer, we talked about it, and he knew I would be going back to work. We were very confident about the day care arrangement that we had chosen. We had looked for a long time for a setting we felt comfortable with.

Before the twins were born, we found an au pair that would care for them while Ethan continued day care. I'm sure some people reading this would feel differently than I did. I always knew that I wanted my career, and I feel that I'm a better mom this way, because I can work and then come home and just adore my children to no end. I really believe that it's a personal choice that people need to make and feel comfortable with. I don't feel any guilt, because I know my children are well taken care of.

If I was home, I'd have a zillion things to do—shopping, cooking dinner, paying the bills, and my children wouldn't get much more time with me anyway. I'm actually delighted with the fact that they are exposed to so many things. Ethan's vocabulary is amazing at age two, and the au pair speaks to the twins in German and other languages, which is great.

One thing I learned from my dad is to try to keep work and home separate if you can. I realize that sounds a little odd coming from a family-business owner, but my dad was good about never wanting my mother involved in the business. Business was never a focal point for the family, and I learned from him to try to keep it that way.

228

So, for example, in choosing care for my children, I chose not to have day care brought into the company, because I didn't want to be a half-time mom and a half-time president. I wanted to be able to commit to the task at hand, whether it was being a mom or being president of a company.

Although it's not like running IBM, the business is always on my mind. Despite that, when I go home to the boys, I can be totally involved with them. I get so little time with them that it's very easy to make sure that I devote myself fully when we're together. When they go to bed, then I can work some more. My employees understand the situation, and they try to cut me some slack. I try never to use the babies as an excuse. I try to be honest with everyone. I tell them if I'm taking the babies to the doctor.

Right from the very beginning we put Ethan on a schedule, and that has worked extremely well for our family. We know when Ethan naps, we know when he eats, we know when he sleeps. Everything is very structured. It took a lot of discipline to stick with this schedule, but we just persevered and tried to keep things consistent. Later, we did the same thing with the twins. We put them on a schedule, and though it may sound cold, it really is like an assembly line. We feed them, diaper them, play with them, one after the other.

I keep a pump at work to express milk. I'm pretty sure that is an unusual item to find in a CEO's office, but you do whatever works. Having three babies and a full-time job running a company is unusual, to say the least. My thought is, "This is the way it is, and this is the way I've chosen it to be." It might sound ridiculous, but I just don't give myself the option of thinking life could be otherwise.

In essence, you just have to deal with it. Every day in the role of CEO or president, you get thrown a curve ball that you don't expect to have to deal with. So what's juggling a baby or three as well? I don't mean to sound cavalier or suggest it's no big deal, but in truth, as CEO, you have so many things going on anyway, you just figure out how to compartmentalize and do the best you can.

I can't let the stereotypes stand in my way. The fact that I am young, female, and have a family has strengths, weaknesses, and opportunities all rolled up in one. I get into trouble when I think "I'm only thirty-six. I can't possibly know how to do all this." When I start feeling sorry for myself, it's a bad week. We all have things that will be hindrances to our careers, but we can't focus on them. Sometimes you just have to realize you need help and go get it. You also have to understand you'll make some bad decisions sometimes. If you want the organization to grow, you have to keep learning from those mistakes.

I actually think that the first time I went on leave, when Ethan was born, it created a sense of independence that was very positive. The management team was essentially the same when I had the twins, and so they had even more of a game plan, more of a roadmap to follow, the second time. I think you become a more effective leader when you go away for a large chunk of time and make sure people clearly understand the expectations. In my case, it was maternity leave. It would be much worse if there was a sudden illness, such as a heart attack. That's something you can't plan for.

My father, who retired in May 1999, has been very supportive, but sometimes the roles get jumbled. He's my children's grandfather, and sometimes he treats me as the company president, when I want him to talk to me as a mother. Sometimes I'd be very involved on maternity leave with Ethan and wouldn't want to talk about the company, and that's all he would want to talk about. I was probably short with him on occasion, but I think he understood. We've never argued about it, and he has never suggested that maybe I ought to stay home with the children.

Though there are times when I wonder how I can do all this, I just tell myself that tomorrow is another day and I'll get through it. The choices my husband and I have made are ones I'm very comfortable with. In order for me to feel that comfort, there is a lot of trust involved—trust in my employees, trust in the day care center, trust in the au pair, trust in my husband. It might be the hardest thing as an executive, but I learned to expect that things may not be done exactly the way I want them done, and I have to be okay with that.

There's always a pull. One of my babies was sick today. He's been in the hospital a couple of times. Today was a hard day to come to work. I left them teary-eyed, and I wanted to hug them all day, but I had an important client meeting. Once I get into work, I'm so committed to this company that I really don't look back. I check in on my family during the day. It's hard. Sometimes you don't get to do what you want to do. I'm content to live with the tugs. I have confidence in my child care providers, and I'm really happy to be working.

Section Six
Rethinking the Norm

Thirty-Two
Hallmark of Loyalty

Wesley E. Cantrell
Lanier Worldwide, Inc.

In 1955, Wes Cantrell, twenty-years-old and fresh from college, turned down a job offer from IBM to work for the tiny Lanier Company, based in Atlanta. Though his family and friends thought he was crazy, Cantrell saw something in the $2-million maker of dictation machines that appealed to him. After forty-four years with the company, Cantrell is chairman and CEO of the $1.4 billion Lanier Worldwide Inc., now one of the world's largest providers and designers of document management solutions and services, with more than 10,000 employees. He was set to retire when Lanier was spun off as an independent company in 1999 by its parent, the Harris Corporation, but was asked to stay on as chairman and CEO, and he did. In an age of job-hopping and career makeovers, Cantrell's loyalty to a single company is rare indeed.

IBM offered me a job as a field engineer in 1955. That was the year it became a $1-billion company. I was supposed to start installing mainframe computers for IBM in September, but I needed a job to tide me over for the summer, and I joined this tiny company called Lanier, which sold copiers and dictating equipment. I never intended to stay past the summer.

During that summer I fell in love with this little company, and when the job offer from IBM came along, I turned it down. My father and mother and everybody else thought I was insane, but if you think about it, it's probably the greatest decision I ever made, because I doubt if I would have wound up chairman of IBM.

If someone had told me then that I'd spend the rest of my career here at Lanier and would become chairman and chief executive officer, I wouldn't have believed that, although I thought that staying with the company was certainly a possibility.

What I saw at Lanier was a great opportunity for growth. Lanier had all these incentive plans, and I liked that. I wanted to make a lot of money, and if you did well, they paid well. If you didn't do so well, they didn't pay you at all. So I did very well and made a lot of money by the standards of that time.

I also saw pretty quickly that the way to management was not through the technical side but through sales, so I switched over in 1957. I went to Baton Rouge with my eye on the district manager's job. Those guys made big bucks. They ran their own stores, so to speak, and that was the job I decided I wanted. In the meantime, I found out that I could sell. I worked on straight commission, and I made a lot of money selling and wound up as one of the top salesmen in the company.

I was twenty-two years old when I started in sales, which is amazing. because when I look at pictures of myself at the time, I look like an absolute baby. I look like I'm twelve, and I wonder who in the world would have bought anything from this twelve-year-old kid? Selling was not my first love; managing was my first love. I saw selling as something you had to be good at in order to become a manager with Lanier.

One of the great things about moving to Louisiana is that I met a beautiful girl down there who I wound up marrying. We've been married all these years. She has stuck with me through thick and thin, and we've produced four children and twenty grandchildren.

We moved around from Louisiana to Mississippi, to Georgia, then back to Louisiana in those years. We went back to Baton Rouge in 1962, and I took the big job and became district manager. I brought that district from $400,000 a year in sales up to $1.7 million in just four years. At that time, the company's total sales were $12 million, so our district accounted for a pretty substantial percentage of Lanier's total business.

What I learned in Baton Rouge was the difference between being a salesman and being a manager. I had not really comprehended how much difference there was. I thought that since I could sell, I could do anything. Then, all of a sudden, I had to go out and hire good salesmen, customer service reps, and administrative people. I had to train those people, manage those people, and motivate those people. It was a different set of skills, and I floundered for about a year. Fortunately, the company was tolerant, and within about a year, I figured out how to do a better job, and we got the engine going.

In 1966, I was called back to Atlanta and became general manager of all the dictation systems sales for the company. I have a vivid memory from that time of a dinner meeting I had with my boss, Gene Millner, the CEO. I was on vacation visiting my parents when Gene called me and asked me to meet him for dinner in Atlanta. Over dinner that night, he shared his dream with me of what Lanier would someday become.

That night, he told me that someday we were going to buy out our suppliers, that someday we would be a national company—and later an international company—and that we would be a very big and extremely successful organization. He laid out for me some of his plans for accomplishing that. There I was, maybe twenty-seven or twenty-eight years old, and I was listening to all this, and I bought it hook, line, and sinker.

I decided right then, "I'm going to do everything I can to make this happen. I believe it's going to happen." So he converted me into a believer of his vision. Gene was not a great one for giving strategic talks or visionary talks. I don't think he planned this, although I'll never know. It seemed like he was just telling me what was in his heart.

I think he chose me for that dinner because Gene knew that I was a guy for the long term. He was always pushing me and promoting my career. I come from a small country town called Hiram, Georgia, and one time, he said, "I drove out to Hiram, the other day, Wes. And right up there on the water tank, it said, "Hiram, Georgia, Home of Wes Cantrell." What he was doing was visualizing big things for me, and he had a powerful way of doing it. Of course, it was a lie; there wasn't even a water tank in Hiram.

I was working for a man who had great natural leadership ability, and I think he decided early on that I was going to be very successful in the company. He made a lot of things happen for me earlier than they otherwise would have. I did my dead-level best never to let him down on that extra measure of confidence that he had in me.

Still, I'm not sure where this degree of loyalty comes from. I do know that different people have a different capacity for loyalty, a different feeling about loyalty than others have. Particularly today, we see a lot of the young men and women whose loyalty index, if you will, to one company is not very great. They're building more dedication and loyalty to the dollar and making money, or to their own success, than to the company.

Back then, I had a different feeling. The way I saw it, if the company made it, I was going to make it as well. Changing jobs seemed like a risky thing, because who knew when you might be jumping out of the frying pan and into the fire. I went through some very hard times. I had some bosses who were terribly oppressive. But I found that if I just stayed there and continued to do a good job, the oppressive bosses were always gone in a short period of time. Every single one of them either committed professional suicide, so to speak, or I was promoted to a higher position.

In fact, the worst guy I ever worked for ended up working for me. I wound up being his boss. I had a chance to get even. I never did, however, because I don't operate that way. I don't think there's any point in that. If someone is a lousy boss like that, he eventually will be gone.

There was only one time I actually thought about leaving the company, and I interviewed for another job. I was working for a horrible boss, and I was very, very depressed. It was when I was going through the transition from being a salesman to being a manager. I needed help and encouragement, but he had a negative style and focused on what was wrong instead of what was right.

I was just looking for a couple of little blinking lights at the end of the tunnel that said, "Hey, here are a few things you did that worked, and if you can do a few, you can many more." I needed to hire one or two salesmen who were successful. I needed to show some sales increases. I needed to have some profits flowing into the Baton Rouge district, so I could say, "Yeah, you can do it." It didn't have to be big; it just had to be a little spark of encouragement.

He was not an encouraging type of leader. So I had to fight my way through that, and that was one of the hardest times of my life. Once I started to see that I could do the job, my confidence soared. I knew that once I'd hired two good sales guys, I would know I could hire two more. I'd be able to say, "I've done this. I can do more of this." So I basically talked myself into it, and from that point on, things just took off like a rocket.

Yes, it was a different world then. Today, I'd probably talk to a headhunter and be gone in a flash. I still believe, however, that with a certain kind of leadership, you can encourage a very high degree of loyalty in a company. I believe we are as good as, and maybe better, than most companies in that regard. There's still a lot of turnover in the sales force here, but when we get sales people into management positions, they almost never leave, except involuntarily. If they can't perform, of course, we will ease them out. You have to do that.

So if I look deep within myself to find what gave me this intense loyalty, one key factor is that I'm a very, very strong Christian. That definitely has an impact on a lot of my beliefs and how I react and feel about things, particularly authority. I have a belief, based on scripture, that God works through the authorities in our lives.

So if you believe that, then it makes the whole aspect of that authority take on a different meaning. If God is at work in this, then maybe I should listen, maybe I should stay, maybe I should do these things. In fact, there's no greater drive or ambition that comes to a man than when he feels he is exactly where God has put him for a purpose.

Of course, the rewards of this long and exacting career didn't come without a price. There are issues you can't take to a consulting firm for help. I think about all the time away from home and away from my wife for the sake of the company. I was blessed with a wife who is a very capable woman—beautiful, intelligent, and very independent. Because of that, I did a lot of things that I couldn't have otherwise done in good conscience. She kept everything going.

I've asked all my children, my son and three daughters, who are grown and have children of their own, if our family life could have been better, if we gave up anything important. Every one of them said they would have liked me to have been home more. My son told me, "Dad, the thing that always amazed me about you is you were a consummate workaholic, but you seemed to be just as committed to getting to my games and stuff as you were to getting to your job. So you always showed up for all the things that were really important for me. Looking back on it now, I can't figure how you did it."

It took commitment—flying home in the middle of the night, making sure I was back in time. But if I am totally honest with myself, my oldest daughter probably couldn't say what my son says. I don't think she could say that. I've never asked her directly. I don't want to, because I feel so badly about it. But I think that she would say that there were a lot of things that I should have been at for her that I wasn't.

There were always pangs of anxiety, not just for my daughter but for my wife. I think of the support and attention I should have shown her. I would say I had more pangs about that than about any of the children, because I thrust an awful lot on her. As you would expect, when you abuse someone in that relationship, when you thrust too much responsibility on them, there comes a time of push-back and reevaluation. We had times like that, where I had to go back and reevaluate my priorities and how I was spending my time. I had to make certain that my actions demonstrated that my wife was still Number One.

In these later years, after the children had grown up, I began to take my wife with me whenever I could. I try to involve her more at business dinners and on trips. She loves the company, and she loves the people. I remember my ex-chairman's wife detested coming to company events, and you could tell. But my wife actually likes it. She feels that these are the people who put the bread on our table and have given us a great lifestyle. We're grateful to these people, and we need to show our gratitude to them. She applauds loudly at awards dinners and pats people on the back, and she genuinely has a good time. She's as crazy as I am. She could have been a very effective CEO herself, and I know she has her own pangs every once in a while about what she could have done.

Though I don't know how long I'll continue as chairman and CEO, I know that the end of my career is approaching. I have spent a good deal of time trying to pick the right moment to step down. The key thing for me is timing. That's what I truly care about. I have good people to replace me. I'm very confident in their ability to lead the company. Before long, they're not going to need me around here anymore.

Thinking about leaving is actually extremely emotional, almost like facing death to some degree. There's a sense that it is the end of life. If you're not careful, you can drift too deep into that kind of thinking. I think a lot of CEOs who face this don't do very well moving through it.

In my case, I have so many other interests. As a spiritual person, I realize that my total significance is not in being Wes Cantrell, president and CEO of Lanier. My total significance is found in being what God created me to be. That belief gives you a real leg up in finding your significance.

When I walk out the door and can no longer say, "I'm the CEO of Lanier," then have I lost my significance or my value as a human being? The answer is no, I haven't lost it. In God's eyes, I'm just as valuable as I ever was. In fact, in terms of what He wants me to do, I may be even more valuable, because He may be able to use me more.

There was a verse of scripture that I came across in the Bible years and years ago. I adopted it as a verse that I would build my life on. It says, "A good name is rather to be chosen than great riches." So what I decided back then was to build my own reputation within the company and in the business community by trying to have a good name, which means keeping your commitments and never breaking promises.

That translated into building a good name for Lanier. A good name for the company is more to be desired than great riches, which would mean that if an employee was faced with a decision to spend some money to make a customer happy rather than putting it on the bottom line, he or she should choose to make the customer happy. We've pretty much stuck with that through the years.

As you can imagine, despite the dramatic changes in the corporate world, I still give young people the same advice. I still lean heavily toward finding a good company and sticking with it—being loyal through thick and thin, and happy with what you do and with the company's value system—as opposed to constantly changing jobs to chase more money. It really makes a lot more sense. You will come out way ahead in the long term, and you'll feel a lot better about yourself too. I think loyalty would create a better world for all of us to live in.

Thirty-Three
Icing a Dream

Byron Osing
Telebackup Systems, Inc.

When he was fourteen years old, Byron Osing was playing junior hockey in Western Canada against players who were four to six years his senior. A goalie on an apparent career track to the National Hockey League, Osing, the son of an Alberta wheat farmer, made some brash and fateful decisions that cost him his National Hockey League dreams. He gave up junior hockey, forsook scholarship offers from two Ivy League schools in the United States, and stayed in Alberta to go to a university. A serious back injury in a university game eventually cost him his hockey career. Osing, with an athlete's determination and intensity, turned to a career in business. He earned a Ph.D. in marketing from the University of Calgary, founded and ran a leading edge, high-technology company called Telebackup Systems, and eventually sold his startup for $130 million (U. S.) to Veritas Software, a high-tech company. Financially secure at age thirty-five, Osing feels as if he is only just getting started.

In 1995, I started a high-tech company with the express purpose of creating a leading-edge technology, taking the company public, and then selling it. We ended up as probably the biggest software acquisition ever in Western Canada. Though, in hindsight, it seems to have been a quick and simple jump from Step A to Step B, it was actually a long and grueling trip. It turned out to be well worth it, but there were many times along the way when I thought we'd never make it.

Of course, when I was younger, I never dreamed that I'd become a successful entrepreneur. I had plans to become a professional hockey goalie, and I had immersed myself in hockey since I was very young.

By the time I was fourteen, I was playing junior hockey, which is a big deal in Canada. I was playing against guys who were eighteen, nineteen, and twenty years old. I was already being scouted by American universities, and I had my heart set on playing in the National Hockey League.

Then, when I was seventeen, I had what I would call the worst day of my life. I was playing Junior A hockey, and I had just been sent down from the top junior league in Canada to a second-tier junior league. I felt I shouldn't have been sent down. The goalie that was chosen wasn't as good as I was, and I felt it was all about politics. I was furious.

Within a few days, I quit playing junior hockey. I knew this would completely screw up my chances of playing pro hockey. I'd worked for this since early childhood, and I'd become so sick of the politics involved in junior hockey that I just walked away.

That was my personality. I felt that if I'd performed and played well, why should I get sent down? I still think back upon that day, with vivid recollections and a lot of regret. If I had stuck it out, put a few months in with a second tier team, then most likely I would have been traded and been playing first tier again quickly. I might have been playing pro hockey within a few years.

But I quit, and I went back home to our farm and told my parents that I'd be going to the university. I knew that university hockey was not the straight path to the National Hockey League that junior hockey was. So I knew my chances were pretty much shot. My father never tried to talk me out of it. He was supportive. He said, "Whatever you want to do, you just do it as best as you can, and we'll support you."

There are always lessons in these kinds of events. I realized later that you have to be more flexible and take a little more aggravation to get what you want. At that point, I was a pretty idealistic young kid. I also have to remember the circumstances at the time. I was so far ahead of my peers, playing junior hockey at fourteen. It was almost unheard of. I figured, "I have the talent, and I have the skills. As long as I'm playing well and not causing any trouble, why should I have to live with this kind of garbage?" That was the attitude I had—indignant, self-righteous. As you mature, reality steps in, and you have to learn to deal with politics and people.

There was also the behind-the-scenes part of the game; young athletes are groomed for professional careers early on, and their parents are usually doing the grooming. I had no career management. My father was a farmer. He didn't know how to make me a professional hockey player. So I wasn't emotionally prepared.

When we got scholarship offers from the Ivy League schools, my dad sat down and said, "What is this university hockey stuff in the United States? If you want to play pro, shouldn't you be playing junior?" So we passed on what might have been an unbelievable educational opportunity.

Instead, I went to the University of Lethbridge in Southern Alberta and played five years of university hockey there. At the same time, I collected a psychology degree that was essentially useless, because I still had dreams of a hockey career. One night in December of my senior year, with contracts already lined up to play in Europe, I was nailed into the goal post by an opposing player and ruptured two disks in my back. I didn't tell anyone how bad it was, and I somehow willed myself to play through the pain to the end of the season. I could barely walk. When the season ended, my career was over.

At that point, my life changed 180 degrees. I thought, "What do I do now?" I ended up going back to school at the University of Calgary and getting an M.B.A. While I was at Calgary, my wife and I started a small business. We leased the entire floor of an office building and opened a business center, a small-business incubator. We sub-leased the independent offices out to small companies and provided them with all sorts of support services. We did pretty well with that and opened a second center two years later.

At the same time, I also decided to take my Ph.D. in marketing. During the Ph.D. process, I met a client in one of our business centers who was selling computer hardware. We started talking about where the computer industry was going and what opportunities might be out there. He was selling storage hardware, such as tape units and hard disk drives, and he understood the need to back up and protect data.

This was in 1994, and laptop computers were emerging as the next big thing. Executives and sales reps were carrying them and using them on the road, but I wondered how these road warriors were backing up and protecting their data. We concluded that a real need was growing.

We found the people to turn the concept into actual technology, and we began to build a system that was able to facilitate remote and mobile back-up and recovery for the growing laptop and mobile market. So, on a shoestring, we started our company, TeleBackup Systems. Along with a third partner, we incorporated in May 1995. We had a total investment of about $60,000, which was all the money we could scrape together. There were two employees—I was one, and we had a programmer. We ran with it from there.

I began with the financing, looking to family and friends and to private placement financing, wherever we could go for money. We had a plan from early on to position TeleBackup as an original-equipment manufacturer, one that didn't have its own sales force or distribution channels but rather developed the technology and struck licensing deals with big companies that could put their own names and brands on the product.

It sounds as if it all happened very quickly, but there were a lot of eighteen-hour days of being immersed in technology—sitting in the office looking at the source code the programmer was writing, learning the technology industry as I went. There was no one to guide me or mentor me and no board to direct me until much later in the game.

I started doing my own research on the technology market and our particular area, and I quickly realized what made a company succeed or fail. Most failures were the result of entrepreneurs with over-inflated aspirations. They all wanted to be the next Bill Gates and create a company that had a high profile and products that every consumer was aware of. But those success stories are extremely rare, because the big players in the industry really do control the distribution channels. The big technology players control and protect their customers—the Fortune 2000 companies—so tightly that to penetrate those markets with a brand-new technology from an unheard-of, small company is just about impossible.

We had a sound game plan, but that didn't mean the stress levels weren't extremely high. We had money from family and friends in a very high-risk, potentially high-reward situation. We operated on a shoestring for the first couple of years and just about failed a number of times. It was tough. I didn't take a salary for eighteen months. But that was part of what I considered the "sweat equity" we were putting into this.

I ended up bridge financing the company myself two or three times, with every nickel I had. There were many sleepless nights, because we were in a make-it or break-it situation, which is typical in a small technology-company. Yet, we got through.

My wife was extremely supportive. She was running our business centers, which generated just enough money to keep us going. It was very tight.

But what carried us through it, every time, was a strong belief that we had a real winner. We had come up with the technology solution to solve an important issue in the marketplace, and none of the big companies had it. We could see the size of the market growing dramatically. In the technology world, it's a matter of being at the right place at the right time with the right technology. Timing is everything.

We could see that the timing was right. We were at the bleeding edge of a market that was just shaping up, and people were just starting to take notice of it. We knew that we were going to be an acquisition target.

It was a strange experience. We were getting ready to take the company public, and I was being asked the same question over and over: "Where are you going to be five years from now and ten years from now? What is your vision?"

I replied, "If we're successful, two or three years from now, we're not going to exist independently. We'll be bought, because that's the nature of this industry. The big guys don't want to build it, they just want to acquire it and run with it."

We ended up with five companies trying to buy us. But before that ever happened, we went through a series of incredible events that might have killed another company. We were all working on the promise of a good idea and that can sometimes be a thin wire to balance on.

A company focused on research and development doesn't generate revenues for a few years. You have to live off your finances. You operate on a very tight budget, and you attract very talented people who come because of the stock options. They were working for half to two-thirds of their market salaries. All of these people had put their time and their lives on hold to come and work for us, for the promise of the upside of the stock price.

What amazed me was that even when things were the bleakest, nobody complained, nobody panicked. Everybody just put their heads down, did their jobs, and put their faith in a couple of management people. It was a real statement of their confidence in us.

I would have expected people to be bailing out, running away as fast as they could, looking for other jobs. No one budged. I think they were influenced by our commitment—or at least my commitment—to make sure this thing was not going to fail. Whatever I had to do, it was going to stay alive and be a success. I think that when you exude that confidence and that mind-set, when you have a pit-bull mentality, it influences people, and they get in the same mind-set: this *is* going to be a success.

What I find, particularly in the technology industry, is that many companies fail, because they end up with a "pure" technology person as CEO. Technology people have a very left-brained orientation; they are very focused on technology development, but they don't know how to set up and run a company. They don't know how to adopt a competitive strategy that will win the game.

Believe me, that's one thing that's made me successful: I have a pretty balanced approach to things and the ability to set strategic direction. That is a must for a CEO, but it goes beyond that. It goes to the question of leadership.

What is it that makes one leader charismatic and another not? Why will people believe in and follow one and not another? I don't know what that quality is. If I could bottle and sell it, I'd be a billionaire, but some people tell me I have that quality. Whatever it is, I seem to have the ability to marshal resources around me—not just financial and operational resources, but human capital. That seems to be the key to building successful organizations: high-quality people who are willing to come work for you and follow your direction.

I honestly believe leadership is something you're born with, not something you can develop. I see people go through all kinds of efforts to try to train themselves to become leaders, by developing skill sets, by learning how to be better public speakers, learning how to make friends and influence people—whatever. They still fall on their faces.

With TeleBackup, I had to use all my leadership skills and then some. There was a very real pressure to be successful, because my family was in it, my friends were in it, and my employees believed in me. When we were getting ready to file our initial public offering, it took three times as long as we thought to turn the deal around. Then, just as we were ready to go public in August 1996, the high-tech sector got slammed, stock prices fell, and suddenly our whole offering was in trouble.

The company here in Calgary that was going to handle the offering received a call from one of the brokerage firms that said, "We can't sell this; you have to reprice the stock. If we can't sell it all beforehand, we're going to drop this." The firm said it had to be "maxed out," so there would be the perception of a fully sold initial public offering (I.P.O.) with lots of demand, which would keep the price stable afterwards.

So we had to go back and redo all the paperwork, reprice it, resubmit it, and we were damn near broke. We were literally down to our last few dollars, and at the end of the day, we were about $400,000 short of closing the deal. I had a call from one of the brokers, who said, "You've got three days to raise that extra $400,000, or we're pulling out, and your I.P.O. and your company are dead."

That day, I just sat there and said, "Well, what do I do? How the hell am I going to raise $400,000?" It was a horrible day. I felt the weight of the world on my shoulders, because my family and friends had put money into this that they couldn't afford to lose. They put it in, because they believed in me. Suddenly I was within three days of losing their money and my company, but I didn't wallow for long. I got on the phone, nonstop, and sold $300,000 worth of stock in three days. One of my partners sold the other $100,000. I called every person that I could possibly think of in the phone book. I basically laid it on the line. "I need your help," I told them. "It is high risk, high return, but we think we're on the right path. We think this is going to be a winner, so if you can put your faith in me, put a little money in, I don't care if it's $1,000 or $2,000 or $5,000, anything you can do to help."

You wouldn't believe the people who came out of the woodwork to help with money. It was very moving that these people, many of them not having much to spare, let alone risk, pulled together and backed us.

In three days, we sold the last $400,000 ourselves, without any help from a broker, and we closed the deal. Of course, that's when the real pressure started.

Now we were public, we had $2 million in the bank, and if I couldn't make this a success, every one of my friends and relatives was going to hate me.

The sale of the company to Veritas for $190 million (Canadian) validated everything I had done. Despite the various traumas, there was never a point at which I gave up or got ready to throw in the towel. I'm certain that strength and determination comes from my upbringing.

I grew up on a farm in Milk River, Alberta. I was the only child of a poor grain farmer. I'm sure my determination came from my dad. He killed himself working, and he scraped and scrimped to get by when he and my mom were first married. He trapped weasels for the fur in the winter, just so they could eat while they paid off their mortgage. I watched how hard he worked to make that farm a success, because he loved what he was doing, and there was just no way he was not going to make it successful.

I was working on the farm from the age of twelve and grew up around the mind-set of "This is going to be a success, and nothing's going to stop it—not drought or bad prices." Whatever you had to do, you did. I watched him and my mom go through incredibly tough times. We never had much money, and they both worked so bloody hard, but they just refused to give up.

My father paid off the mortgage when he was sixty-nine years old, the year before he died. There was no notion of failure. He wanted me to take over the farm, but he understood that was not what I wanted to do. I didn't like farming, because there was so little control over your success. You could work yourself to death, but you couldn't control the weather, and you couldn't control commodity prices; you just weren't the master of your own destiny.

Ironically, he loved what he was doing, because he was working for himself. He said, "I'd rather make ten dollars a day working for myself than a hundred bucks working for somebody else." So, I grew up with that mentality.

The big payoff from the sale of the company certainly represents a long leap from where I came from. The feeling of financial security is the best part of having money. That's what we were really striving for. Otherwise, my wife and I are still fairly simple people. We went ahead and bought a slightly bigger house. We drive a slightly newer car. At the end of the day, it's not the possessions that really motivate us. It is not the desire to spend a lot of money. Frankly, I don't think we will. My wife's Dutch; she still rubs her first nickels together. I tell her that every day, and she's proud of it. She comes from a farm family as well.

It will be strange, but I don't think there are going to be any dramatic changes. It's a wonderful feeling to have financial security for the rest of your life. You don't have to do anything you don't want to for the rest of your life. If I chose to retire, I could, but what would I do for the next forty years? I'm already involved in starting a new company.

So I'll always be an entrepreneur, starting new things, building new companies, but the feeling of freedom, the freedom to choose what you want to do and who you do it for and with, is probably the nicest part of it. At least ten or twelve out of our forty-five employees and associates also became multimillionaires, which is a great feeling. They all contributed heavily. They came here and worked for very little and took the risks too. The people who are coming out of this so very well deserve it.

The other great part of it is I can now help out my family, my in-laws, and my good friends. When they need it, I can help give them a leg up. These are the people who put their faith in me and put in their money. I look forward to returning the favor.

I only wish my dad could have lived to see all this. He died in the early 1990s, and it saddens me that he couldn't be around to see what happened. It would have meant an awful lot to him. If I have any other regret at this point in my life, it's that I failed at my one big goal: to play professional hockey.

Thirty-Four
Rethinking the Priorities

Peter Fontaine
Discount Auto Parts, Inc.

Some CEOs travel to the beat of a different drummer. Peter Fontaine is certainly one of those. As CEO of the publicly traded $515-million Discount Auto Parts, a retail auto-parts supplier with 540 stores and 5,000 employees in six states, Fontaine more than doubled the size of the company in the five years he has been in charge. As devoted as he is to the company that his father Herman founded in 1971, Fontaine decided in 1998 to hand over the day-to-day operations to Bill Perkins, D.A.P.'s president. Fontaine then moved his family from Lakeland, Florida, where the company has its headquarters, to Asheville, North Carolina, and became a part-time CEO and full-time father. In his second marriage, the forty-five-year-old Fontaine has four small children, ages seven, six, three, and one, and he decided that he wanted to be much more involved in their lives than he would have been while running the company full time. An experienced pilot, he flies from Asheville to Lakeland several times a month and maintains a visible role within Discount Auto Parts. But a family tragedy and the importance of his wife and children are what lead him to reconsider his priorities.

I can't say that it was just one thing that made me change my lifestyle so dramatically. I'm one of those late bloomers. I'm forty-five, with four young children. I wanted to be very involved in their lives and what they were doing. As CEO, I was struggling with that.

Before I made the move, I worked a typical CEO workweek. I'd be in the office by 7:30 or 8:00 A.M. and leave at 6:30 P.M. I'd work most Saturdays, attending store openings or other events. I realized that if

I'm at work, I've got to be in the heat of the battle, and my family takes me away from the heat of the battle.

With my new arrangement, when I'm in Lakeland, I'm in the heat of the battle, and I'm there alone. So it's not unusual for me to get to the office at seven in the morning, and stay until eight or nine o'clock at night. It just doesn't bother me for a few days. Then I come back to Asheville, and I can spend time with my family.

A CEO's life is about setting priorities, and you spend a great deal of time planning. You look at your calendar and try to put in as many family things in as you can. I think I balanced work and family as well as anybody could for six years. But your day is consumed with planning and actuating the plan and putting out fires. CEOs who say they don't spend a lot of time putting out fires are not telling the truth, because there's always another fire right over the horizon.

You're just inundated. About the time you've put one fire out, there's another one cropping up, and a lot of the plans you make with your family play second fiddle to putting out fires. That's just the way it is. That is why so many older CEOs who are retiring or near retirement look back with regret on the time they missed with their families, time they can't get back. I didn't want that to happen to me.

There was no single event that triggered my decision to move my family to Asheville. It was something that had built up over several years. The company was facing yet another fire—some litigation in the organization—and I'd been down that road before. I knew that we would overcome it, but facing the prospect of a difficult legal battle, along with the fact that our third child had just been born, let me see the writing on the wall. I just wasn't comfortable playing both roles.

There was another factor. My older brother, Denis, who was my partner here for twenty-six years, died of cancer in 1994. To watch somebody I'd worked with for more than twenty years go through all that misery and die at age fifty-four, leaving behind his own young family, was very powerful. I not only grieved for my brother, I had to take over the company and move forward without him. It made me reconsider just how I wanted my own life to be.

Denis had been the CEO of the company for over fifteen years. I was the chief operating officer. My dad had really just got the ball rolling with the company, and Denis and I and one of my sisters took over early on.

Although we argued about a lot of things, my brother and I had a pretty good relationship. He was an attorney and an hard-driving numbers guy, a "Wall Street Journal"-type CEO. He came in and took over the organization and did a great job. He was very competitive. He had never worked in the nuts and bolts of the company. I had grown up in the business. After business school at Florida State University, I started out as an assistant manager in one of the stores. I worked in the stores selling auto parts for years before taking on an executive role.

So his perspective was different from mine. I had a strong sense of the team, the people, and what the essence of the business was about. His perspective was on a grander scale, a business-oriented view. As time went on, we began to understand each other's views more. We both had to. I also understood his hard-driving personality, but there was a downside to it.

You miss a lot, even if you are not aware of it. To that kind of CEO, they are not missing anything, because their whole lives are oriented around their companies. The company is everything. That's what they live and breathe for, and most of their happiness comes from that. I'm not that type of animal. A lot of my joys come from other places. I like to say that I balance three or four different things that give me pleasure.

Though my brother had been sick for a while, when he died, it was a shock. As I took over the company, I knew I had a lot of work to do on the Wall Street scene, representing the company to financial analysts. Other than that, I had been involved in everything in the organization. I had started running things while he fought his illness. But truthfully, being CEO was not something that I had ever wished for. I was not driven to be a CEO as my brother had been.

So my decision to scale back and move to North Carolina was not a sudden one. There are many things that affect a decision like that; you'd almost have to go back to childhood to find the answers. It's still hard to say what truly motivated me. I probably never would have made such a decision if I didn't have four kids. If I had only two, I may not have made the decision. It's hard to say.

Of course, you've got to be financially secure to make this kind of decision and to do it the way I did it. Money for me is not a big issue. I was financially secure, and I knew my decision wasn't dependent on income. I couldn't have done it if I was worrying about the next paycheck.

But I need to be clear: I am not retired. I'm still very involved with the organization. I'm not involved with many of the day-to-day operations, but I do play a role in our strategic planning. My wife would tell you that I'm still very involved. I missed one of my son's soccer games the other day, and she let me know about it. She also let me know that I was going to miss my son's kindergarten graduation, which couldn't be avoided. Even with my stepped-back role, I can't be everywhere.

So after mulling things over for several years, I finally said to myself, "Once I get through this particular legal issue within our organization, I'm going to change my lifestyle," and I did.

When I told my dad, who is now eighty-six years old, he said, "I understand entirely." It's actually amazing. When I speak to him and my mom, the first questions he asks are, "How are the kids? What are they doing? How is school? How's soccer?" Only after the family questions does he ask about the company. That shows where his head is at.

My mom and dad were not in the auto-parts business while I was growing up. He was in the restaurant business and worked from 8:00 A.M. to 6:00 P.M., six days a week. When he came home, my mom went in and worked from 6:00 P.M. to midnight or 1:00 A.M.

He never talked about missing my childhood or anything like that. He and my mom were Depression children. They just knew that you worked as hard as you could. You saved every penny you had, because tomorrow the world was going to end. They still feel that way today, but they also place a very high value on family and being with your kids and watching them grow up.

The directors on my board also understood. We have a small board and the members knew me intimately and had been around me for a long time. I explained my position, and they were very understanding and really did not question it that much. They said, "Okay. We know you're going to be here, and you're not going to let the wheel fall off this thing."

I am sure most CEOs find it difficult to understand my decision. If I was ten years older and my kids were much older, I would be doing things differently. But because they are so young, there is much to be done with this young family. It just became clear to me that this is my highest priority. After my relationship with God, my family is right there at the top, and I just have to accomplish certain things with them. I have to do it right.

I looked at my work habits from the past twenty years and saw that it was unlikely they would change dramatically. I'm pretty driven, and when I see something that needs to get done, I typically go for it with blinders on. I'm a very narrow-vision, tunnel-vision type of a person. Once I get on track, I have a hard time getting off the track. That is as much a strength as it is a weakness, because I'll be involved with something in business, and it's damn to everything else—family and friends and other priorities.

When I'm in Asheville, I get up at 5:00 A.M. and spend an hour praying or doing motivational reading. I exercise until 7:30 and then shower and have breakfast with the kids. I take them to school in the morning, which is a special time for me.

Then I come back to the house, where there is usually a line of projects. We live in an old house, and I like tinkering around with it. I serve on several boards here in Asheville that I'm very involved in. I pick up the kids and get them to soccer and gymnastics and play dates. The rest of the evening is homework and getting kids bathed and helping my wife get them to bed. I suppose it is an unusual day for a CEO of a company.

I'm also on the phone with Bill Perkins, our president, a few times every other day. We send faxes back and forth, and I have meetings with people about company business pretty regularly.

I believe this new lifestyle works for me because of the dramatic transition between my home and my office. When I'm in Asheville, I'm really with the family, and I think I'm doing a pretty good job here. Then when I go back down to Lakeland, I put on my blinders and I go to work. I can commute in an hour and twenty minutes—some people drive further than that to get to work. It's working for me. It enables me to have the best of both worlds.

I am clear about one thing: this is what I have to do now, but I don't know what the future holds. I don't have a long-range plan. My comment to myself and others was, "If I hate it, don't worry, I'll be back. I know that you'll let me come back into any role that I want to play. I have that option. But if I love it, I'm probably going to stick it out." So far, I must say that I've liked it more than I've hated it. I'm also lucky in that the company is doing very well. If there were a major crisis, obviously I would be there a lot more.

What is interesting is that I've not felt any guilt. My biggest concern was about losing touch. I don't feel like that has happened either, but I worry about it. You know, when you're out of the day-to-day rhythms, you've got to be careful about losing that kind of instinctive sense of where the business is and where the problems are. There are certain things you've got to do to make sure that doesn't happen.

One thing I continue to do is teach a class in our Discount Auto Parts University, which is our internal training and education program. I teach a class for upcoming assistants who are about to run their first store.

I tell them that as part of our mission statement, we as a company are responsible to them and to the families that they support. That's how our mission statements reads. I tell them that if it's taking them more than fifty hours a week to do their jobs, if they are working seventy hours or they find themselves just about living at their store jeopardizing their family life, then I suggest they find other careers. I tell them that up front. I also say that there are going to be times when that's going to happen, when things in the store require a lot of time, and they're going to have to sacrifice certain family things.

But on a day-to-day basis, if they look at it over a year or two years, they should be able to balance the two, and family should take a higher priority than your work. If it doesn't, and it's jeopardizing their family, they should consider doing something different.

It may seem like harsh advice, but I really believe in it. I'm not sure where all this will lead me, but it is enough for me now. I think of it this way: my children are my $500-million company. I'm watching them grow. I'm trying to divide my time up between them and my other $500-million company. I try to keep my finger on both. I want to instill that moral fiber that runs between me and my family into the company as best I can. I believe that's a big part of the CEO's job—to make sure the foundation remains strong. You're always incorporating things in the organization to make sure it stays strong, just like you do in your family. In fact, they run very parallel.

Thirty-Five
Road to Rejuvenation

Mary Roberts
Rejuvenation Inc.

At forty-five years old, Mary Roberts is the CEO of Rejuvenation Inc., a twenty-year-old, $15-million, company based in Portland, Oregon. It is the country's leading maker of reproduction lighting fixtures. Roberts became CEO at Rejuvenation in 1995 after a long tenure at Hanna Andersson, the mail-order children's clothing maker, where she had been president and chief operating officer for three and a half years. In 1997, Rejuvenation was named by Oregon Business magazine as the best company to work for in Oregon. At both Hanna Andersson and Rejuvenation, Roberts has worked with entrepreneurial founders who have stayed involved with their respective companies, and at both places Roberts has encountered entrenched corporate cultures, instituted when the companies were founded, that had become obstacles to running a successful business.

I joined Hanna Andersson in a management position in purchasing and merchandising and eventually became COO and then president. I loved Hanna Andersson, but I wasn't really able to implement my vision of where the company was going. There was nothing more for me to do, so I decided to leave.

As CEO at Rejuvenation, I've discovered something similar to what I found at Hanna Andersson—paradoxical statements that get people charged up about a company. At Hanna Andersson, it was, "Do the right thing and the money will follow." The founders really espoused that from the very beginning, well before I worked there. Similarly, at Rejuvenation, the founder Jim Kelly espouses the phrase, "Employees come first."

Those are both ideas that I personally find inspiring. So I'm not critical of the statements in and of themselves. Unfortunately, in a company, the difficulty arises when business decisions must be made that appear to be contrary to those statements. That's where a gap can emerge between employees and management, between an individual and a manager.

Because there is so much ambiguity in those statements, issues inevitably arise. From a CEOs perspective, "do the right thing" means to survey all the stakeholders who are invested in the company's success. One does the right thing mindful of all the stakeholders, knowing full well that what is most important is to keep the company running, or else everyone loses.

So for example, as president of Hanna Andersson, I decided to take certain benefits away, and even worse, I initiated a layoff. When the company got started, the founder gave very generous benefits, because the company could afford to do it and her Swedish background said it was the right thing to do. Hanna Andersson had been first on the American scene in selling children's cotton clothing. It had no competition at the time, and because all the clothing came from Sweden, the exchange rate was incredibly favorable to the United States, and the profit margins were tremendous. With that combination, the company said, "We have more than enough money; we can provide generous benefits, and profit looks great."

Well, ten years down the road, these kinds of benefits were completely unsupportable. Competition arrived, for one thing. The Gap had come on the scene, several large national cataloguers had come in with their own children's cotton-clothes line, and the national children's wear chain Gymboree was just taking off. Hanna Andersson was suddenly under incredible competitive pressure. Exchange rates, over the years, swung against us. Our business could no longer support such benefits. So I made the decision to pull excess benefits, which was very unpopular. It was also necessary to lay off about 30 of our 350 employees, and that was an extremely painful experience for me.

Our employees were disappointed, and one in particular was very angry. She went so far as to call *Inc. Magazine* and tell a writer how wrong everyone had been about how great a company we were. It was bad enough to layoff people I cared about without making my way into a national magazine story about how wrong I was.

At Hanna Andersson, the founder and CEO, Gun Denhart, essentially agreed with my decisions, but it was even more difficult for her. This was her baby. She had birthed this fabulous company. These wonderful benefits had earned the company a very rich reputation, and her generosity was heartfelt. It wasn't just lip service, it was very real for her. Suddenly reality hit, and she had to see that many things had to be changed. She liked it less than I did, but she was resigned to make changes in order to perpetuate the business.

This is all part of the CEO's job, and it is incredibly hard. The CEO always has to keep the long-range vision in mind and continually put it in the front of other peoples' minds, including the founders. From a personal perspective it was also very hard for me, because I had the bad cop's role. And it was very hard for others, especially for employees who felt things were changing and they didn't have control.

Ironically, this all happened while I was being promoted to president. I have a very vivid memory of the day that my photograph was taken for the publicity shots to announce my promotion. I remember sitting in the photographer's studio at the time, knowing what I was up against and knowing that I had a very unpopular and unpleasant decision to make. I remember thinking, "This is the last time I'm going to smile for a long time."

One of the ways I handled the stress was by walking. I've always been a walker, and I walk an hour a day with my husband Mark. We walk at six o'clock in the morning in the pitch black in the winter. The physical exercise helps me process things. I put together a list of things to talk about with him every day. He's a great listener, and he's really incredibly supportive. He's always been there for me.

I also walked with Gun Denhart. She's a walker too, and there's a wonderful park in Portland that is really twenty miles of forest. We would go walking and just talk. I felt that a big part of my role was to support her, and looking back, sometimes I wonder if that was a mistake, that maybe I should have shouldered less and, instead, asked her for more help, asked her to share the burden more. We probably could have supported each other better had we talked more honestly about our feelings.

One thing I've learned is that a company's vision has to be kept vivid and be renewed. I felt the original vision at Hanna Andersson had run its course and was no longer providing direction. There were interesting options for how we could renew ourselves, but we couldn't agree on which to follow. This created confusion and chaos.

I also learned that I needed to have more courage to speak up in my relationship with Gun. I waited for her as CEO to drive our future, not realizing that she wasn't quite clear herself about what to do. I learned to have more courage, which I've come to exercise here at Rejuvenation. Part of my job is to broaden the founders' existing notions by balancing their original vision, what led them to found a company, with my more diverse experience. It requires great listening and trust on both sides to realize a collaboration.

What that means is that I have to really listen to myself and check frequently how I feel about what's happening here. At Hanna Andersson, I relied on my analytical skills. I've realized that for me to be a true leader, I must also listen to my feelings. I think this is true for all leaders. For example, we have a very vivid vision of the business here, and it is renewed frequently through discussions. We commit ourselves to it. If a decision or course of action doesn't feel right, boy, I'm right there saying, "Let's look at this. What are we really doing here?"

It's very tempting, for example, to consider making light fixtures that aren't exact, authentic reproductions. There's a huge market out there for fixtures that are more interpretive. We see companies come and go all the time in that market. Pottery Barn is selling such light fixtures. They are interpretive and lovely, but they aren't authentic. So it's tempting for us to move in that direction. It's at these moments, when we're having this kind of conversation and thinking about opportunities for the company, that I have to check how it squares with our mission. I say, "No, that's not what we're about. It's not our niche. It just doesn't feel right." We lose our competitive edge when we wander into other people's markets.

Now don't misunderstand me. I'm incredibly profit-driven. I have conversations with employees here all the time about that. Some people think we either make money or we do what we love. I don't think it's one or the other. I say we absolutely have to make money, because money is oxygen, money is breathing for a company. If we can take in big lungfuls and have a bunch of money to expend for exploring new business opportunities or investing in equipment, then we have a healthy company. It's the base from which we operate. Of course, we have to be highly profitable. Now how are we going to do that? Well, I'm going to choose to do it by doing something I love. I hope other people make that choice as well.

But people can interpret something in many ways. When I left Hanna Andersson, I walked into Rejuvenation and read "The employee comes first." Well, let's just say, I knew this was a problem waiting to happen. From the very beginning, I said, "I think this is going to be trouble." And here I am three years later, and I'm still saying, "I think this is trouble." We've altered and rewritten the vision statement and added some more explanations around what the founder really meant. But we're still struggling with this.

When we say, "The employee comes first," we have to think about the implications of that statement. Jim Kelly, who founded this company, is enlightened and very smart. And when he says that, he means it. The trouble is, people both inside and outside the company just hear the first phrase, "employee comes first," because it is catchy and sounds great and enlightened, and that's what really sticks.

But when it comes down to making a decision that an employee doesn't like, the first thing out of his mouth is, "Well, I thought the employee came first here." When, in fact, what we mean in that statement is employees *collectively*. In other words, our community of employees needs to be healthy and happy and engaged and excited about what they're doing. That makes sense to me, to put the collective first, not just an individual. You can just imagine the trouble we have with everyone thinking that he or she, as an individual, comes first.

At one point, for example, I was not satisfied with the results that we were getting out of our manufacturing plant. I was working closely with one of the managers there and questioning him about what was happening. I could see some obvious changes that would bring an immediate improvement. But his reaction was, "That's not the Rejuvenation way." I said, "Where did you get that?" He said, "Well, the employee comes first." I said, "Whoa, whoa, wait a minute here. Let's talk about this, because I think that you're misinterpreting that statement." And, in fact, he was.

I was talking about controlling our inventory and tracking it through a computer system accurately so we could fulfill commitments to customers. One of the problems is that our craftsmen walk into the storeroom and take parts for fixtures they are working on, and no one is accounting for these parts in inventory. So our customer-service suffers, our purchasing people have to jump through hoops, and it creates a chain reaction through the organization.

One obvious solution was to secure the inventory control area so that when people need a part, they have to ask someone for it, and it can be accounted for. What would employees think of this? The manager said, "They'll think that we don't trust them, and they'll be unhappy."

Now, of course, I don't want my employees to think I don't trust them. Just the opposite is true. But I am looking at the big picture and suggesting we are a company that satisfies our customers by being able to make commitments to them and deliver on those commitments. By doing that reliably, we're profitable and able to pay our employees well. At the end of the year, we give bonuses. That's really what's going to make our employees come first.

Not surprisingly, we're really wrestling with this. We're trying to communicate to people that putting employees first means setting high expectations, engaging employees to make a commitment to those high expectations, and getting there together. My challenge and work is empowering employees to embrace the challenge of the greater good. We have 200 employees now. What happens when we grow to 2000 employees or more? It is hard work.

The guidance for me comes from within. It always comes back to integrity, to listening to myself. It sounds a little too easy? Believe me, it's not. Knowing what is right is a process. I have some information. I have some time to think about that and reflect on it. Maybe I engage in another conversation or another experience, and I process it again. It takes time. Truthfully, I don't always know where I'm going. What I do know is that whatever path I take, it will not be a success unless it's a win for the company *and* the employees.

Thirty-Six

Darkness Visible

Ron Huston
Advanced Circuits Inc.

In 1989, at age twenty-five, Ron Huston was working at the McDonnell Douglas Corporation in Long Beach, California, designing black boxes for commercial airplanes. With an electrical engineering degree from Wichita State University in his native Kansas, Huston had been at McDonnell Douglas for four years when he got a call about an ailing circuit board shop that was up for sale. The tiny company was all but defunct, having lost all of its customers and all but two part-time employees. Still, some entrepreneurial spirit lured Huston. He gathered some family money and took over the struggling business. Two weeks before he would have been forced to close up for good, Huston and his wife picked up their lives and the company and moved to Colorado, deciding it was a better place to raise a family. A decade later, Advanced Circuits Inc. is a thriving $11-million manufacturer of prototype printed circuit boards with eighty employees and 3,000 customers, including the International Business Machines Corporation, the Hewlett-Packard Company, and Apple Computer Inc. The turnaround was painstaking and treacherous, but Huston, now only thirty-five years old, feels he has learned a lifetime-worth of leadership lessons.

I was twenty-five years old, so I didn't know any better. I didn't know a company in this condition wasn't supposed to stay in business. It was a total sweat-equity startup for me. The first year, I probably worked twenty hours a day, seven days a week. I slowed down a little bit when we had our first child, thanks to my wife's encouragement. I slowed down to twelve or sixteen hours a day.

I had a partner at the beginning, and neither one of us had any particular interest in being the CEO. In fact, when we were about to meet with the bankers for the first time to talk about money, we realized that one of us had to be in charge, so we flipped a coin. I won, and I became president and, later, CEO. Obviously, it was never my driving ambition to be a CEO.

Our company is a build-to-order custom manufacturer of printed circuit boards. We focus on the smallest of quantities. Usually our customers are in the development stage of an electronic-circuit design. The customer might create a brand new design, and then we will build the first bare board. The client buys two, five, or ten from me to test it, debug it, and improve it. Then I'm sent new design data, and I build it again. Once a design is stable, we might do preproduction quantities of fifty to five hundred. Meanwhile, the client is taking the prototype offshore to produce it cheaply. By then, another engineer with a new design comes in, and we start the same process again.

In order to make the business work, we need a lot of customers. We add over a hundred new, first-time customers every month. We have to have a lot of customers buying small orders; our average invoice is only $500.

Of course, that's the way it is today. When we first moved to Colorado, it was a very different story. We had no money. I basically made phone calls all day to people around Colorado, until I found somebody who needed something. When I'd find a prospect, I'd get directions, drive there, and ask for the order. I always landed the order, because I told people that price and delivery were no obstacles. I said, "If somebody comes in and offers to do it cheaper, you call me, and I'll match the price."

When I was done building the boards, I would take them out to the customers and tell them that their credit was great but I needed cash. I'd ask for another order on my way out. That was my startup survival recipe. I did that, day in and day out, during business hours. During non-business hours, I was either estimating jobs, or I was building product. In fact, on weekends, all I did was build product.

Some might call this the passion of the new entrepreneur. The passion was actually an acute case of fear. When I decided to buy this company, I wrote a fourteen-page business plan with help from a college textbook on technical entrepreneurship. I basically formulated a business plan with just enough information to show to family and friends and get them to lend me $1,000 or $5,000.

I raised about $100,000. Of that, $30,000 was to make the down payment and buy the place. The other $70,000 was what I thought I needed for working capital, because I knew I was going to be C.O.D. with every vendor. The balance of the purchase was a note to the seller.

I needed to produce $40,000 worth of product the first month. Fear is the reason I've never used an alarm clock since I started this business. I woke up at four o'clock every day that first year, no matter what time I went to bed. I'd told everyone who'd lent me money, "If I don't make it, I will pay you back $100 a month for the rest of my life out of my engineering salary." That was the driving force.

I'm not sure where that fear comes from, but I've been a very avid saver my entire life. I grew up in Kansas, the oldest of three boys. My grandpa would slaughter a cow, and that was our meat for the year. Our best meal, our free meal, was steak. We never ate in restaurants when I was young, and usually all the vegetables we had were things we'd grown. So it was a very humble upbringing, and my frugality probably comes from that.

Whatever its origin, this fear drove me from the beginning. We were profitable from the first year. When I said I was going to ship $40,000 the first month, I shipped $44,000. The business grew by $5,000 a month every month thereafter. It was the maximum the cash flow would allow.

The first two years, we hit every number every month. It was grueling and grinding, but we were profitable. We grew from about five or six people at the beginning to close to forty-four at the end of our second year. Then we landed one very big customer, and it became 50 percent of my business in the course of a month. We went from selling $100,000 a month to $200,000 a month in no time at all.

Six months later, that company dropped us. Just like that. We were giving great delivery times, because we had the capacity, but I was hiring so many new people that I lost control of the quality. Not everything was as perfect as it should have been. So it left as easily as it came.

I was stunned. I was twenty-seven years old, totally growth-oriented, and I ran out of cash. The banks had just lent me money. I had my first line of credit and working capital, and I'd spent all of it. I was in my third year, and I was deeper in debt than I had been when I started. Instead of owing $300,000, I owed $500,000, because we'd taken a loan from the Small Business Administration.

I'd spent my entire line of credit, and I'd stopped calling to collect money. Remember those aggressive collections I mentioned that I'd made in the first months? I stopped doing that. I had money in the bank. Here's where my inexperience in cash management showed. So the lesson I learned was to manage the business the same way, whether your cash account is zero or $200,000. You've got to be aggressive on collections—always!

Meanwhile, I had to face the reality of being nearly out of business. It is a traumatic and humbling experience and one you never forget.

Soon after our one big customer left, I simply ran out of cash. There was a day I vividly remember when I said, "We're not going to be able to make payroll if we have all these people. We have to let some go." I had never thought about ever letting go of an employee, because I had so carefully rezruited each one of them.

I had to spend a day making a list of who was going to go. On that one day, I had to lay off twenty people. I let each person go individually. I talked to each one and said how sorry I was. Ironically, most of them weren't surprised. They said, "Jeez, we've had no work for the last several weeks. We knew it was coming." So it was probably harder on me than it was on them, because they'd experienced it before.

For me, it was very tough. I went home and cried for hours. It is tough even to talk about it now. I had no real guidance or anyone to turn to. I remember thinking that I was really alone, the only one going through this experience. Today, I have quite a few consultants around me for various business reasons, but back then I never even thought to pick up the phone and call my tax accountant. I had no mentor or business advisor. I literally paid payroll until I ran out of cash, and then I had to let people go. It was gut wrenching.

In some ways, it felt like one of those near-death experiences. It felt like I saw the light. I saw how close to the edge I had reached. I was going to run out of cash and go out of business. I recognized that feeling, because I had felt it at the very beginning, when I'd started the company and realized what it was going to take to keep it going. Now the problem was that I had far more debt to consider, and worse, the industry was collapsing around me.

In the early 1990s, this industry was in a major trough, because offshore pricing on circuit boards was so cheap that United States manufacturers were getting badly squeezed. The U.S. went from 2,000 to 700 board shops in a very short time. I received three auction notices for equipment every week. My third and fourth years of business were real hell.

All I could do was keep going. I regularly rallied what few troops I had left. There were about ten of us at that point. We had shrunk from forty to ten. I followed the layoff with a 10 percent across-the-board pay cut, but I did it in a positive way. I said, "As soon as we bounce back, I will reinstate it." They all bought in and were working hard. I had to rethink my entire approach to business and customers.

First, I had to reinvent my business. I decided that I would never get dependent on one big customer again, because you can lose that account and face bankruptcy. I had to have a lot of small customers, so I decided to go into direct-mail advertising and contact thousands of engineers around the country about what we offered. Once I sent out that mailing, we just started growing again like crazy.

I had thought about what my customers wanted, and I spent the entire year analyzing what it would take to be profitable in terms of products and pricing. I ran spreadsheets in my living room for two straight months. I had spreadsheets all over my living room and looked at every possible angle. How often will customers buy? How many units will they buy? What size boards would they need? I over-analyzed it, but I'm still using the same price list six years later.

But when it came to managing, I was a different person after the layoff. I realized that nobody was going to make the tough decisions except me. Not one of my employees, including my partner who ran operations, ever came to me before the layoff and said, "Ron, we need to let some people go."

After the fact, some of them said, "I knew you were going to need to do this. I don't know why you didn't do it sooner." I said, "What do you mean you knew? Why didn't you say something?" These were my core people, the people I kept in order to keep the business going. They didn't say anything. So I learned a hard CEO lesson. I have to make the tough decisions. Nobody is going to come in and tell me.

What I also learned is that as gut-wrenching as firing somebody may be, I know now not to wait. Having had to do it a few times now, I've learned that no one ever says, "Gee, I wish I would've waited to fire that guy." What you often hear is, "I should have done that sooner." So I'm pretty strict on the probationary period around here. After a few weeks, I talk to a manager about a new hire, and if I get a sense from that conversation that a person is not working out, I make the manager let that person go before getting emotionally attached. I used to tell the managers, "If you don't let them go, I will, and then I will come and let you go after that." So I have forced some of my key managers to be able to cut the string early when they have to. It never gets easy, but it's a required discipline.

Since that crisis, I've found a new way to approach my business. I have two small children now, and I only work four days a week. I decided that I can accomplish only so much in a week, so I chose to do it in four days instead of five. Plus, there isn't much more my employees can absorb from me on that fifth day. So it hasn't hurt the company at all.

I spend time in school on Fridays or doing some other activity with my wife and children. I feel that those first few years in business earned me this time now. I also feel that this business is really mine in a way that it never was before. In the beginning, I always believed there was nothing to lose. I could always get a job as an engineer and pay everyone back slowly but surely over time.

Now, I have a real stake in this. I had estimated the maximum this business would ever do would be $3 million a year, and now we are up to $11 million. I thought my old facility was the biggest I'd ever need. Now we've more than doubled that space. I think to myself, "How did we do this?"

I played a lot of sports growing up, and I'm competitive by nature. I'm a bar-raiser, and now the bar is raised again. I see the opportunity to be Number One nationally in my market. I can see hitting $50 million in sales and even $100 million in sales. Five years ago, I would have never said that.

Even as we do well, I never forget the early trauma of having to lay off so many people and almost losing the business. In hindsight, I'm glad it happened so early and not when I had a bigger company. You just want to make sure you have the systems and the disciplined "guts" in place, so you don't ever have to go through it again.

Thirty-Seven
Getting the Lead Out

Jeff Zelms
Doe Run Company

Jeff Zelms, fifty-five years old, is vice chairman, president, and CEO of the Doe Run Company, a privately owned mineral extraction and processing company based in St. Louis, Missouri. Founded in 1867, Doe Run began as a small, family-owned lead mining company and gradually expanded into a worldwide enterprise that today boasts 7,000 employees. In addition to mining lead, copper, and other minerals, Doe Run makes a variety of products, from lead walls in hospital X-ray rooms to copper bullet casings. An aggressive manager and leader, Zelms has built the company from $300 million to $900 million in annual sales. Yet he brings a down-home, people-oriented approach to an often cold, dark, and mechanical business.

I always knew I wanted to work in Doe Run. One of my earliest memories is of my father (who spent most of his career as an executive with the company) leading me by the hand deep into a mine shaft. I must have been seven or eight years old. I can't recall the exact time or place, but I can still feel the darkness, smell the pungent earth, and sense all the activity going on around me. The memory has a magical quality that transcends my ability to explain it. I didn't know it at the time, but that first trip underground hooked me into this profession.

I never set a goal of becoming CEO of the company. As a young engineer, that was the furthest thing from my mind, because I loved going into the mines and getting my hands dirty. I still do. But I never shied away from hard work, and slowly but surely I moved up through the ranks. It seemed like every time I started to get bored, things just happened, and I'd be promoted to another level. My father always told me, "Keep your head down and your rear up, and you'll get ahead." I followed his advice and—to my complete surprise—one day found myself sitting behind the CEO's desk.

Not too many people get the opportunity to run a 132-year-old company. As you might expect, having to manage that much history has its advantages and disadvantages. On the one hand, we have a stellar reputation in the community that goes back for generations. People still talk about how Doe Run let their families farm its land during the Great Depression and how we kept people on the payroll through the toughest times. We have plenty of second- and third-generation employees, which makes for a loyalty in our work force that you rarely see anymore.

On the other hand, we do a lot of things around here without knowing why we do them any more. Plus, our work force still expects us to provide things like first-dollar medical insurance and protection against layoffs. In a different day and age we could, but we can't do those kinds of things any more and remain competitive.

I like to describe myself as a hands-on manager. With so many different operations around the world, that means I get to travel a lot. I wouldn't go so far as to say I live on airplanes, but I probably spend at least two weeks of every month on the road or overseas. I don't believe in sitting behind a desk and managing by just the numbers (although they are important). I like to get a feel for things, so I go down into the mines at least once or twice a month. When I put on that hard hat and descend into the darkness, I feel like I'm really in my element. The little boy inside of me comes alive, and I remember why I have stayed in this business for my entire life. Most people, especially if they have any traces of claustrophobia, recoil from the dark, close quarters, but I always say that I do my best work in the dark.

When I go on-site to check out a mine, I like to talk with the foreman or general manager, to take his pulse and see how the place looks. I don't expect to add much to the situation, but I quickly get a feel for the workings of a particular operation. I never stay down for very long, so I can't really get into the innards of everything that is going on. But after thirty years, you develop an intuitive feel for what is happening, and the fact that I have enough interest to make a personal visit has a big affect on the workers. It shows them that I care enough to give the mine my personal attention. That's true even in other countries. I haven't found running our overseas operations to be that different from operating in the United States. Of course you have to deal with cultural differences and other obstacles, but the secret to success is still hiring good people, telling them what you expect, and giving them the support they need to get the job done.

For me, the language barrier is usually what causes the most frustration. I recently went underground in a copper mine in Peru, and I was ticked off about something or other. After several unsuccessful attempts to convey my displeasure, I complained to the foreman, "I feel so damn inadequate, because I can't talk to you in Spanish!"

There's a lack of a sense of urgency to get things done (in some countries) that has also caused a few hairs to turn gray. It's not that the workers don't want to get the job done. They do. Often, they just don't have the resources and infrastructure to respond in a timely manner. When you have a problem in the United States, you can marshal an army of resources to resolve a situation within twenty-four hours. In South America, you can go back a week later, and nothing much has changed. People there don't have our sense of urgency, because they don't have the power to make things happen as quickly. I don't like it, but I've learned to live with it, because there's not much to do about it.

One of my biggest pet peeves as a manager is failure, especially my own. I despise the times we've had to downsize and reduce our work force. With Doe Run's history of not having layoffs, it brings out a lot of memories in the second- and third-generation employees. They say, "I remember when if something like this had happened, they wouldn't have laid anyone off," or, "I remember back when that occurred, and nobody lost a job." And it's true. But we can't conduct business like that anymore and stay competitive. On the other hand, if I did a better job of running the company, I wouldn't have to stand in front of them and give them the bad news, which I insist on doing in person.

Fortunately, we've only had one round of layoffs under my watch. It was in the early 1990s, when our industry took quite a hit. You do it for the good of the company, and you have all the numbers and all the logical reasons to back up your decision to cut personnel, but that doesn't make it any easier. When you look people in the eye who have worked long and hard for you and tell them they no longer have a job, it feels like hitting yourself in the head with a hammer. Still, when you sit behind the desk with the sign that says, "The buck stops here," you remember that it comes with the territory.

My worst failures are those very rare occasions when we've suffered a fatality at one of our operations. We work in a very unforgiving business, and if you make a mistake, it can cost your life. We put a premium on safety, as evidenced by the fact that we have won the industry's most prestigious safety award more times than any other company. But we're not perfect, and occasionally we lose one of our people.

When that happens, it just consumes me. Part of me says, "There's nothing personally that you could have done." I never seem to get past believing that if I just had more ability or more talent, somehow I would have been able to influence the management, the training, the application, the selection of people, or done *something* that would have avoided the tragedy. In the old days, before Doe Run became so big, I used to contact the family personally. Today I'm too far removed from most cases, but we have a system that immediately steps in and takes care of the family. I make it a point to attend the funeral whenever possible. It's a horrible thing to lose an employee. I would give anything for the ability to ensure that it would never happen again.

I've never been one to reflect much on my own performance, preferring to measure my success by the successes of those around me. For some inexplicable reason, I seem to have a talent for leading people and an ability to feel what is going on and sort out whether something should or shouldn't affect a decision. Franklin Roosevelt once said, "A good leader is the guy who can step on your toes without messing up your shine." I think I can do that. I can give people a kick in the pants without them resenting me for months at a time. I can also read people with some accuracy. Having been there in the blood, the guts, and the beer, I can tell when people are trying to give me a bunch of bull, and I don't have any problems calling them on it. Fortunately, that doesn't happen very often in this company. I tell it like it is and expect others to do the same.

Despite the fact that I've risen from junior engineer to the top of the food chain, I don't feel like I've changed much over the years. I started out as a "what-you-see-is-what-you-get" kind of person, and I've tried to maintain that quality. I've found that when you walk your talk, when you treat folks with honesty, dignity, and respect, they will respond in kind. It makes the job of managing much simpler.

I have changed in one important area: I have a lot more patience than I used to. As a youngster fresh out of engineering school, I probably had a bit more salt in my britches than I was entitled to. Back in those days everyone punched a time clock, even the salaried people. Quitting time rolled around at 3:30 P.M., and if you stood in the hall at 3:25 you ran the risk of getting trampled to death. I can remember standing in front of the clock—with no authority or license to do so—and telling people with more seniority and rank than I that if they weren't so anxious to get home, this company would be doing a darn sight better! I chuckle when I look back on those days. I've never had any trouble speaking my mind, but now I give things a lot more consideration before opening my mouth.

Sometimes I still want to get too much done too soon, but I have learned restraint. That has come by recognizing my limitations and appreciating the skills of others. A few months ago, while visiting one of our smelting plants, I told the general manager, "I can't tell you what to do anymore. There was a time a while back when I sure as hell could, but not anymore." Thirty years ago, I could never have uttered such a statement, but we've grown larger, and I have too many responsibilities on too many fronts to keep up on all aspects of the business. Fortunately, I no longer have a problem admitting I don't know it all. Besides, if I tell you what to do, it gives you an out. If you screw up, and I've told you what to do, you're free and clear. I have no intention of giving my people that out, and they know it.

The funny part is when you've been around this long and done as much as I have, people think you see infinitely more than you do. It's like the grade school teacher writing on the chalkboard and all the kids thinking she has eyes in the back of her head. If I could do a fraction of what my people think I can, I would retire to my luxury estate and clip coupons all day long. Seriously though, I've had the good fortune of being surrounded by a magnificent group of people. Like the Energizer Bunny, they just keep going and going and going. They make everything I do look ten times better than it actually is.

When I leave Doe Run, I hope I'll be remembered as someone who took the time to get involved, as someone who never let his position come between him and others in his organization. I think I'll be remembered as an empathetic and, at times, sympathetic person, but also as someone who couldn't easily be taken advantage of. Most of all, I hope to be remembered as someone who knew how to have fun.

Part of our strategic plan calls for having fun, and I think that has to be an essential component of work, no matter what you do. Until I made vice chairman in January, I jokingly called myself a failure, because I hadn't received a promotion in fifteen years. When you consider that the average life span of the a CEO term in the United States is five years, that doesn't look too good. I've had a good, long run at Doe Run, and I intend to keep plugging away until they drag me out of here. If it all ended today, I would say it's been a great career.

Thirty-Eight

A Malaysian Turnaround

Ong Boon Kee
GB Industries

In December, 1990, when Ong Boon Kee became general manager (or CEO) of GB Industries, a rubber glove manufacturer in Kuala Lumpur, Malaysia, he was just thirty-one years old and had no experience running a company. An accountant, Ong was working for a trading company importing goods for the gas and oil industry when GB Industries' managing director, a college schoolmate and friend, contacted him about turning around the struggling rubber glove manufacturer. At the time Ong took over, GB Industries had sales of just 5 million ringgit ($1.3 million) and was losing money. Today, GB Industries has become profitable and sales have soared to 30 million ringgit ($8 million). For Ong, the turnaround required years of seventy- to eighty-hour workweeks and some unconventional management thinking. Now aged forty, he has had remarkably similar experiences to his American counterparts in the executive suite. Even in Malaysia, he has found it can get very lonely at the top

When I was being interviewed for this job by the board of directors, they asked me quite bluntly, "Are you able to make this company profitable? If not, let's shut it down." The managing director, in particular, was quite impatient. He kept asking, "When is it going to happen?"

I didn't have an answer. This was a new industry to me. Malaysia is the rubber glove capital of the world, and there are several huge glove makers that compete with GB Industries. GB was an original-equipment manufacturer. We exported our gloves to big suppliers, mostly in Europe, who put their own brand labels on them. In order to grow and become profitable, we needed to expand into new markets and compete effectively in terms of both quality and cost. It wouldn't be easy.

In Malaysia, with a company this size, it is usually a shareholder who runs the company. My friend who brought me here was that person, but he had other things he wanted to do. The members of the board all have other businesses elsewhere. They invested money here and assumed my friend would be running the show. They didn't want to have to employ a general manager and pay him a lot of money to run the business. So the fact that they hired me as a professional manager made our situation rather unique.

Add to that the fact that I was an accountant by training and that the highest rank I had achieved was as a middle manager at a trading company and you can see this was a very big step for me, especially at age of thirty-one.

To be frank, I wasn't really aware of what I was getting myself into, but I had always cherished the idea of being the CEO of a company. I even told job interviewers that my goal was to become a CEO. They were skeptical at first; if I was so good, why wasn't I running my own company?

In a way, I had. I was the first employee of the trading company, and that gave me a chance to gain experience setting up the whole organization, from recruiting and hiring sales executives and accountants, to setting up the systems to run the company. I had two solid years of that.

I also don't fit the typical accountant's profile. They tend to be more introverted and focused on numbers. My friend from the university hired me, because I was on the more aggressive side, even back in our university days. I was very active in extracurricular activities, and I organized several events, including a study tour of Europe. I had always been ambitious, despite the fact that I hadn't grown up in the city.

I grew up in a distant and remote state called Kelantas, in a village on the southern border of Thailand. My father ran a motorbike repair shop, but the town was so isolated that there were hardly any bikes to repair. We were very poor, and the idea that I could one day end up a CEO was nothing more than a dream.

But even when I was a teenager, I had always wanted to come to Kuala Lumpur to study. I always thought, "If I can study in the city where the competition is stronger, I will be much better off." In rural areas like where I grew up, few young people are interested in studying. I was fortunate, because when I was in high school, I managed to get a transfer out of that town, out of that state, to another state not far from the capital city. I have four brothers and sisters, and they all stayed in Kelantas. I was the only one to leave.

I actually lived in a residential school, and it provided more than accommodations. It provided good discipline and proper guidelines. There was a time for everything, just like in the military: a time to wake up, a time to go to school, a time for games, a time for review, a time for homework. This discipline helped my studies greatly.

The discipline has also helped me later, when turning around GB Industries. When I first arrived, the company was investing in a new manufacturing machine, and the machine didn't work. We ended up making additional installments of repayments of loans, and we had a serious cash-flow problem. There was little additional work coming in from the investment, so there was a tremendous stress on the company.

I had to work extremely hard during that period to solve the cash flow problem, and at the same time, I realized we had to make a change to the marketing and production strategies. The pressure was very intense, because I was in a one-year grace period before my predecessor finally phased himself out. I remember clearly how I won him over.

We had a particular glove that was pink. Most rubber gloves are yellow. But we had this one pink glove, and when I looked through the reports and records, I realized that the pink coloring that we were using seemed to be causing five or six defects in the glove. The cost was also exorbitant.

I talked to the lab people, and I said, "Why don't we do something about it?" It turned out that the problem was caused by heat sensitivity. So I said "Why don't you change the pigment to one which is not heat sensitive?" They replaced the pigment, but of course, there was a slight difference in the color. The shade of pink would be slightly different. We tried to blend it as closely as possible.

When I spoke to my predecessor about it, he said, "No. You can't change the color, because the customer won't want a different color."

So I threw him a challenge. I put six or seven pairs of pink gloves on the table and said, "Since you know the difference so well, tell me which is our present color and which is the new color?" He said, "All right. This is our existing color. And these are all the new colors." I said, "Wrong. I never put the new color on the table. You can't tell the difference, even if you look closely."

That won him over. He said, "You make the decision." That was my first major decision in the company. After that, I had no doubt that I could do the job. From there, I made more changes. The company had been manufacturing eight different colors of gloves, and I decided that we would make just two colors. It was considered radical and risky, but when we made the switch, we saw immediate benefits in our economies of scale. There was less downtime, and we were able to lower prices. We started getting a lot of new customers, but of course, in the process we lost some customers who wanted the old color range.

I called it the consolidation phase; we could reap more profits and reinvest in the company. But it was a most stressful time. We were living hand to mouth. Like any company going through stressful times, I was worried that we would lose people, but I was very fortunate. In fact, I retained most of the staff. I met with the staff and said, "I can't promise you wealth, but I can promise you a great experience. If we can make it through this phase together, each of us will definitely be a better person."

Today, some of those people are my key managers. We have secretaries and other rank-and-file employees who have been retrained and are now managers or executives. They didn't have high qualifications in terms of educational backgrounds, but they have the right attitude. If you get the right people, the training can come later.

I've found that those who come in with the right training but without the right attitude end up leaving. We actually switched our recruitment model to look first for attitude and then for skills. And so far, it's been working.

In fact, when I took over, I created a new culture in the company. Most of my senior staff left within the first twelve months, because they didn't like my style. My predecessor had been involved in multiple companies, and he was pretty "hands off" in his management style. When I came in, I could see what was going on and could see people's weaknesses. I could see the mistakes that had been made. When I brought my observations to these managers, a few of them were not too happy. They are what I call the "dead wood."

Their departures opened up opportunities for the lower level staff, and they all moved up very nicely. I didn't have the luxury of employing a new staff, even if I'd wanted to. At that point, in the early 1990s, Malaysia was experiencing a boom, and unemployment was extremely low. People had good, high-paying jobs, and it was difficult to recruit. So I had to work with the resources that I had.

Despite the difficulties, it never crossed my mind to give up. I had a great bunch of directors who had entrusted me with the business. They allowed me to run the business the way I wanted, and I knew that in any other company, I would not have been given such an opportunity.

The directors had money to put into the business, and all I had to do was put my heart and soul into reviving it. If I could do that, I would earn their trust. That's why I am still able to run it the way I want, and there continue to be great opportunities.

I never got discouraged, but of course, there are times when you don't know whether you are doing the right thing. Sometimes you'll be digging, and it looks like there is no light at the end of the tunnel. Those are the times when you have to believe in your instincts.

For example, I would tell my accounting staff, "Our costs are too high. We are going to bring them down another 10 or 20 percent." They would look at me in disbelief, but because I was so passionate and enthusiastic, they made it happen.

My wife was always supportive and a great sounding board for me. She understood that I had to work seventy to eighty hours each week to turn things around. She is a product manager in a publicly traded company, so I can bounce ideas off her and get good feedback, but there have been sacrifices.

When my wife was expecting our first child, I was supposed to show up at the hospital for the sonogram to see what the baby's sex was. Some problems crept up at the office, and I completely forgot about the appointment. She called me later and said, "I thought you were supposed to be here." I said, "Oh gosh, I'm leaving right now." And she said, "It's too late. It's over." Fortunately, it was a boy. In Asia, boys are favored, and she was quite happy and forgot that I wasn't there. She forgave me instantly, and I made sure I was there when the baby was born. His timing was good. He was born on a Sunday morning.

CEOs, even in Malaysia, must have supportive wives. Today, I won't work from Friday evening until Sunday evening. That is strictly family time.

After a decade, the hard work has started to pay off. When I started, we were just talking about survival. Now we talk about wanting to be the best in the industry. All the big glove-makers are in Malaysia, because it is the rubber capital of the world. They are much bigger than we are, but they have started to notice us.

I set up a vision and a mission for the company. We have five critical success factors, the first of which is to be the cost leader in the glove industry. We want to be the lowest cost manufacturer in the world, and we push our people. I tell them, "We want to be the best in the world." I'm always encouraging our people to be better. I've insisted that we do benchmarking. I say to them, "Why do you think Motorola is so good? Let's be the Motorola in this industry."

So we benchmark. We go into education. We go into training. We are starting to invest more in training. I want to double the size of the company in the next two to three years and hopefully take the company public. We were rewarded in 1998 by being selected as one of the top fifty enterprises in Malaysia.

Unlike my counterparts in the United States, my financial rewards are much more limited. I get a good salary and profit sharing, but I don't have equity in the company—not yet anyway. When we take the company public that will change. Still, I run it as if I owned it. I tell my people that I am an employee here, just like they are. At the same time, my success has come, because I think of the company as my own.

Thirty-Nine

Transplanting the Dream Every Seven Years

Ken Saxon
Farm Capital Services, L.L.C.

Ken Saxon has traveled a very different career path than most entrepreneurs. Fresh out of Stanford Business School, he and a partner purchased a tiny records-management company, which grew to $10 million in annual sales, eighty employees, and twelve facilities up and down the West Coast. Along the way, the company earned an Arthur Andersen Best Practices Award for its innovative management and compensation practices. At the age of thirty-three, after serving as co-CEO for only seven years, Saxon and his partner decided to turn over the day-to-day management of the business and explore new territory. Far too young to retire, Saxon used the transition to open the door to a more diverse, rewarding, and personally fulfilling life.

I don't think I fit the profile of the "typical" entrepreneur—not so much because of the way I run my company, but because of the way I have designed and laid out my career and my life. The standard model for entrepreneurs is to devote your whole life to your company, cash out at the right time, and then ride off into the sunset. I can't imagine anything less interesting. In fact, the thought of having nothing more to show for my career than thirty years as the CEO of a records-storage company makes me cringe. I need more from life.

I also differ from most entrepreneurs in that I did not found my first company. My partner and I bought First American Records Management (FARM), a small company in San Jose that had eight employees and $500,000 a year in sales. Over the next decade, we proceeded to expand it to twenty times that size. We had a lot of fun and experienced a lot of success, but we both went into FARM with no intention of winding up our careers there. We agreed to get out long before it got stale.

My partner expressed the need for a change first. I could have bought him out and stayed in the business, but our partnership meant too much to me. I had achieved my two primary goals—becoming an effective CEO and building a company based on human relationships as well as the bottom line—so it seemed like the right time to move on. We brought in a professional manager to round out a two-person Office of the President, promoted ourselves to co-chairmen of the board, and pulled out of the operational aspects of the business.

Our decision raised a lot of eyebrows among friends and colleagues. Why would we make those kinds of changes at an age when most entrepreneurs are just getting started? I can't speak for my partner, but my answer is that I've always had a different paradigm for how my career and life should flow. Part of my vision has always been to have four ten-year "careers," although lately I have adjusted my thinking to more along the lines of seven-year cycles.

I also have a very strong desire for continual learning, and in the last year or two at FARM, my learning curve had flattened out. I don't mean to imply that I had learned everything there was to know about running a company; that would take at least two or three lifetimes. But the kinds of things I was learning no longer punched my ticket. I found myself growing less excited about coming in to work every day.

I could have chosen to ramp up and find a new challenge, such as making the company ten times bigger, but that didn't motivate me. Instead, my partner and I formed a venture capital company, FARM Capital Services. We coach and mentor young entrepreneurs and take a minority stake in their companies. We've become involved with several companies over the last few years. I absolutely love the work, because it still takes place in the entrepreneurial world, but from a different perspective.

Most entrepreneurs make lousy venture capitalists, because entrepreneurs want absolute control. They have to own everything and run the whole show. My partner and I have chosen a very different approach. We look for young, talented, raw entrepreneurs in certain industries, and we invest in them as well as in their companies. We take a financial stake in the business, but the core of our work involves coaching, mentoring, and supporting entrepreneurs. We tend to build strong relationships with the entrepreneurs, partly as a result of the empathy we feel for them. They know we've been there.

This kind of work gets me going like nothing I have done before. The entrepreneurs we work with are out there hustling every day and making things happen, and I thrive on that kind of energy and enthusiasm. I also find it very rewarding when we help to make their growth paths less bumpy. For example, one of our first investments involved an emerging high-tech company run by two bright young guys out of Stanford.

Nine months after our initial investment, it became clear that their accelerating burn rate might cause the business to go under within a year. We gave them our assessment of the situation and suggested some adjustments in their strategy, which they quickly executed. Two years later, the company has grown several times larger and continues to expand at a rapid clip. The owners say that had we not put our foot down at the time, the whole enterprise might have collapsed around them. I take a lot of pride in what their company does and how they do it, so it felt great to help them through a critical period in their growth.

As an investor and coach, you sometimes get involved in ways you don't anticipate or enjoy. In late 1998, one of the young entrepreneurs I worked closely with died in a terrible car crash. As the most hands-on board member, I jumped in to help the management team. I also brought in some grief counselors and escorted a group of employees to and from the funeral. Since then, I have spent many days at the company, supporting the partner of the departed entrepreneur. I also discovered that throwing myself into the mix with the entrepreneur's family and co-workers helped with my own mourning process.

When you work closely with someone to build a company, you develop a deep sense of friendship and mutual respect. To have that violently snatched away shakes up your whole world and painfully reminds you of your own mortality. Fortunately, keeping the company going and supporting each other gave us all a positive outlet for channeling our grief.

One of my primary goals in this cycle of my career is maintaining a greater sense of balance in my life. For now, that means devoting as much time as possible to my four-year-old twins. Now that I'm no longer saddled with the responsibility of running a company, I have the freedom and flexibility to be present with my children, and I treasure my time with them. I feel like I know my children better than most dads, and I hope that will translate into close relationships with them as they grow older.

Fatherhood definitely ranks among the most challenging things I've ever done. It's also one of the most humbling. I'm learning that the big things don't make the difference. It's the little daily activities— being there at breakfast and dinner and bath time—that give you the chance to bond as a parent. I have dinner with my children every night and have been surprised (and dismayed) to learn how few parents do. I find it ironic that in the early years, when our children can most benefit from our presence, we often have the least amount of time to give them, because we're in our peak productivity years. I feel very fortunate to have a lifestyle that allows me to share this formative time in their lives.

From a business standpoint, probably the biggest lesson I've learned is that the company should be your vehicle for getting what you want from life and not vice versa. An early mentor constantly pounded the message into my head that, "If you aren't having fun or you're not getting what you want, sell the company and leave. Otherwise, change the vehicle to make it more of what you want." Fortunately, I listened, and it sank in.

Most entrepreneurs get stuck, because they never learn to think like an owner. When you only think as a CEO or manager, you always think of the business first. As a result, you become a slave to it. I learned early in my career that my business should serve my life, not run it, and that has made a huge difference in how my career has unfolded.

I've also learned that you can run a company in a positive, ethical, people-oriented way and still achieve success. Conventional wisdom states that you have to manage hard and aggressively and pay attention to the bottom line first in order to get ahead. I know a lot of CEOs who still think that way, but I don't subscribe. In fact, my experience has been just the opposite. Running a business has actually increased my idealism—not decreased it. I firmly believe that when you put people first, good things will happen.

For example, when my partner and I decided to turn over the daily operations at FARM, we had to make some tough management-succession decisions. One of our senior executives—only twenty-nine years old—had superb sales and sales-management skills, but no experience in financials or operations. Had we taken a purely bottom line approach, we would never have given him a second thought, especially since all our advisors recommended bringing in an experienced pro from the outside. But he had tremendous potential, and he lived and breathed the firm's values and culture. The idea of installing him as keeper of the flame appealed to us a great deal. So we searched long and hard to find a partner who could complement his areas of inexperience. We found an older, more experienced manager who embraced the idea of partnering with our young executive, and four years later the two co-CEOs are doing a great job at FARM. Today, given his experience at FARM, I think our young manager could make an excellent sole CEO.

Some would say we took a huge risk promoting our young neophyte, but it felt safer to me than hiring a president from the outside. Sure, you need someone who can read a balance sheet and manage inventory and all that, but you also need someone who can communicate the vision, mission, and values and has the same passion for the business that you do. If it hadn't work out, I was prepared to step back in and try something else. I'm not afraid to try something new, and if I don't get the results I want, I learn from it and move on. To me, the only "sin" in business is making the same mistake over and over again.

How long will I stay with FARM Capital Services? The answer is as long as I find it stimulating and rewarding. I don't have any preset time frame. When I find myself starting to wonder about the next phase, that probably means the time has come to begin exploring something new. I love to build, so maybe the next itch will involve diving back into building myself. My current vision is to "repot" myself every seven years, so I can experience as much as possible and develop all that I have within me. I can't tell you where I will be five years from now, but I plan to be learning and having a lot of fun doing it.

Forty

No Longer Lonely at the Top

Kent Griswold
Griswold Special Care, Inc.

Kent Griswold's mother founded Griswold Special Care, a nonmedical home-care provider, in 1982 after she learned that she had multiple sclerosis. When she tried to get a job, no one would hire her because of her illness. At the same time, an elderly woman in the local Presbyterian Church where Griswold's father was the minister died, because no one had taken care of her in her home, despite the fact that she was wealthy and her family lived a mile away. So Mrs. Griswold decided she would work for herself and fulfill a need for providing home care for the elderly and disabled. She founded her company just outside Philadelphia. A few years later, after falling and breaking her arm and shoulder, Mrs. Griswold called her son Kent, a Harvard and Wharton Business School graduate living and working in Australia, and asked him to come home and help her run the business while she mended. Griswold, now president, extended his initial six-month stay into twelve years and counting. Now forty-one years old, he has built the family business into a $50-million company with offices in nine eastern states and 6,000 full- and part-time employees. Despite his success, Griswold put everything on the line for true love.

Sometime in the mid-1990s I decided to take a six-month leave of absence to write a novel. At the time, the company wasn't as big as it is now, but it was still a growing company and needed a fair amount of management. I needed to find a temporary replacement who had the skills to handle this kind of job.

We interviewed people from all over the country and finally found a woman in California who had her Ph.D. in social policy and a

287

master's degree in gerontology. Her name was Lori Rosenquist, and she was very well connected on the national level and had served on a number of important boards. She was a very talented person.

We were lucky enough to catch her at the right moment, kind of between things, and she agreed to come serve as acting president of Special Care for six months while I took a leave of absence to write my book. I actually came back after a little over four months, and she had developed the business and had endeared herself to a lot of people in our various offices. We had about thirty-five offices then. We decided to make her an offer to stay on as our vice president, and she accepted.

The following summer, because she was here and so capable, I was able to take a second leave of absence to write a second book. I hadn't had the first book published, and I decided to write a murder mystery that took place in a nursing home. I figured that would be good for business. After reading it, people would want to stay at home.

So Lori stayed through that second summer. We had gotten to know each other the previous year, and we just started doing things as friends. I had a lousy track record with romance, and my globetrotting to Australia and Sweden had precluded any serious relationships. I had just broken up with the person I had been dating, so Lori and I began to spend more time together, and we shared a number of interests. I ended up coming back to work after just three months. The novel would have to wait.

As we moved closer to romance, we faced a serious obstacle: our company philosophy and policy prohibited dating people in the company. From a more practical point of view, as the president, I might be putting the best interests of the company in jeopardy by getting involved with a person who reported to me. This person was a key vice president who had some tremendous skills and would be very difficult to replace.

If I dated her and, inevitably, ended up breaking up—which was the story of my life—it would be very uncomfortable to continue working together. The odds were, she would leave. So I was really torn.

Here was someone I really wanted to date. Working long hours as a CEO, you don't get a chance to meet a lot of other people. Finding someone who has similar interests and is a very caring, genuine, talented person is a rare occurrence.

So we had a discussion about it. I remember that it was on January 31, 1995, at her apartment. We had this very serious conversation, and we decided that life is too short and sometimes you just have to take some chances. While it was probably a very foolish move from a business perspective, from a personal point of view it was something that I really needed to do. So we both agreed to start dating and to keep it completely secret. Not a single person in the company knew that we were doing this.

On Friday afternoons, Lori would leave the office at five o'clock and she would tell everyone to have a nice weekend. She would go home to her apartment, which was actually walking distance from our office. I would hang around and work a little bit longer, and then if any employees were still around, I would say, "Have a nice weekend," and I would leave. I would get in my car and drive off in a different direction and loop around to her apartment. Then we would go off and do whatever we were going to do that evening.

On one occasion, as we were walking back from lunch together, we had been holding hands in the parking lot, and then we stopped, because we saw someone who we were afraid would see us together and start speculating. But that person just assumed that we were out to lunch together.

Most amazing was the fact that we had a manager of development whose office was between ours. Both of us had to go through her office to get out of our own offices. And she didn't have a clue that we were dating the entire time. We actually attended her wedding the day after we got engaged, and at that point, she still didn't know we were dating and was quite surprised when she later found out. We were good actors.

I do believe that despite our strong emotions, we did a pretty good risk assessment from the business side. We had been doing things as friends, and we'd known each other for a couple of years at that point, so this wasn't a quick romance. There was also the realization that she was too a special person for me to walk away. I had a zero success rate up to then, but I had never ever wanted to marry somebody before. I felt that the odds were good enough here that it was worth the business risk. With that said, given my personal track record, I was still being very selfish, because the odds of it working out were not great.

I also didn't tell my parents at the outset. That was wrong from a business perspective, but part of the romance was the fact that it was a secret. It added to the intrigue and mystery. But from a purely business perspective, it was the wrong thing to do.

Eventually, we told my parents as well as her parents. But that was the extent of who knew within the company. As time went on, I talked to a number of my friends from high school, college, or business school. Many of them were attorneys, and they, along with my non-attorney friends, strongly advised against our relationship because of the risk in dating someone who reports to you.

If we broke up and it was acrimonious, there could be wrongful termination suits, sexual-harassment suits, or whatever. It could have been highly risky. Every single one of my attorney friends said, "Don't do it. It's just not worth it." Of course, I didn't listen to them, which is a good thing.

Instead, we moved forward quickly. We had our first discussion about dating in January, and I was ready to make her my wife by May. And it isn't in my nature to do things in a subtle way. All this mystery and intrigue made me want to do something outrageous and very visible when we got engaged.

I had been active in community theater. In fact, that year, I was doing a community theater production in Berwyn, a small Pennsylvania town, called "Woman of the Year"—an old Spencer Tracy/Katharine Hepburn film. Lori was very supportive and came to see the show three times.

I had originally agreed to do a small chorus part with a friend of mine who was in the show, but the person playing the Russian ballet dancer, which was a minor lead role, dropped out. They pressed me into the part, despite the fact that I don't speak Russian, I don't dance ballet, and on top of everything else, I'd sprained my ankle playing volleyball. I showed up at rehearsal in a wheelchair one night. It was a series of fiascoes.

Still, I had a plan. After the show on the second from last night, I was going to propose—right from the stage. I was so nervous about the whole thing that I almost blew it before the show began. Lori asked me to go to dinner with her before the show, and I sort of snapped at her with a "No!" I had too many things to get done before the show. She thought I was so rude that she almost didn't come to the show that night. Fortunately, she did come with two friends of ours.

That night, I was so nervous, I got nauseous. Not only did I have to sing a solo number, "Happy in the Morning," but also I wanted my marriage proposal to go flawlessly. During the show, I couldn't find her in the audience. I searched frantically from the wings when I was off stage and finally located her. But then she and our friends moved their seats after the second act, and I had to find her again.

I was so nervous, I told the three ballerinas in my song-and-dance number that they might have to do it without me. They got very upset, so I pulled myself together and did the song.

After the show, during the curtain call, I started to make an announcement. I explained that I had sung this song called "Happy in the Morning," but there was someone in the audience who made me happy in the morning, happy in the evening, and every time in between. I said she was *my* "Woman of the Year." They brought out a giant engagement ring that had been used as a prop in the show. Our friend Claudia was sitting next to Lori, tapping her on the leg, saying, "What's he talking about?" She was completely baffled.

I had spoken to the production staff ahead of time, and they had left the curtain up. One guy brought out a large bouquet of flowers that I had bought before the show. Then another fellow came out with a bottle of champagne. I came down off the stage and out into the audience, and they had the spotlight on Lori. I got down on my knee and asked her to make me the happiest man on earth. She said yes, but the problem was that I couldn't hear her, because the entire cast was screaming and the audience was applauding. The women all around her were weeping. I was crying, and I had to ask her three times before I could actually hear what she said. It was bedlam.

The whole idea was a big risk. I wasn't sure whether she would be completely furious with me for doing this in a public forum. This is a very private moment, after all. Worst of all, what if she said "No"? I wanted to make it a very special, memorable moment, but I didn't know how she would react to it at all. How demoralizing and embarrassing if she turned me down, in front of everyone. But she did say yes, and I was completely thrilled.

Later that night, as I was walking out to the car, one of the cast members came up to me and said, "Where's your fiancée?" I had never even thought about that word, and it just didn't click in. Who was she was talking about? I was in a state of shock. I remember driving home with my hand on my mouth, just thinking, "Oh my God, what have I done?"

In fact, what I did has turned out to be wonderful. We were married on October 7, and Lori was pregnant with our child by December. Today, she is still vice president, and we're in a new set of offices now—she's directly next to me. Our daughter comes in every Tuesday and Thursday afternoon and naps while we work.

We're together essentially day and night, and it still feels like a Tracy/Hepburn movie. We're past the three-year mark, and in some ways, we're still on our honeymoon. We've been very blessed in getting married a little bit older, when it really was the right marriage. So we don't have a lot of personal problems, and the fact that we're married actually makes this a much stronger leadership team, in part because the office does interfere a lot with our home life.

We find ourselves, late at night in bed, talking about the office, and we have at times had to say, "Okay, after ten o'clock we're not going to talk about the office any more." But because we are around each other so much, we are able to talk about different issues at different times, and we get to feel the confidence you feel when the person you're talking to supports you, even when that person doesn't agree with you.

We've also discovered that we're a more effective management team, because people feel comfortable talking to Lori about issues they don't want to present to me. A lot of people felt very close to her when she was running the company in my absence, and that feeling has carried over. I think I'm a very likable guy, but I'm told that I can be intimidating. Lori helps ameliorate that when it happens.

It's ironic that we're together so much and so happy about it. When I was single, I'd tell my friends that I'd love to find a part-time wife and part-time children, because I really valued my independence and being alone. But now that I'm married, the thought of not seeing Lori every day, all day, is actually kind of frightening. I would hate for her to not be here. We're thinking about having a second child, and if we do, then she might cut back her hours, and I don't look forward to that.

What I learned from all this is that even a CEO must follow his heart every once in a while and leave conventional business wisdom by the side of the road. In our case, the reward turned out to be well worth the risk.

Forty-One

When the Core Is Passion

Rob Gordon
W.A.R? Ltd.

After an unsatisfying, four-year stint at Thorn EMI Records, one of the world's biggest record companies, Rob Gordon decided that the only way to retain his passion and love for the music industry was to start his own label. In 1991, at age twenty-five, Gordon founded W.A.R.? (What Are Records? Ltd.) in his New York City loft. He relocated the company to Boulder, Colorado, in 1994. With just over $1 million in sales, W.A.R.? is a tiny, independent label featuring artists including The Samples, Maceo Parker, and Melissa Ferrick. Gordon, an iconoclast who has always chafed against traditional music-industry practices, is attempting to build his label by changing the rules and offering better deals for established as well as emerging artists. He hired his sister Jan to help run the day-to-day operations and oversee the company's fourteen employees, which frees Gordon up to manage his other employees, the artists themselves.

I started the business out of my loft in downtown Manhattan. I put my small amount of money into technology—not into furnishings or other things that would have made life more comfortable. We had upside-down milk crates for chairs and sheets of plywood on sawhorses for tables. But we had computers, and we had a phone system. I figured that nice desks wouldn't help us sell records.

One of my first recollections about becoming CEO is the feeling of isolation it brought with it. There wasn't anyone to talk to about a lot of the issues surrounding the daily running of a business. Most of my peers in the industry have gone on to higher positions at major companies, but they are vice presidents of specific areas in big companies. I had to figure out everything for myself.

First of all, my industry is very strange. It has its own book of unwritten rules. I had very strong opinions about how it *doesn't* work. I also had to figure out what I was going to do to compensate my modest funding, when I had no desire to depend on radio hits.

So I had to constantly reinvent every wheel. I had to pull apart every rule that I came up against and put it back together. If some of it made sense, that part stayed. Whatever didn't, I redesigned.

On top of that, I had to formulate a vision and follow through with it, which is difficult, because we are so different from most other labels, both major and independent. I have broken a number of industry rules, and that was really hard. Even my own employees would tell me that no one else was doing it like this.

For example, radio tends to be the main focus of this business, but not for me. Touring sales and grassroots marketing have been my primary focus. We use our sales and marketing successes to encourage radio to support our releases, but we don't depend on radio. For 99 percent of the record companies in this country, if they don't get radio air play, they aren't going to sell any records, period.

We also sell direct to retailers whenever possible, instead of selling exclusively through one distribution company. We didn't want to flood record stores with our records. We wanted to put only the number of records in that would sell through. We wanted to create an audience ourselves, instead of catering to the industry and having the industry create consumers for our music. The concept is very simple: create the demand yourself, the supply takes care of itself.

Our industry is not known for that. Our industry is known for push-marketing. The idea is to supersaturate the single on radio, get placement everywhere, and make it so visible that consumers think they're missing something if they don't buy it—even if they don't really know or care who the artist is. Even when this works, the unfortunate outcome is the "one-hit wonder," a successful song by a still unknown or undeveloped artist.

So I couldn't just go out and hire people with a lot of major-label experience, because they are used to doing business the way that major labels do it. I would have to spend a huge amount of time reprogramming them. So I tend to hire younger people with a passion for music. In fact, over the years, some of the people who have worked for me started as unpaid interns and rose to such key positions as head of sales and head of marketing. It was just a matter of finding smart people who had common sense.

Most of the ideas that formed this company are just a series of little ideas I gathered while working at EMI doing A&R, which is basically talent scouting. I spent endless nights in clubs listening to music, talking to artists, managers, and lawyers—people who were stimulated by many issues. Most of the people I encountered in the business early on didn't agree with the system either, but very few people felt ready to go up against it.

I was a musician before I got into the business. That is where my passion comes from, and I still play the guitar to relax and step away from the intensity of the business. When I was in New York and needed to clear my head and get away from the frenzy of the business, I would go up to a summer camp that my family owns in Connecticut. I was almost born at the camp, so I know every route around the grounds intimately. I would just walk around with my eyes closed, feel the earth, and feel my way down roads or across fields. The summer camp season lasts just eight weeks, so there was plenty of time for me to go there in the off-season. I would listen to music a lot, particularly the bands I was interested in. I would listen to their music and visualize different ways to market them. I'd come back from Connecticut refreshed and ready to go at it again.

Sometimes, when I'm just lying down in bed at night or when I'm waking up, I'll create a reality, a scenario, and just think about the way things can unfold. I'll think about the entire pathway, from making a record, to the timing of the release, to the campaign in advance of a release. I'll try to figure out what we are going to do and what the band could be doing to better our chances. This visualization technique works very well.

I have fourteen people on staff and each band has at least ten people involved, so there are a lot of people to think about. This process of visualization helps me see how we're going to work together, step by step by step, over a series of months, to more than a year ahead. Part of my role is to see far forward. I always have to be planning for the future.

I'm sure that I raised a few eyebrows being a CEO at age twenty-five. The way I look at it is that although I didn't put in many years, I worked so many hours when I was at EMI—seventy to ninety hours a week— that I really have twice my number of years of experience. I was always inquisitive as well, always trying to learn something from every person at the company. I observed that many people only knew their one specific area. I was down the hall from the business affairs department and the accounting department, from finance and marketing and other departments, and I spent a lot of time asking everyone in every department about their jobs. How did it relate to my job, how did it influence things in the company? That was the beginning of my CEO education.

Also, watching my father be an entrepreneur and run a family business was a very big inspiration to me. He owned and ran the summer camp in Connecticut. I watched how he managed things. He had had three jobs when I was a child, and then when the camp started doing very well, he ran that full-time. The camp was a wonderful inspiration. Years after my father died, I actually ran the camp for a few years. I continued to run the camp after I started the label, but the camp was never my passion. That was my father's passion. My passion was music.

When I got into the record business as an unpaid intern, my first reaction was, "This is not a business." It was so haphazard, and people just didn't seem to know what they were talking about. They tended to talk with their wallets, and it was about the money, not the music or the ideas.

A lot of how I act as a CEO I learned from my father. I expect myself to be a fair leader, to work very hard, and to lead by example, which was always what my father did. I've taken a lot of his best qualities; the way that he ran his business was very inspirational.

Most importantly, I try to treat my artists with a lot of respect. There's a rush to working with artists, even an unknown artist. There's an excitement to new music as it's being made, to being in the studio and hearing the genesis, sometimes being there when the song is actually being written. Then there's an incredible pressure to try and make that music successful, to get that music out to people, so that they at least can hear it and decide for themselves whether they want to buy it or patronize the band.

I have already met some of the people that I grew up idolizing. It's an absolutely awesome feeling to be talking to this person about the music business, their music and their lives, and what they want to see, because that's what I have to satisfy. I have to offer a better lifestyle for musicians than a major company does. I have to offer them not only more money, but more attention and better opportunities from a marketing point of view than these big companies do. I have to convince them that I really can deliver on what I'm offering.

Obviously, in this business, the highs are tempered by a lot of rejection, and you need to be able to deal with that. The biggest rejection I've ever felt was when I wanted to sign the Dave Matthews Band. I was about nine months ahead of RCA records in the pursuit. I was trying to sign the deal, and I just couldn't get the deal done. My company was less than a year old. It would have been my second signing. I offered a bad deal and made a very unconvincing pitch. I reread some of my correspondence just recently and understand now what I did wrong, but the rejection was terribly visceral. I couldn't see Dave Matthews play a concert without getting emotional. It felt like someone choosing to marry someone else. It hurts, especially when you hear someone, and you know how good they are.

I don't believe in "should haves" or "could haves." It was an emotional blow not to get to work with them. And that is something I have to live with. I was the first record company to find this guy, and I had a clear opportunity to work with him. I was in there negotiating before anyone else. The ultimate irony is that my friend and former assistant at EMI was the guy who signed them at RCA.

In the long run, it's just a situation I've had to learn from. My attitude is to take any bad experience and find something positive, to try to grow from every experience. It's difficult to be a CEO in the music business, however, because there's no longer a balance between finances and art, and I believe the business needs to get back to that balance. The music business has lost track of the music. The core is now about money. I made a pact with myself very early on that if the business ever jeopardized my love for the music, then the business had to go. Thankfully, that hasn't happened.